VARIETIES OF

AFRICAN

AMERICAN

RELIGIOUS

EXPERIENCE

VARIETIES OF

AFRICAN

AMERICAN

RELIGIOUS

EXPERIENCE

Anthony B. Pinn

FORTRESS PRESS
MINNEAPOLIS

VARIETIES OF AFRICAN AMERICAN RELIGIOUS EXPERIENCE

Cover design: Brad Norr
Cover photo: Woman Profile ©1992 Mark Harmel. Used by permission of FPG
    International
Interior design: Julie Odland Smith
Index: Eileen Quam

Library of Congress Cataloging in Publication Data

Pinn, Anthony B.
    Varieties of African American religious experience / Anthony B.
Pinn.
        p.   cm.
    Includes bibliographical references and index.
    ISBN 0-8006-2994-9 (alk. paper)
    1. Afro-Americans—Religion.   2. Voodooism.   3. Afro-Caribbean
cults.   4. Black Muslims.   5. Humanism, Religious.   I. Title.
BL2490.P46 1998
200'.89'96073—dc21

98–44408
                                                                                    CIP

The paper used in this publication meets the minimum requirements of American National Standard for Information Sciences—Permanence of Paper for Printed Library Materials, ANSI Z329.48-1984.   ∞ ™

Manufactured in the U.S.A.   AF 1-2994
                                        3   4   5   6   7   8   9   10

CONTENTS

FIGURES

For the Ancestors, among them
Jesse Howard III

Gods ought to exude out of the pores like sweat.
They had to well up from the inside.

—S. Naipaul, *Love and Death in a Hot Country*

We need more studies about the voiceless people who want to
be heard in the councils of the world. We need more action in
terms of the truths that are already known. We shall have to
hurry, I think, if we hope to pass on to our children a world in
which there is reasonable hope for creative survival.

—C. Eric Lincoln, *The Black Muslims in America*

ACKNOWLEDGMENTS

Many individuals assisted me in very important ways during the process of writing this volume. Readers should know who they are. I must begin by thanking my editor, Michael West, for his commitment to this project and his work to help me polish it. I would also like to thank other staff members of Fortress Press: David Lott for his encouragement and Julie Odland Smith for the final production work.

Closer to "home," I am grateful for the kind words from the chair of my department, Calvin Roetzel. The other members of my department also helped to create a comfortable environment in which to write. I must also thank Macalester College, in particular Dan Hornbach and Wayne Roberts, for helping in numerous ways. Those in Macalester's library, most notably Danette Roach and Jean Beccone, worked hard to make certain that needed materials arrived in a timely fashion, and they graciously put up with my research "idiosyncrasies." Also at Macalester, several friends—Richard Ammons, Ramon Rentas, Ahmed Samatar, and Alexs Pate—provided needed moments away from the computer screen. They are friends indeed. And, of course, I am grateful to all of my students who challenged me and pushed me to refine my ideas during several semesters of "African American Religions." Much of what is contained here grows out of my work with those students. I thank them all. Several students, in particular, who worked as research assistants, merit special recognition. Thank you to Gregory Colleton, Gretchen Rohr (recently named a Rhodes Scholar!), Mary Kate Little, Leif Johnson, Sean Palmer, and Minh Ta. In terms of research assistance, I am also grateful to Steve Farmer and Eli Valentin.

Without the cooperation of the various communities represented in this book, the project would have failed. I owe a great deal of gratitude to them and the various representatives of those communities: Priestess Miriam Chamani, H.R.H. Oba Ofuntola Oseijeman Adelabu Adefunmi I, Adenibi Edubi Ifamuyiwa Ajamu, Medahochi K. O. Zannu, Minister James Muhammad, Norm Allen, Jr., Timothy Madigan, and others who contributed to making my time with each community so very productive and rewarding. These are those who gave me entry into their religious traditions, and the members of their communities also made me feel welcome and graciously provided information. I thank you all. I am also grateful to

Mary Ann Clark, Robert Barnett, Amos Nascimento, Margaret Guider, Rosa Marina de Brito Meyer, Cecilia Loreto Mariz, Carlos Hasenbalg, Jether Ramalho, Clovis Boufleur, Robert Adams, Iain Maclean, Geraldo Rocha, Claudio Ribeiro, Paula Cristina da Silva, KOINONIA, and Yasmur Flores Esamur, for helping me to understand (and sharing with me) the manner in which religion is explored and lived.

In addition, the members of the 1997 Association for Religion and Intellectual Life colloquium provided invaluable critique and suggestions. The members of the Theology and Cultural Criticism conference held in October of 1997 also gave me needed encouragement and ideas for refining my thoughts. Helpful comments were also provided by James H. Cone, Dwight Hopkins, Victor Anderson, Dennis Dickerson, William R. Jones, Emilie Townes, Cheryl Townsend Gilkes, and many other colleagues who participate in the Black Theology Group of the American Academy of Religion as well as the Society for the Study of Black Religion. And several churches and other organizations in the Twin Cities gave me an opportunity to further develop my ideas: St. Paul Branch of the American Association of University Women, the Minnesota Valley Unitarian Universalist Fellowship, the Humanist Association of Minneapolis and St. Paul, St. James Episcopal Church, the Unitarian Universalist Church of Minnetonka, the First Unitarian Society of Minneapolis, Grace University Lutheran Church, and the Minnesota Atheist Association. Thank you.

I also continue to learn a great deal from Gordon Kaufman and Charles Long. Friends outside of the Twin Cities were extremely encouraging, and I thank them: Benjamin Valentin, Stanley Bernard, Theresa Davis, and Kimberly Connor.

My family, as always, provided much needed support and encouragement. Thank you, Linda, Joyce, Raymond, and especially my mother—Rev. Anne H. Pinn—who also helped transcribe interview materials. Finally, my companion, Cheryl Johnson ("CJ"), has been a blessing. I marvel at her thoughtfulness, kindness, and concern for me and my work. She is truly a wonder, and I am grateful.

Others certainly contributed to the success of this project, and although not mentioned by name, I hope they see themselves reflected in the following pages. All those mentioned here, whether by name or not, have helped me in countless ways to make this project rich; however, I alone must take responsibility for its shortcomings. Oversights and misinterpretations are bound to occur, and I ask for patience from those who have helped with this project.

NOTE ON ORTHOGRAPHY

Maintaining consistency with respect to terms that have undergone the transformation marked by the middle passage is difficult. However, I have attempted to address this by presenting names and terms as they appear in the various contexts with which I am concerned: Africa, the Americas, the United States. When quoting other sources, I attempt to maintain as best I can the spelling used by the various authors. In most cases, this entails presenting simultaneously several possibilities. Some will find my method tiresome. Where this is the case, I apologize to members of the various communities represented in this text. My dilemma, I think, is one experienced by the interested "outsider." Nevertheless, my goal is to present the complexity and movement of religion within the context of the diaspora not only in the material I discuss but also in the "roughness" of the words I use.

INTRODUCTION
Theology and the Canon of Black Religion Rethought

Black (Christian) church centered dialogue dominates academic Black religious thought. Consequently, much additional religious ground needs to be covered in order to recognize Black religious expression's full complexity. . . . Exploration and dialogue must eventually encompass traditions beyond those presented if a full spectrum of Black religion—in its broadest sense—is to surface.[1]

The above rethinking of African American religious experience's content, scope, and meaning is the challenge I posed in *Why, Lord?* Having thrown out the challenge in that book, I attempt to address the demands of this challenge in subsequent efforts, most notably this volume.

It is my contention that African American religious experience extends beyond the formation and practice of black Christianity. That is to say, historically African Americans have participated in a variety of traditions, such as Yorùbá religious practices (attention to the *orisha* or deities), Voodoo (Vodou), Islam, and humanism. Much of the discussion concerning these traditions has been conducted by anthropologists, sociologists, historians of religion, and those in the arts. African American theologians have not, in large measure, understood the ritual structures of these and other traditions as anything more than resources for the construction of a syncretic black Christianity, sources whose dynamic nature was lost to the fervor of the two Great Awakenings. This is tragic in that theologians are best equipped to explore the theological issues underlying the practices of these traditions. Without attention to these traditions by theologians and others scholars of religion, our understanding of religion within African American communities contains an unhealthy limitation on its scope and vision.

The narrow agenda and resource base of contemporary African American theological reflection troubles me because it limits itself to Christianity in ways that establish Christian doctrine and concerns as normative. It has considered the church its sole conversation partner. Resulting from this is a problematic allegiance to Christian churches and their doctrine and dogma as theology's benefactor. One notices this in James Evans'

words, in *We Have Been Believers,* concerning the nature of black theology.
Evans says, "Theology is essentially the church's response to the autobiographical impulse, and it grows out of the need to proclaim with authority
and commitment the identity and mission of the church in the world. . . .
The important factor, however, is that the theology that results must coher-
ently interpret the experience of black people and the Gospel. . . ."[2] The
identity of theology and theologians is too intimately tied to the Christian
tradition as opposed to the exploration of life-altering questions that arise
within the various formations of African American religiosity. An unfortunate consequence of this link is the assumed threat to "black" identity associated with critiques of black churches. Comparative study is often considered intellectual adultery and critique is too often equated with treachery.
Consequently, I understand African American theologians, by and large, as
displaying the same provincial and defensive attitude espoused in Shiva
Naipaul's novel *Love and Death in a Hot Country.* In this text a school teacher
whose daughter has questioned the existence of God says the following in
response: "I've built my life on faith in Christ, he said. If there was no God
there would be no reason for anything. Life would be one big joke. . . . Is
my life a joke to you?"[3]

There is, nonetheless, a richness to the religious terrain of African
American communities that should be explored. Having critiqued current
treatments of African American religions that I find problematic, it is my
responsibility to offer an alternate approach. That is to say, there is a fundamental question that I must, in this text, address: How does theology
address traditions that fall outside the Christian context, traditions that are
contrary to, if not hostile toward, the basic claims of Christian faith?

The purpose of this volume, as is further explained at the end of this
Introduction and in the final chapter, is to provide an initial exploration of
four underexplored traditions: voodoo (vodou), Yorùbá religion (or devotion to the *orisha*), the Nation of Islam, and humanism. These are just a few
of the religious traditions alive in African American communities. Others
will be explored in a second volume of *Varieties* I am committed to producing. I begin with these traditions because of their vibrancy and their
"marginal" status based, in large part, on their cosmological structures.
They are linked, I believe, by this cosmological marginality and also by
their long presence in African American communities stemming from the
early period of slavery. I am convinced that theological challenges posed by
these traditions and their various structures can greatly enhance constructive theological reflection and ethics. In short, there is much to learn from

these traditions because of the ways in which they push theological boundaries and force a reevaluation of what the term *religion* describes.

To set in place some necessary terminology, I must briefly discuss my
understanding of religion. I have made use of Paul Tillich's dynamic
notions of ultimate orientation and ultimate concern. Yet the latter entails
a singularity that does not fully capture the religious plurality and diversity
within African American communities. To better express my sense of religious plurality, I now make use of Gordon Kaufman's recent work. Simply
put, religion is that which provides orientation or direction for human life,
"for life in the world, together with motivation for living and acting in
accordance with this orientation—that is, would gain, and gradually for-
mulate, a sense of the *meaning* of human existence."[4] In terms of praxis or
movement through the maze of life (e.g., the problem of evil), religion
helps individuals and groups live in beneficial ways, in light of life-altering
(hence theological) questions that are not easily addressed through skills
and resources associated with the patterns of actions learned and acted out
from infancy through adulthood.[5] Through the ritual structures and symbolic sources provided in various religions, humans give their thought and
actions meaning. Therefore, religion at its core is a process of meaning-
making. I am not suggesting that this orientation moves us toward the
"sacred" as conceived in traditional ways. Instead, this is orientation toward
"reality" conceived in very general and broad ways. Because of this framework, both "theistic" and "nontheistic" forms of religious expression and
experience are religion because religion, simply understood, spreads
beyond traditional boundaries of Christian formations. In short, religion
entails "underlying resources of meaning and ritual that inform and fund
the ongoing living and dying in a culture as a whole."[6] With religion so conceived, there is no need for religious traditions to fight for supremacy
because the needs of various human communities are complex and varied
enough to allow for a plurality of religious traditions. One tradition does
not "replace" others. Instead each contributes to the diversity that charac-
terizes the religious terrain of the United States.

I acknowledge, however, that this definition is broad in ways that allow
for inclusion of structures and activities that few are initially comfortable
considering religious. In response to this, I argue that there is no real benefit in guarding the gates, so to speak. If we are the slightest bit pragmatic
and liberation-minded, is not the *function* of religious practice more important than definitions and arguments that are semantic in character? What is
the real benefit of narrowing the parameters of recognized religious prac-

tice? Is the myopic identity that narrow definitions allow "mainstream" communities to achieve worth the effort and isolation entailed? Should not the quest for liberation and healthy life options take precedence over labels and stilted definitions? I think so.

With this said, it is still necessary to think through the type of theological reflection that can embrace such a fluid definition of religion. The undertaking I propose is possible once the nature of theological discourse is rethought, in part using the work of Gordon Kaufman and Charles Long. African American theology's approach to traditions such as those discussed in this text is presently based upon a soft version of what Kaufman has labeled "first-order theology." Kaufman writes:

> In this sense, it may be held, theology always presupposes a certain faith, namely the faith that God has in fact revealed [Godself]; and this faith is not itself subject to theological questioning or doubt. Theology [understood in this way] is thus a work of the church and for the church; it is an analysis and interpretation of the faith of those who already stand within the "theological circle."[7]

This perspective, with Christian meanings and forms as normative, limits the relevance of sustained engagement with other traditions. These traditions are not understood as dynamic and complex—they merely point beyond themselves to the ultimate revelation of God in the message of Christ.

I want to suggest that the task of African American theology, and other constructive and liberation theologies by extension, is more in line with Kaufman's "third-order theology" and Charles Long's reflections upon theology of the opaque. That is to say, theology is deliberate or self-conscious human construction focused upon uncovering and exploring the meaning and structures of religious experience within the larger body of cultural production. It is, by nature, comparative in a way that does not seek to denounce or destructively handle other traditions. Conceived in this way, African American theology's only obligation, then, is the uncovering of meaning and the providing of responses to the questions of life that explain experience, assess existing symbols and categories, and allow for healthy existence. It may find itself engaging churches, but that does not make theology the sole possession of churches. That is to say: "Theology, thus, has public, not private or parochial foundations. It is not restricted either to the language and traditions of a particular esoteric community or to the peculiar experience of unusual individuals."[8] Theology must address religious experience without concentrating on a particular tradition. Kaufman and Long agree on this point. Both it seems, understand the difficulty if not impossibility, of actually being a "theologian." Kaufman argues, however, and I agree, that those who call themselves theologians must continuously seek to perform this possible impossibility.[9]

What is required is methodical stretching and openness. Without this alteration, the structure of theology as valuable discourse is hopelessly undermined. That is to say, "extrachurch" traditions (a term used by Charles Long and one that is less problematic than "non-Christian") must be looked at not as sources for strengthening Christian faith and its theology but rather as means by which to understand better the larger complex of African American religious experience. In this way, the conceptualization and study of African American religions moves outside their current static phase within the discipline of theology. How do theologians involve themselves in this reconstructive enterprise? I suggest that the problem of evil provides a starting point.

These traditions can be explored theologically based upon the assumption that their appeal and practices rest upon a response to moral evil. Could religious traditions forged in the arena of "contact and conquest" avoid this issue? My intention here is not to provide a critique of their particular responses to the problem of evil. Rather, I see the problem of evil as simply an entry point, a category of investigation that allows the theologian to make a contribution to the exploration of these traditions currently underway by sociologists and others. The problem of evil allows the theologian to locate these traditions in time and space, in the same way that the notion of progress has been used to locate and understand certain developments in U.S. intellectual and institutional history. The problem of evil in my first book was used as a point of critique—deconstruction and reconstruction of responses to the existential realities of black life. Yet, because I have argued in this introduction that these religious traditions are under-recognized, I must first present them in their historical, theological, and ritual forms before critical analysis can be undertaken. Therefore, this volume's major thrust is by necessity descriptive. Again, the problem of evil is used as an organizing principle. It must also be noted that the central concern here is theological in nature, therefore, the traditions are not presented in their full complexity. Not every aspect of their ritual, thought, practice, and historical development is discussed.

With the theological agenda defined, the call for a comparative theological approach made, and religion redefined, I would like to quickly turn to my reasons for believing that this call and redefining are necessary. That is to say, I would like to provide a few comments concerning the "evidence" of this religious complexity before moving the reader into fuller discussions. This is important because this "evidence" serves as the rationale or basis for the following chapters.

Prior to the aggressive introduction of slaves to Christianity during the Great Awakening revivals, there was a roughly one-hundred-year period during which complex African traditions could have taken root. Hinting at the value and validity of such a connection, Theophus Smith, in *Conjuring Culture*, argues that African Americans have made use of African-based and "New World" adopted religious techniques to make sense of their experiences in the United States. He argues that using conjure—the harnessing of power and authority through ritual and magical means—allowed African Americans to maintain the vibrancy of their traditions within their new religious context. In this way, African Americans conjured the Bible—applied principles, signs, symbols, and magic—in a way that made it speak to their liberation. Accordingly, God became the first conjuror through the creation of the world out of raw materials and magical words. In like manner, Moses becomes a conjurer who, in very real ways, resembles the trickster or messenger *orisha* (deity) commonly called by the name Esu or Eleggua.[10] Smith's argument, although on one level resembling traditional statements concerning slave reworking of Scripture, is important and provocative because it suggests the maintenance of African practices in the United States beyond simply a philosophical outlook. That is, the harnessing of nature's power and authority is maintained through available materials and powerful words. The difficulty is that Smith places this practice within the service of black Christian formulations.

Others suggest a vitality and dynamic nature of conjure and like practices extending beyond Christian expression. Both Albert Raboteau and Yvonne Chireau suggest that these practices may not have been empty of ritual meaning. Albert Raboteau has noted that some "conjuring objects were symbolically 'fed' by black practitioners, hearkening back to their identification as personifications of powerful spirits in traditional African religions."[11] The work of Yvonne Chireau suggests that conjure and other "extrachurch" (to use Charles Long's term) practices were viable and complex and provided the type of meaning that Charles Long argues is essential within any system labeled religion. Yet we are unaware of a great deal of the complexities of these religious practices because of the secrecy surrounding them (to avoid punishment) within secret hush arbor–like meetings. Accounts do exist, however, as Chireau points out, of practitioners providing valuable services:

In the latter part of the eighteenth-century, there are further, scattered hints indicating the presence of supernatural traditions among Black bondspersons in the South. A 1784 advertisement of a runaway female slave in Savannah, Georgia, for example, suggests that not only did popular interest in clairvoyance, divination, and fortunetelling circulate widely among whites and African Americans, but to some extent such ideas functioned as marketable goods for resourceful Black bondspersons: 'Runaway from the subscriber, an elderly Negro woman named Luce, of a thin visage, and rather a small stature. . . . She . . . pretends to be skill[ed] in fortunetelling, by cutting of cards, whereby she imposes on young people.'[12]

Lawrence Levine, in *Black Culture and Black Consciousness*, provides accounts indicating that "extrachurch" practices were known within pre-emancipation African American communities. Levine records the words of one Anthony Dawson: "We didn't have no voodoo women nor conjure folks at our 'Twenty Acres,' Anthony Dawson of North Carolina testified. 'We all knowed about the Word and the unseen Son of God and we didn't put no stock in conjure. 'Course we had luck charms and good and bad signs, but everybody got dem tings, even nowadays.' "[13] I must note that beyond conjure, hoodoo, and voodoo mentioned explicitly here, the religious landscape of African American communities includes, and has since the arrival of Africans to North America, Islam. In addition, this religious landscape also includes the nontheistic tradition known as humanism. Again, Christianity is not the only expression and representation of African American religious life. According to Charles Long:

> To be sure, the church is one place one looks for religion. . . . But even more than this, the church was not the only context for the meaning of religion. . . . The Christian faith provided a language for the meaning of religion, but not all the religious meanings of the black communities were encompassed by the Christian forms of religion. . . . Some tensions have existed between these forms of orientation and those of the Christian churches, but some of these extrachurch orientations have had great critical and creative power. They have often touched deeper religious issues regarding the true situation of black communities than those of the church leaders of their time.[14]

The lack of direct evidence should not prevent an acceptance of "extrachurch" practices as viable, in the same way that a lack of direct knowledge of Christian hush arbor meetings has not resulted in a dismissal of the vitality of pre-emancipation African American Christian organizations and practices. But even on this score, archaeological evidence, for example, provides a fuller depiction of religious practices within these secret slave meetings.

And out of this archaeological work emerges the plausibility of both African-based and nontheistic religious practices in the United States. By extension, continuity between antebellum "extrachurch" practices and twentieth-century religious manifestations is also possible.

Gayraud Wilmore's discussion of the "de-radicalization" of black churches helps with this latter point. In the words of Wilmore,

> During the 1920s and 1930s most black churches retained a basically rural orientation and retreated into enclaves of moralistic, revivalistic Christianity by which they tried to fend off the encroaching gloom and pathology of the ghetto. As far as challenging white society, or seeking to mobilize the community against poverty and oppression, most churches were too otherworldly, apathetic, or caught up in institutional maintenance to deal with such issues.[15]

At this point, many African Americans lost interest in the teachings and practices of black churches and joined alternative traditions. The God of the Christian faith did not provide acceptable resolutions to the African American plight. Consequently, the Christian God appeared foreign, the property of the oppressor. Again, Naipaul's novel, which explores the meaning of life and liberation within the context of the "third world," provides shocking insight into the point I am making. Mrs. St. Pierre, after a frustrating conversation with her idealistic and unjustifiably optimistic husband concerning the possibility of liberation for the oppressed of his nation, finds solitude in her bedroom and begins to reflect on the nature of religious experience for the oppressed. Her reflections are telling:

> Gods ought to exude out of the pores like sweat. They had to well up from the inside. They could not be borrowed from others or imposed by others. Such gods were no good at all. They had no magic, no potency. Borrowed gods erased the soul and left you with nothing you could call your own. It was the most terrible form of robbery. . . . But where were her gods? Who were they? Christianity did not belong to her. It had never oozed out of her pores. She had never experienced the Christian god as a living presence within her: because he belonged to others, not to her.[16]

Many left Christian churches in search of the gods who ooze out of the community's collective pores, gods that respond to the existential reality of African Americans. In some cases, such as humanism, "god" was replaced by a concern for community itself and individual advancement. Thus, one begins to see the groundwork had been laid, through the de-radicalization of black churches and the hunger for identity felt by many African Americans, for the embracing of "extrachurch" traditions. This hunger for alternate religious meaning and symbol systems continued during the Civil Rights movement, in part, sparked by the dissatisfaction of black power advocates with the tone and program of the Christian-dominated movement.

Although material has been presented by figures such as Joseph Murphy, George Brandon, and Karen McCarthy Brown on the complexity of the U.S. religious terrain, this volume is one of the only treatments that looks explicitly at the participation of *African Americans* in this religious complexity and from the standpoint of the theologian. I am interested in bringing to academic light the explicit involvement of African Americans born in and contextualized by the United States. The following chapters are based upon a reading of relevant primary and secondary materials, limited field work, and interviews with practitioners of four traditions.[17] The first chapter addresses the historical development (from Africa to the United States), ritual and hierarchical issues, cosmology and the problem of evil as developed in voodoo (vodou). The next chapter makes use of the same structure to discuss the development of *Santería* and other forms of Yorùbá religion in the United States. The third chapter explores the development, structure, and theological underpinnings of Islam in the United States, in the form of the Nation of Islam. The final study concerns the presence of humanism within the African American religious landscape, giving attention to the same structural and theological issues addressed in the first three chapters. The final chapter explores methodological questions and possibilities sparked by this study.

Although the structure of each chapter is similar, differences in the transmission of these traditions and the character of the various "case-study" communities force certain differences in presentation. The nature of oral transmission as well as the secret nature of many activities results, undoubtedly, in contradictions between my study and information presented in other studies. This is unavoidable, yet it does not render this study nor other studies fundamentally flawed. When a difference between the terminology and thinking of those I interviewed and academic treatments of these traditions occurred, I made an effort always to give preference to the interpretation offered by those I interviewed. In so doing, I tried to demonstrate a preference for the "lived" quality of each tradition. In addition, before the final proof pages of this text were ready, each community represented in the case study section of each chapter was asked to review the respective chapters and offer comments and corrections where necessary.

It should be noted that this text does not provide an explicitly comparative study of the various traditions and their points of epistemological origin. The point of this project is to provide general information concerning these practices within communities of African Americans in the United States. I am not concerned with demonstrating or denying the legitimacy of these traditions with respect to their "parent" forms.

The reader will also note that a glossary is not provided. This is because uncommon terms are explained in the text and indexed. Available space is given to pictures and a bibliography.

Finally, some may raise questions concerning an "outsider" presenting these traditions. This, I suppose, is a legitimate concern. Yet I do not claim expertise; rather, I claim an interest in and profound respect for the various forms of religious expression alive in African American communities. I am in no way attempting to provide definitive treatments of these traditions. Rather, I am attempting to bring my theological tools and sociohistorical sensibilities to bear on vital and viable religious traditions in communities of concern to me. Other scholars must also stretch and respectfully learn about traditions. Although, in the process, mistakes are inevitable, it is my hope that the strengths and weaknesses of my presentation will inspire others to venture forth and explore these uncharted religious waters. In this way, we allow the sundry ways of being African American and religious to enrich our vision of the religious horizon before us.

1

▲▼▲▼▲▼▲▼▲▼▲▼▲▼▲

SERVING THE *LOA*
Vodou, Voodoo, and the Voodoo Spiritual Temple

DAHOMEY AND VODUN

The small and independent groups that lived in what is now Benin were replaced by a complex system headed by a king. It is said that the royal line, the first ancestor of the royal dynasty, originated in Adja-Tado (1300). The royal family moved from Adja-Tado before the beginning of the seventeenth century. In the genealogical story, the daughter of Adja-Tado's king was impregnated by a leopard. The child was named Agasu and is remembered as the ancestor of all the Fon of Dahomey. The children of Agasu ultimately attempted to rule Adja-Tado but were forced to flee, and through their travel, the holy city of Allada was founded.[1] From this line emerges the leaders of Dahomey.

The relocation to Allada resulted in prosperity and tranquility until a feud between the king's sons resulted in a triadic split within the community: one group went north (founding Dahomey's capital city of Abomey), another south (taking control of Ajase-Ipo or Porto Novo), and the third remained in Allada. In roughly 1625, Dako became the king of the Agasuvi and undertook expansionist goals within the region. This activity successfully continued under several additional kings, who were even successful against the powerful Yorùbá kingdom and interior groups.[2] One of the greatest of these leaders was Wegbadja, who is said to have given Dahomey its name. In fact,

> a famous story tells how he demanded land on which to build a palace from a chief called Dan. His demands were considered excessive, and Dan asked him, "Do you want to build in my belly?" Wegbadja killed Dan for his resistance and built the palace on his grave. The palace was called Danhome ("in the belly of Dan"), whence the familiar version, Dahomey.[3]

11

Dahomey was never a centralized kingdom but was composed of a loosely connected, yet highly organized, grouping of people using agriculture and the market for its major forms of economic support. Socially, it is composed for the most part of three structures: the family, the extended family, and the geographically decentralized sib groups or groupings of families.

The cultural exchange that comes along with contact through trade and war shapes the religious development of Dahomey. Its complex pantheon, ritual structure, and theological system are marked by contact with Yorùbá, Mahi, and Ketu. Robert Farris Thompson observes:

> The deities of the Yorùbá had already made their presence felt in Dahomey over hundreds of years. Yorùbá deities were served under different manifestations in Allada before 1659. Therefore, the Abomey conquests brought together Yorùbá deities already transformed into Ewe and Fon local spirits, in addition to deities from Ketu and Anago Yorùbá. . . . Fusion and refusion of Yorùbá spirits, first in Dahomey and then all over again in Haiti, go a long way toward explaining the phenomenon of multiple avatars of the same Dahomean-Yorùbá god. It also helps explain the persistence of the concept of the orisha in the black New World.[4]

Dahomean religion is composed of a high God, lesser deities who are concerned with the daily dealings of life, spirits, ancestors, humans, other animals, and objects (see Figure 1). All of these elements are connected through an energy that gives shape to daily life. Maintaining balance of this energy involves the complex structures, information and rituals that comprise the religious tradition and entail the way of service to the gods (*vodun*).[5] The following story of creation puts this into perspective:

> The world was created by one god, who is at the same time both male and female . . . named Nana-Buluku. In time, Nana-Buluku gave birth to twins, who were named Mawu and Lisa, and to whom eventually dominion over the realm thus created was added. To Mawu, the woman, was given command of the night; to Lisa, the man, command of the day; Mawu, therefore is the moon and inhabits the west, while Lisa, who is the sun, inhabits the east.[6]

For the Dahomey, Nana-Buluku does not figure prominently in worship; rather, attention is given to Mawu-Lisa.[7] This "deity may have been of Adja origin. . . . The cult was probably known in Dahomey before the reign of Tegbesou, for the name Lisa was used by the Capuchin monks to translate 'Jesus' in their version of the Doctrina Christiana prepared for their mission at Allada in 1658. Perhaps the safest conclusion is that the cult of Mawu-Lisa was not widespread in Dahomey proper until Tegbesou encouraged it for reasons of his own."[8]

There is debate concerning whether or not Mawu-Lisa receives direct attention from devotees, or whether Mawu-Lisa is too distant to care for the daily affairs of humans. Regardless of one's position, it is certain that Mawu-Lisa provides the energy that is the essence of life—the essential ontological energy for the human soul and all other forms of existence. Mawu-Lisa gave birth to many children, who can be divided into three major groups corresponding to earth, sky, and thunder. Each child was given control over some segment of existence. Among them, Gû was given control over metal and war. Age was to rule the wilderness and its animals. Djo was given control over the space between earth and sky—atmosphere and human destiny. Sakpata (Sagbata) was given control over earth. (Dada Zodji and Nyohwe Ananu, children of Mawu and Lisa, descended to earth and produced children that control various aspects of life on earth. In this connection, Sakpata is a term for a group of smallpox or earth deities.) Hebiosso owns the sky and punishes wrongdoing with thunder. Sogbo, who has power to create, remained with Mawu and Lisa in the sky and gave birth to several children, including Agbe and Naete. Agbe and Naete were given control over water—the oceans and the seas. Wete and Alawe, Aizu and Akazu are "storekeepers" for the original creators. Adjakpa is associated with water used by humans for nourishment and as a result has a valued place within the cosmos. Ayaba is also valued because she is associated with fire.

Legba was made the mediator between the gods and humans. Each child of Mawu-Lisa was given a particular language which is indecipherable by the other vodun, or deities, "mysteries." It is for this reason that Legba, who provides communication between the various realms, is so central to the workings of the world. Legba has no element of the cosmos with which he is associated, yet the workings of the world and the relationship between vodun and humans are impossible without him. Because of this, Legba must be approached prior to any of the other vodun if tasks are to be successfully fulfilled and rituals performed. Thus Legba has no place of his own, but his presence is required in all places. Because of Legba's communicative importance, it is natural that he would have associations with Fa, the system of divination associated with Dahomean religion, which is at times referred to as the voice of Mawu.[9] Legba, through this connection, is responsible for communicating human destinies. Although Legba is important, the principal figures among the children are Sakpata, Sogbo, and Agbe.[10]

Da (force) marks an important aspect of the universe, the powerful nature of combinations. As Robert Thompson remarks, "The good serpent of the sky, Da, is a metaphor for this primary sign of order. Like Mawu-Lisa, Da combines male and female aspects and is sometimes represented as twins. Many are his avatars, but principal among them is Da Ayido Hwedo, the rainbow-serpent. Coiling a resplendent bichromatic body about the earth, Da shaped its globelike form and sustained its balance and existence."[11] Da or Ayido Hwedo guarantees the movement of the celestial elements and is discernible to the human eye in the rainbow.

Theological anthropology is discernible through the outlining of the human soul (se), which is composed of numerous nonvisible elements: three souls (Selido, Semedo, and Semekokato), and the djoto or ancestral guide. It is believed that when a person passes away, Mawu uses the body to create another human, but the soul continues through a variety of possibilities and in a variety of locations. This, as Herskovits notes, highlights the concept of multiple souls. The djoto, often referred to as the ancestral guide, is the soul (or the eternal substance) inherited from one's ancestors. Prior to being the djoto, or the individual's given soul, it is the Semekokato, or the element that seeks out the body it will guard during life on earth. Once the Semekokato finds the clay out of which the body will be formed, the second soul or semedo inhabits the molded body and becomes the person's individual or personal soul. The next soul, the Selido, is the portion of Mawu residing in each person. Conceived in another way: the Semekokato is the biological representation of the person; the selido is a person's mind and instinct, which is responsible for reporting the person's deeds to Mawu; and the semedo is the person's personality.[12]

Dahomeans understood that life force is not ultimately extinguished with physical death but, through the presence of one's ancestors, remains a vital link with the universe and one's place within the universe. Ancestors, when remembered and taken care of, provide guidance and protection from harm. In addition to family ancestors, there are the ancestors (tohwiyo) of the various clans who provide connection to the first people, animals, and cosmic powers. It is also clear that ancestors and the larger cosmology provide epistemological and ontological legitimation because they explain the recognized and respected lines of authority. Through individual and family actions and the complex rule of priesthood, Dahomeans maintained balance with the cosmic forces that shaped their existence. Memories of such stability and ontological legitimacy were vitally important in light of the slave trade that would mark the existential reality of the Dahomey in the years after the fifteenth century.

Figure 1. Partial List of Dahomey Vodun

African Name	Function
Mawu	God Almighty
Lisa	Creativity God (usually understood as combined with Mawu)
Legba	Trickster and messenger between the gods and the gods and humans
Gû	Iron God and God of war
Age	God of the hunt and the bush
Sakpata	Ruler of the earth (who punishes with smallpox)
Hebiosso	God of the sky who punishes with lightning
Da (Ayido Hwedo)	Divine Serpent represented by the rainbow; assisted with creation
Loko	Associated with the Loko tree
Agbe	God of the waters
Sogbo	God of the sky, parent of Sakpata

Adapted from Robert Farris Thompson, *Flash of the Spirit: African and Afro-American Art and Philosophy* (New York: Random House, 1983).

HAITI AND VODOU

In 1492, Columbus caught sight of Hispaniola (referred to by the Arawaks as Haiti or "land of mountains") and was bewildered by its beauty and, what is more, its potential for increasing Spain's wealth through gold. After initial difficulties with the inhabitants, Spaniards set about achieving their economic goals through forced Arawak labor. Cruelty combined with hard work resulted in high death rates, however, and the need for a new source of labor.[13] In addition, Bartolomé de las Casas (a conquistador turned priest) spoke to the Spanish crown on behalf of the indigenous population, criticizing harsh treatment and advocating missionary efforts. Yet the economic interests of settlers and Spain required workers. De las Casas, although he later repented, suggested the use of Africans as a ready-made labor force.

Although the first African slaves in what became Haiti were brought from Spain by Governor Nicolas de Ovando, by the early sixteenth century,

Africa provided chattel labor. By 1504, the Spanish crown allowed the importation of two hundred slaves per year; this was repealed in 1516 but later revived. By 1517, natives from West Africa were being imported wholesale. In the words of C. L. R. James, "As they devastated an area they moved westward and then south, decade after decade, past the Niger, down the Congo coast, past Loango and Angola, round the Cape of Good Hope. . . ."[14] By the beginning of the sixteenth century, slave ships were making their way to Hispaniola, depositing chattel taken from the Foulas, Poulards, Sosos, Bambarras, Mandingos, Fon, Ibos, Yorùbá, and so forth, and claiming wealth.

With new potential for wealth in locations such as Peru, much of the western portion of the island (modern Haiti) was abandoned. Raids by French pirates also made this section of Hispaniola less attractive over the course of time. In large part Bertrand d'Ogeron's ability to dominate these French *boucaniers* and develop more organized towns resulted in French control of western Hispaniola. By 1675, many of the former boucaniers were planters and Saint-Dominique was established. Spain was not in a position to conduct a successful fight against French aggressors and so, in 1697, the Treaty of Ryswick gave official control of the western half of the Island to the French.[15] Although the Spanish and the French both had economic gain in mind, their attitudes toward the cultural and religious development of slaves differed.

Slaves on the island did receive religious attention from Spaniards. Both the Spanish Crown and the Catholic Church actively encouraged missionary work. The geography of the island, however, combined with a relatively limited number of religious leaders, hampered the complexity and depth of missionary work. With the Treaty of Ryswick the difficulty in providing solid religious training for slaves was reinforced by a lack of interest on the part of French planters and businesspersons who now controlled the area. This, combined with intense interest in economic gain and advanced production capabilities, resulted in slaves receiving a great deal of religious "free space."

While the population of Africans increased on the island and economic success marked the day, religious missionary zeal waned. This zeal was artificially revived through the Code Noir (1685), which regulated "the social, political, and religious life of all the French colonies throughout the world." With respect to slaves, the Code required forced baptism and doctrinal education and outlawed African religious practices and superstitions. Regulations imposed in 1758 and 1777 further enforced the

Christianization of slaves by controlling the space in which slaves moved: under penalty of death, slaves were not to meet except in the presence of a priest, and were not allowed to gather near the home of their master and in remote spaces.[16]

The religious leadership of the island underestimated the "staying power" of cultural beliefs and activities. And so, regardless of the church's efforts, Africans from Dahomey and elsewhere maintained their traditional rituals, beliefs, and theological posture. In the words of Father Jean-Baptiste Labat:

> The Negroes have no scruples. . . . They intermix Dagon's ark and secretly keep all the superstitions of their ancient idolatrous cult with the cere-monies of the Christian religion. All the Negroes have much devotion for the communion wafer. They eat it only when they are ill, or when they are afraid of some danger. In regard to the holy water, the little bit of water that is consecrated during the Sunday Mass, it is rare that one finds one drop of it when the ceremony has ended; they carry it in little calabashes and drink some drops when they rise (in the morning) and pretend that it will guarantee their welfare against all the witchcraft that might befall them.[17]

Africans in the "New World" had to make sense of their surroundings, to center themselves and respond to the pressing questions forced by enslave-ment. What can be said about the gods, ancestors, spirits, and self in light of enslavement? For them, the problem of evil that was the basis of their questioning was not best addressed through the Catholic Church, nor could suffering be understood in this context strictly through traditional practices. Rather, the blending—what some have called syncretism, cre-olization, or dissimulation—of Catholicism and African beliefs provided the best working resolution. In this way, the vodun (gods), ancestors, and other energies were revised or re-empowered to address a foreign and harsh social context. What emerged is Haiti's vodou.[18]

The Catholic Church in time found it necessary to give at least "unof-ficial" recognition to vodou as a flourishing religious tradition. Yet during its early years and for much of its history, vodou practitioners had to exer-cise great care and secrecy to avoid persecution. Consequently, slaves made use of celebratory times to keep alive a core of African-based practice. Although there is debate on this point, it seems reasonable that Catholic signs, symbols, and elements served as a convenient cover for a deeper real-ity based heavily upon the "blending" of religious traditions and world-views of the Dahomey, Yorùbá, Congo, and other Africans brought to Saint-Dominique, as well as elements borrowed from the indigenous population.

It should be noted that the term *vodou* properly serves as a generic covering. In the same manner that "the black Church" is used as a term denoting the various black denominations in the United States, "vodou" is a term used to catalogue the decentralized and various forms of vodou practice or "nations" found throughout Haiti.[19]

The attempt to replace vodou with Catholicism was not consistently maintained. Friction between Haiti and Rome resulted in the irregular arrival of priests to the island due to the Pope's reluctance to recognize Haiti as an independent and legitimate entity capable of developing its own priesthood. Although the tension between the Haitian state and the Vatican was resolved in 1860 with the appointment of church officials for the West Indies and Santo Domingo (Dominican Republic), the religious landscape was firmly developed and vodou was a vital component of Haitian culture.[20] In 1896 the Bishop of Cape Haitian had this to say about the apparent problem with vodou:

> It is certain that we cannot heap enough dishonor on these presumptuous and shameful observances, unworthy of civilized people, sinful to Christians. This insane confidence in practices and objects devoid of any virtue in themselves, much less any conferred by God or his Church; this overblown or ridiculous power attributed to saints, to images, to relics, and invoked, often enough, to achieve criminal ends; these claims to create supernatural effects by methods condemned by religion and common sense, these are so many violations against the purity of the faith, so many offenses to the saints, so many outrages against God himself.[21]

Catechism-based religious indoctrination was used by religious leaders to associate vodou practices with the demonic:

> 31. Who is the principal slave of Satan? —the principal slave of Satan is the *houngan* [vodou priest].

> 32. What are the names given by houngan to Satan? —The names given to Satan by *houngan* are *loas* [the term for the gods], angels, saints *morts* [venerated ancestors], and *marass* [the divine twins].

> 33. Why do *houngan* give Satan the names of angels, saints, and *morts*? —*Houngan* call Satan after saints, angels and *morts* in order to deceive us more easily.

> 34. How do men serve Satan? —In sinning, casting spells, practicing magic, giving food-offerings, *manger les anges, manger marassa.*

> 37. Are we allowed to mingle with the slaves of Satan? —No, because they are evil-doers; like Satan himself they are liars.[22]

Such recitations were often accompanied by coerced oaths of allegiance to the Catholic Church.

> I before God, stand in the Tabernacle, before the priest who represents Him and renew the promises of my baptism. With hand on the Gospels I swear never to give a food-offering (*manger loas*) of whatever kind—never to attend a Voodoo ceremony of whatever kind, never to take part in a service to loas in any way whatsoever. I promise to destroy or have destroyed as soon as possible all fetishes and objects of superstition, if any—on me, in my house, and in my compound. In short I swear never to sink to any superstitious practice whatever.[23]

As Laguerre comments, "what ever the content of the religion brought by the slaves from Africa might have been . . . it was evidently influenced by several factors: the ecology of the plantation, the slave's daily schedules, their acquisition of new friends or comrades, a new language for communication, new types of housing, new diet, new patterns of social organization and political power, new kinds of work specialization (domestics, field slaves, craftsmen, overseers, musicians, preachers), and a new calendar of events that included Catholic religious feasts and national holidays."[24] It is commonly said that the term *vaudoux,* later *vodun,* was first used by Mederick Louis Moreau de St. Mery, who described a dance he witnessed in Saint-Dominique among slaves.

> In 1768 a black man of Le Petit-Goave . . . taking advantage of the credulity of the black smith superstitious practices, gave them the idea of a dance analogous to that of the vaudoux, but in which the movements were more sharp and sudden. To give the dance even more of an effect, the blacks mixed well-crushed gunpowder in the cheap rum they drank while dancing.[25]

This is an early account of "vaudoux" practices among the Africans of Saint-Dominique, recorded by one of the few nonpractitioners to witness vodou religious practices. What Moreau describes is, with many flaws, the Petro division of vodou described later in this chapter. Often associated with the success of the Revolution, Petro is not the largest segment of practice. Rada claims this position.[26] The term *Rada* is widely held to emerge from the name of the Dahomey holy city of Allada, referring to the Africans taken from Arada, on the coast of Dahomey.[27] Because of this connection to Dahomey and because Rada is the major level of vodou practice, many closely associate vodou and Dahomey. The Rada *lwas* (deities) and rituals, signs and symbols are considered "cool." Vodou, in this case Rada, involves service to the *lwa* through which the energies of the uni-

verse, residing in Africa or, more specifically, Ginen, are brought into harmony with human life.[28] The goal is to keep the natural forces in balance,
to tap into these forces, and in this way to center oneself, one's family, and
one's community; in short, to live. This economy of energies is composed
of several elements: Bondye (the supreme power), the manifestations of
Bondye, the *lwas (loas)* or *mysteres* (of which there are over one thousand),
ancestors *(les morts)*, other spirits, earthbound humans, animals, plants,
and other objects.

Bondye is responsible for the creation of the universe and maintaining
the cosmic balance that allows for the continuation of the world.
Consequently, Bondye, rather like Mawu-Lisa, is not actively involved in
human affairs, yet is understood as just. According to some of those who
live in the Plaisance region, God does not come to humans but rather meets
the gods *(loas)* between heaven and earth and responds to the requests that
the *loas* bring from humanity. God either grants the petition or rejects it.[29]
The *lwas* or *loas,* also referred to as *les invisibles* or *les mysteres,* are directly
involved in human life. These beings are the manifestations of Bondye and,
in many instances, correspond to elements of our physical environment or,
in the words of Maya Deren, "archetypal representative[s] of some natural
or moral principle."[30] Although often manifested in the physical realm, they
are metaphysical, and what receives the *serviteurs'* (believers') attention is
the energy behind the symbol—*les invisibles.*

Vodou practitioners made use of Haiti's Catholic environment and associated or masked the *loas* with catholic saints in order to avoid persecution.[31] As mentioned earlier, a large number of *lwas* play a vital role within
Haitian life; however, this chapter is limited to a brief discussion of ten
widely recognized *loa,* and this discussion focuses on overviews of generic
attributes without reference to the particular manifestations of the *loa,* and
without extended attention to regional differences (see Figure 2).

The centrality of Legba, associated with Christ or Saint Peter, is undeniable. Legba has various manifestations within vodou. Referred to as Papa
Legba he is, like many of the *loas,* depicted as Haitian—to use Desmangles'
and Laguerre's term, creolized. In keeping with his creole status and identification with the rural location of many practitioners, Papa Legba is often
pictured with typical attire—jeans and work shirt. He is also understood as
having a crutch or cane and smoking a pipe, with peasant bag in tow.[32]
Legba is an intermediary and keeper of the gate and the crossroads. In this
capacity, Legba is responsible for relying messages between the *lwas* and
between the *lwas* and humans.[33] Because of these functions, Legba is essen-

tial to life and ritual. Without his assistance the "gate" remains closed, communication with the cosmic powers is impossible, and, consequently necessary resources and health are denied. In order to assure his cooperation, he must be approached first with thanks, praise, and gifts. In addition to his function as keeper of the gate, Legba punishes those who fail in their obligations. He also has the potential to trick devotees, hence his depiction as the Trickster. Because he is a trickster, Christians often associated him with the biblical figure Satan. Yet he is not evil in the Christian sense. Each *loa* is associated with a *veve* or sacred drawing that centers the energy and represents the *loa*. For Papa Legba, the *veve* entails the crossing of the two worlds and is represented by two crossed lines with a staff on the horizontal line's right side.[34]

Also of tremendous importance is Erzulie, associated with the Virgin Mary. She is responsible for taking care of the temple. Erzulie is also associated with love, beauty, and the sexual self. Within the realm of nature, Erzulie is associated with the waters, but she can also be found in the woods. She is known for her tremendous number of lovers and is thus referred to as Mistress (Maitresse Erzulie). She is often depicted as a young and beautiful woman; however, like the other *lwas*, she appears in many forms, including that of an old woman.[35] Erzulie is known to be very jealous and requires devotion. For example, men who are selected by her must set a room or space aside for her in their home, a space for loving her. The *veve* for Erzulie represents her relationship to love and love-making—an elaborately drawn heart.

One cannot forget Damballah,[36] the *loa* associated with the rainbow and often manifest as a snake. Damballah is often referred to as the "Father" (the first member of the Christian Trinity); yet his representation is not limited to this. He is also seen as Saint Patrick (because of Saint Patrick's connection with the snakes of Ireland). Because Damballah (often associated with Dan addressed earlier) dwells in water, each temple *(oum'phor)* recognizing him builds a shallow pool or basin for his use. Although he has been one of Erzulie's lovers, he lives with his wife A(y)ida Wedo (Our Lady of the Immaculate Conception). Due to his grace and strength, his presence speaks to stability and harmony. The security his grace provides also stems from Damballah's age: he is as old as humanity. Unlike other *loas*, who communicate verbally with devotees, Damballah's only sound is the hissing of a snake. His communication is based solely upon dreams and psychic "knowing." The *veve* for Damballah consists of two snakes—one on the right and one on the left side with a goblet between the two snakes (with the mason emblem) and an egg (one of his foods) above the goblet—and thereby highlights his existence as the primordial snake.

The imagery generated by Damballah or Danbala's representation as a snake extends beyond this particular *loa*. The sign of the snake as rainbow, for example, speaks to Bondye's means of communication between the two worlds and, according to Milo Rigaud, the machete (*ku-bha-sah* or "the greatest has destroyed all material") held by Ogou is symbolic of Damballah in the form of a serpent. Ogou, associated with St. James on a white horse battling unbelievers, is Vodou's *loa* of iron and battle, protecting devotees as they fight forces opposed to their survival. He is also, at times, linked with alchemy and herbal work. This association with alchemy and herbs is important, because many hold that the iron worker, Ogou, is responsible for providing humans with the secrets of vodou.[37] In some areas of Haiti, the *veve* for Ogou is dominated by the depiction of Ogou's machete; above this instrument is a design housing two dissecting lines (with perpendicular lines and diagonal lines intersecting) curled at their ends. And on either side of this is a flag containing various symbols.

Agwe (Agoué) is the *loa* of the sea, the protector of the sea. He is one of Erzulie's lovers (others say husband), and his symbol is a boat or a fish. With respect to Catholicism, he is associated with Saint Ulrich. According to Desmangles, the connection between this Catholic saint and Agwe stems from Saint Ulrich's depiction with a fish in one hand.[38] Those who have dealings with the sea by occupation seek the assistance of this *loa*.

Haitians are not only dependent upon the waters; they also have a strong relationship with the land because of the agricultural occupation of most practitioners. This aspect of life, this component of creation, is controlled by Cousin Zaka, the *loa* of agriculture, associated with Saint John the Baptist.[39] Cousin Zaka's identification with the country and the peasant class is represented by his traditional attire—a straw hat to protect from the harsh sun, shoulder bag, and machete for work. He can also, however, manifest himself as the Minister of Agriculture—refined and sophisticated.[40] Zaka's connection with the land is also suggested by the sound of his voice, which resembles the cry of a goat. Furthermore, just as Erzulie is associated with many loves, Zaka is considered desirous of many women. He is depicted symbolically in a *veve* containing a rectangle with two horizontal lines dissected by five vertical lines. On the outside of this rectangle are: on the left a machete and on the right a sickle. On top is another sickle and below the rectangle is an arch over a box covered with various symbols.

Cousin Zaka's brother is Gede (first of the Guedes or Gede deities), the lord of the cemetery, associated with Saint Gerard because both are concerned with family. Whereas Legba is often related to destiny and therefore life, the Gede *loas* are associated with death, the underworld, and the dead. Those who seek the counsel of the ancestors must first address Gede, Lord of the Dead. Interestingly enough, both Legba and Gede are associated with fertility. This becomes obvious in the sensual and sexual gestures and word-play many Guedes engage in with devotees. Because of their strong connection with sexuality, women look to the Guedes for sexual prowess and fertility. As with other *loas*, Guedes, too, have many manifestations, the chief of which is the most "American" of the *loas*, Baron Samedi. Sensual gestures and rude comments are not lost with Baron Samedi, who is often associated with control over death and reanimation of humans as zombies. The Baron's wife, Gran Brigit is also associated with the sexual aspects of life. According to legend, Gran Brigit was a ritual prostitute who performed for Baron Samedi, and from their sexual activity the Guedes were born.[41] Those who are possessed by a Guede (in the form of Baron Samedi) seek out the traditional clothing of these *loas*—black clothing, black hat, and sunglasses. Associated with hungry beggars, Gede *loas* are not afraid to appear during rituals not intended for them. And whereas rituals begin with respect paid to Legba, they end with acknowledgment of the Guede; hence, the intimate link between life and death is acknowledged. Also of interest is the fact that their rituals take place between Rada and Petro ceremonies and as a result they are not ultimately connected with either.[42] The *veve* for the Guede is a cross upon a grave-like mound.

The importance of the earth and agriculture is present not only with devotion to Cousin Zaka, but also in the attention given to Papa Loko, guardian of fields and "king of vegetation." Because of this close relationship with the land and its produce, Papa Loko plays a central role in healing and health issues. This control over the land and its produce also relates to his sense of balance—justice and equality. It is easy to understand the importance of this *loa* because of Haiti's need for the land's produce and communal cooperation: ritual activities are not strictly individual in nature but are communal and relate to the land. As a result of this, Loko—represented by a butterfly—is also understood as the protector of ritual space, and patron of the priesthood.

With Haiti's high infant mortality rate, it is not odd that the Marassa (Dosou Dosa)—divine twins—are extremely important. Within the cosmological story, the Marassa are twins who died early in life and now appear during ritual activities requesting goods, a request that must be met to ensure ritual success. According to Deren, the twins symbolize human nature: half matter and half soul. Furthermore, the twins are said to be the first of God's children and are often, in this respect, related to the Christ figure—half God and half human—divine offspring. In addition to this association, they are also connected to Guede as the first dead.[43] The *veve* for the Marassa consists of three circles connected by a horizontal and highly stylized line, with each circle cut through the middle by a vertical and stylized line.

The context of slavery involved an absurdity and fostered an anger that could not be handled through the gentle and balancing attributes of the Rada *loas* discussed above. In response, Petro (or Pethro) rituals and *loas* emerged as a "New World" development. These *loas* are aggressive and exacting, capable of supporting violent activities. The benevolent nature of the Dahomean *loa* had to respond to a threat against the moral order of life. And so "the traditional defensive, protective attitude could not suffice where there was no longer anything organized or solid to defend. It was a moment of specific and urgent need: The need for action."[44] These new "American" *loas* had a more aggressive approach to problem solving and allowed Haitians to match the violent and aggressive nature of a social order bent toward domination. Whereas Rada rituals and *loas* are "cool," providing balance, Petro rituals and *loas* are aggressive and angry. The distinctions are symbolized by the use of ritual water with Rada *loas* and ritual rum with Petro *loas*—coolness and heat. This is not meant to imply that Petro *loas* are dangerous for devotees and are limited to aggression, or that Rada *loas* are restricted to generosity and coolness; nothing could be further from the truth. The manifestations of the *loas* in daily life depend in great part upon the devotees. That is to say, the direction and intent of cosmic energy is guided by priests, priestesses, and devotees who petition for certain effects. In this way both *nanchons* (groupings of gods) are capable of help and harm. Energy is amoral.

The Petro *loas* are not, for the most part, distinctive or separate from Rada *loas*. Rather, they are alternate manifestations of the same *loas,* the same energy bent in another direction and meeting divergent needs. Because the relationship between the *loas* and humans is pragmatic and somewhat utilitarian, nation status (petro and rada being the two central *loa* nations) does not create barriers with respect to ritual use. Nevertheless, it is worth noting the Petro manifestation of some *loas* discussed above.

Those who seek Legba in Petro rituals call for Kafou (Carrefour) Legba.

Manifested in this way, Kafou Legba is at the height of his magical and trickster abilities and aggressively protects and monitors the crossroads. Unlike the Rada manifestation described above, Petro Legba is young, physically fit, and strong. Kafou Legba maintains control over destiny and demons, but a control that can result in misfortune for those who are not careful in their service to Kafou Legba. Nonetheless, careful devotees stand to make tremendous gain through the power of Kafou.

The intensification of certain character traits noted between Papa Legba and Kafou Legba is mirrored in the Petro Erzulie served in the form of Ezili Je-Rouge (red eye) or Ezili Danto. Within this Petro "mode," Ezili is a woman of rage who can inflict destruction on those who fail in their obligations to her. She can also provide protection and guidance for those who must act aggressively in order to survive an ordeal or painful situation. Here Ezili remains the exemplar of womanhood, but womanhood extending beyond sensual allure by embracing the ability to act for preservation. It is this Ezili who fights alongside warriors—sensuality combined with the instinct of a soldier.

The battle savvy and aggression of a warrior is found in the Rada Ogou and is intensified in the Petro manifestation named Ogou Ferary. Through Ogou Ferary practitioners have contact with and protection from a supreme strategist and military might. He is recognized by the iron that protects him from harm and with which he inflicts punishment on his (and his devotees') enemies. Those who seek his assistance must do so with great care; misconduct of any kind can result in tremendous loss and physical harm. In this *loa* is the balance between the pleasures of life (i.e., consumption of rum) and survival/defiance (i.e., expertise in battle).

The care shown in addressing Petro's Ogou Ferary must also be displayed when petitioning Petro's manifestation of Gede energy—Baron la Koa, etc. The relationship between Legba and Gede—life and death, destiny and destruction—is heightened here. Baron la Koa and the other Petro manifestations of the more than thirty Gedes are represented by a black cross, and they viciously guard the cemetery and the access to Ginen it symbolizes. The Petro manifestations of Gede more sharply unleash cosmic forces—spirits to harm enemies and punish the disobedient. They also display an even greater hunger than the Rada manifestations, seeking food constantly and turning on devotees who fail to satisfy this urge. In this way, Petro's Baron la Koa, Baron Samedi, Baron La Croix, and other manifestations impose on themselves rituals and thus emphasize the inevitability of life's connection to death.

Although found in both Petro and Rada, the next *loa* is often approached only through the Petro. Simbi serves as keeper of springs and ponds. Like Damballah, Simbi is associated with snakes and, like Legba, he is believed to facilitate communication between Petro deities and humans. He is connected to both Ginen and the earth—the two worlds. Although reluctant to involve himself in ritual functions, Simbi is still capable of great magic and as such is associated with magicians. In essence, he embodies all *loa* energies. His *veve*—a snake among crosses—points to his primal position and relationship to the crossroads, the balance or meeting of all things.

Whereas Damballah and Legba serve to center Rada rites and Simbi links the two "major" *nanchons,* Dan Petro (or Ti-Jean Petro, Escalie Boumba, Makaia Boumba, Palman-nan Boumba) grounds the Petro rites. Some argue that Don Pedro (Dan Petro) was a maroon responsible for the Petro rites. This is highly debatable. What one can safely and reasonably say, however, is that Dan Petro is associated with the earliest manifestations of Petro energy and as such is considered the "father" of the Petro *loa*. Hence, he is an essential component of any discussion of these rites and *loa*.[45] Furthermore, because of his central role as the head of the *loa* pantheon, Dan Petro is intimately associated with the Haitian Revolution and the energy that made it possible. In keeping with his role as energy toward transformation, Dan Petro helps devotees pay back mistreatment.

Despite some disagreement over the genealogy of Petro *loas,* it is safe to say that they played some role in the Haitian revolution and earlier revolts.[46] Those who rely on Mederick Louis Moreau de St. Mery tend to assert that the Petro cult stems from the activities of one Don Pedro, a black Spaniard and possibly a member of a maroon community. The off-beat dances initiated by this figure were aggressive and violent and are said to have sparked rebellion in the hearts of slave participants. Yet it can be argued that the Petro cults arose not with Don Pedro but from Indian and African contact during the Spaniards' control over the island. Furthermore, many dances and names found within Petro rites are undeniably of Indian origin.[47]

With respect to the Revolution many argue that Boukman, a plantation slave who used Vodou ritual and dance, gathered African slaves empowered by the *loas*. According to George E. Simpson:

> In order to produce greater unity among the rebels. . . he [Boukman] conducted an impressive ceremony during the night of August 14, 1791. After an enormous crowd had assembled a violent storm arose, and in the midst of thunder and lightening an old Negro woman appeared, danced

wildly, sang, and brandished a huge cutlass over her head. Finally, the silenced and fascinated crowd saw her plunge the cutlass into the throat of a black hog. The slaves drank the animal's blood and swore they would execute Boukman's orders. . . .[48]

Although Boukman's efforts were not successful, the link between religion and rebellion was forged, and revolution would eventually—with the help of vodou—liberate enslaved Haitians.[49]

In addition to the Petro and Rada *loas* there are "lesser" spirits whom devotees contact for specific tasks. Within this group are those relatively weak spirits such as Congo Ouangol and Congo Zando. These spirits are members of the Congo (Kongo) *nanchon,* those *loas* of the Congo who have remained distinguishable from Rada and Petro manifestations.[50] Congo spirits are known for their joviality and fine dressing. They tend to be gregarious and rather good-natured, and are regarded as responsible for returning Haitians back to Africa when desired. There are also several Igbo *loas* who have continued independent of Rada, Petro, and Congo *loas.* Unlike Congo spirits, Igbo spirits tend to be aggressive and angry. The major spirit of this group is Igbo Lele, who is "a capricious spirit" yet concerned with the overall welfare of Congos in the "New World."[51]

There are spirits, referred to as *baka,* who do the bidding of the *loas.* Within the cosmic hierarchy they come below the *loas. Baka* (malevolent spirits) are also at the service of humans (referred to as *bocor* or magicians) who "buy" them for select tasks. Such purchases have great benefit, but *baka* are exacting spirits who easily and quickly turn on those they serve. The *baka,* are actually capable of operating under good or evil energy, depending upon the nature of the request made by the baka's employer. The *loas,* as a general rule, are served in order to foster healthy community as an extension of individual requests, whereas the *baka* are manipulated to provide individual gain at the expense of community values and health.

Vodou's cosmological framework is not limited to the *loa* and spirits "for hire." The ancestors are also important. Many devotees believe that those who die as a result of Bondye's will—that is, naturally—ascend and reap the consequences of their earthly actions. Some ancestors, because of their importance and their tremendous activities (for good or ill), become *loa* while others are reconnected to the extended family through reincarnation.

Ancestors must be remembered because of the link they represent between the two worlds. And with this in mind, devotees say: "I believe in the power of ancestors who watch over us and serve us before the lwas; that they must be remembered and served faithfully."[52] Vodou understands itself as responsible for maintaining the memory of the ancestors—their home, deeds, and words. Respect and appreciation for the ancestors maintains epistemological and ontological connection with a life that extends beyond existential hardship. Memory and reverence, then, remove geographical and chronological distance between Haitians and Ginen.

Humans comprise the next level within vodou's cosmological design. It is useful to define the human in terms of the two "souls" or "angels" that make up the essential self. These two components are housed within the human head. The first is the *ti-bon-anj*—the little, good soul—which allows for self-evaluation, ethical and moral conduct. It is, in essence, the personality. It is the spirit (*espri*) or guardian.[53] The *gwo-bon-anj* (or *gros-bon-ange*) corresponds to human intelligence and historical recollection and is commonly depicted as the soul.[54] It is the further development of this latter component that some suggest separates humans from *loas*. The latter, of course, are more developed and refined. The little soul (*ka*, or *ti-bon-anj*), if not properly cared for after death, stays with the dead body and feeds off it. This neglected soul becomes the baka and can be used by religious experts as mentioned above. The grand soul (*ba* or *gwo-bon-anj* or *gros-bon-ange*) is associated with the essence of the human that ascends, at death, for "judgment" and "reward." In some cases the *gwo-bon-anj* gains *loa* status through communal memory and through close association with a particular *loa* by means of shared attributes and manifestation. Vodun rites and knowledge, in essence, help devotees to develop their *gwo-bon-anj* and thereby live a good and responsible life.

A ceremony held for the dead, the *retirer d'en bas de l'eau*, allows the *ka* to find peace and union with the ascended *ba*. This entails the third birth (the first two being physical birth and second birth through religious initiation). Ancestors "reclaimed" in this way gain new status, not merely as family members but as powers who influence physical health and happiness. The reclaimed spirit is housed in a clay jar referred to as a *govi*. Ancestors who are not reclaimed remain in Ginen and take the form of animals and insects. It is understood that after a true death (as opposed to one caused by magic), the *ti-bon-anj* remains close to the body for nine days prior to removal to heaven. Ultimately the death rituals, which are cleansing rituals, prevent the *ti-bon-anj* from reuniting with the body. The most prominent ritual serves ultimately to separate the *gwo-bon-anj* and the *loa* of the head (*loa mait-tete*) from the physical body. The final contact with the dead occurs roughly one year after death, when the soul is ritually collected and housed in the *govi*.[55]

Figure 2. Partial List of *Loas*

African Name	Rada/Saint/Petro Name	Functional Identification/Color
Mawa-Lisa	Bondye Creator	
Legba	Papa Legba/St. Peter/ Kafou Legba	Trickster, Messenger/red
Aziri	Ezili/Virgin Mary/ Ezili Je-Rouge	River Goddess, Goddess of Love/blue, pink
Da Ayido	Damballah/St. Patrick	Primordial Serpent/white
Gu	Ogou/St. James/ Ogou Ferary	God of Iron and War/red
Agbe	Agwe/St. Ulrich (Ulrique)	Protector of the Sea/ white, green, pink
Zaka	Zaka/St. John the Baptist/St. Isidore	God of Agriculture/ blue, red, green
Gede	Gede/St. Gerard or St. Expedite/Baron	Lord of Cemeteries, Death/black
Loko	Papa Loko	God of Agriculture/yellow
Hohovi	Marassa	Sacred Twins
	Jean Petro	Leader of Petro *Loa*
	Petro Simbi	Guardian of Ponds/black, grey
	Petro Bosou	Spirit of Military Might

Adapted from Robert Farris Thompson, *Flash of the Spirit;* Milo Rigaud, *Secrets of Voodoo,* trans. Robert B. Cross (San Francisco: City Lights Books, 1953); and Laennec Hurbon, *Voodoo: Search for the Spirit,* trans. Lory Frankel (New York: Harry N. Abrams, 1995).

The energies and cosmic realities discussed above are held in balance through ritual structures that allow for mutual benefit. The world is kept orderly, human needs are met, and the *loas* as well as the ancestors receive the respect and admiration they require. For this to occur, ritual space, ritual experts, ritual activities, and doctrinal schemes are necessary.

It has already been stated that vodou is rather decentralized, without an overarching governance body. This allows for doctrinal, ritual, and theological differences between various locations of practice. The spaces in which ritual is acted out, however, the spaces used for fellowship between humans and the *loas*, are relatively similar. The ritual space—which houses ritual instruments, areas, and ritual participants—is the temple *(oum'phor* or *hounfor*).[56] The inner area of the *oum'phor* typically consists of a space in which the *veves* are drawn and the *loa* manifest themselves. These sacred drawings are made around the center post of the *oum'phor* referred to as the *poteaumian* or *poteau-mitan* ("solar support"), connected to the courtyard known as the *peristyle*. In some respects, the central post is symbolic of Legba in that both represent the link between worlds, the connection between Ginen and earth.[57] There are separate peristyles for Rada (the larger of the two) and Petro rites whenever the finances of the *oum'phor* allow.[58] One may also find on the walls of the *oum'phor* drawings designating the *loas* served by the temple's members. Other ritual items housed in the *oum'phor* are a continuously burning fire with a metal rod in it (representing Ogou) and a whip attached to the poteaumian that signifies the service-gain relationship upon which vodou is premised. One also finds the mound and cross associated with Guede and the pool used by Damballah, among other significant objects. On the main wall one sees the symbol of the *loa* who "owns" the temple and the temple's coat of arms. There, too, are hung the vodou flags associated with the *oum'phor*. These flags tell a great deal about the *loas* associated with the *oum'phor;* the colors of the flags correspond to the colors of the *loas,* and the detailed designs signal the importance of properly recognizing the *loa* with beauty and allegiance. Also of importance is the sword, Ogou's machete (the *ku-bha-sah*), carried and used during ceremonies to kill the sacrificial animals. Other common items are stones and trees understood as dwelling places for the *loas* and spirits.

Off the central area are smaller rooms, some dedicated to particular *loas,* and the *djevo* (*ghuevo*) or room used for initiation ceremonies. Because initiation in Vodou represents death and rebirth, the *djevo* is symbolic of the tomb in which the old self gives way as knowledge and spiritual insight are gained. Housed in another room of limited access is the pe or altar—the altar room.[59] This room is of limited access because, unlike the *oum'phor's* outer areas, nonritual activities are never conducted in the altar room. On this altar are the symbols of certain *loa,* the *gejo* pots mentioned earlier, and the *pots-de-tete* (pots containing the spiritual essence of those initiated in the temple).

Also of undeniable importance as ritual tools are the vodou drums (the voices of the *loa*) used during the course of every gathering. Drums are interesting components of the *oum'phor* because they enjoy status close to that of the *loa,* with a degree of independence not associated with other items. In addition, they are fed and put to bed in order to renew their strength daily. Each *nanchon* has its own set of drums. Beginning with Rada, there are three drums named in descending order based upon size: the *Manman,* the Second, and the *Bou-Lah.* They represent the three layers of the atmosphere: chromosphere, photosphere, and the solar nucleus. In this way they are also related to Legba, who centers ritual structures because he is the means of communication between two worlds. Because these drums are not used for Petro rituals, another set of drums is required. The two Petro drums are the *Quebiesou Dan Leh* (the larger of the two) and the *Sakbha Lah Tha Vovo Lih Vo.* These two drums are considered "hot" because of the *loas* they call; consequently, they are "thunder," an energy difficult to control by all but the most talented drummers. The final set of drums is for the Congo *nanchon;* the *Manman* (the largest), the *Grondez,* and the *Ka-Tha-Bou* (the smallest). It should be noted that when financially necessary, Congo or Ibo rituals can be performed using Petro or Rada drums.[60] In addition to these drums, the most powerful drum is the large *Assato* drum, which, because of its power, has restricted use extending beyond what was outlined for the Petro and Rada drums. Spiritual power that operates through and is embodied in the drums must be periodically renewed if the drums are to continue their usefulness.[61] This is true of every element related to vodun worship; every object and every space must be baptized in the name of the *loa* and thereby opened for infusion with divine energy. There now arises the question of who uses these ritual tools and ritual space.

Levels of participation in Vodou are premised upon levels of knowledge and expertise—levels of initiation—which correspond to degrees of involvement and responsibility. The highest level of attainment is that of *houn'gan* (priest) or *mambo* (priestess). The *houn'gan* (or papa-loa) and the *mambo* (mama) have the most direct contact with the *loas* because of their attainment of knowledge and training.[62] They have learned the likes and dislikes of the *loa,* how to call them to work, and how to "control" their activities for the good of the petitioners. In addition to this knowledge, they are well versed in the use of tools such as palm reading and fortune telling with tarot cards. The treatments given by the *mambo* or *houn'gan* address physical illness caused by environment and by psychological destruction. In essence, although referral to doctors is not uncommon, the *houn'gan* addresses the holistic healing of clients in a way that "modern" medicine does not. The balance between this knowledge and action is delicate because the priest or priestess "is dependent upon the continuity of a circular, or rather spiral process by which his control over the *loa* gives him access to greater divine power; this he must in turn properly serve in order to control it, and he must constantly demonstrate achievement."[63] The distinguishing marks of the *mambo* or *houn'gan* are the *asson* and *clochette* (bell) they carry. Together, the *clochette* and *asson* represent the cosmic powers of Africa and are used to summon these powers. Inside the *asson,* made from a calabash and wooden handle, are snake vertebrae and other items that, when shaken, make a rattling sound. This rattling is the sound of the ancestors and *loa,* it is cosmic speech. The beads found on the outside of the *asson* represent the rainbow and its power. The possession of the *asson,* obtained by means of an *asson* taking ceremony, symbolizes the connection with the eternal powers.[64] The *oum'phor* members are not only trained by oral tradition, but they also learn by observing manifestations of power. Thus there is constant competition to keep practitioners within one's *oum'phor* by both spoken knowledge and demonstrated ritual prowess.

The next level of authority within the *oum'phor* contains the various assistants to the *houn'gan* or *mambo.*[65] These include the *houn'sih ventailleur,* a member of the société who is responsible for obtaining sacrificial animals; the *houn'sih cuisiniere,* who cooks the sacrifice remains; the *reine silence,* who serves as the sergeant at arms, maintaining order during ceremonies; the *houn'torguiers,* who are the drummers, and the *ogantier* who plays the ogan. In addition, the *houn'guenicon quartier-maitre* distributes sacrificial meats to members of the *oum'phor* after the completion of ritual activities. The *houn'guenicon caille* maintains the *oum'phor,* while the *mam'bo caille* is an apprentice to the *houn'gan* or *mambo.*[66] The *hounsi carzo*—*hounsi* who have gone through the trial by fire—have some control over the *loa* due to their initiation and thus they have important ritual responsibilities.

The remaining members of this group are described in more detail because of their large ceremonial roles. The first is *la place,* the bearer of Ogou's sword, who begins ritual activities by leading the salutations to the key elements of the *oum'phor,* such as the center-post, drums, *houn'gans* and *mambos,* as well as the four cardinal points—north, south, east, and west. In this way, the proper order of ceremonial activities and the various relationships are maintained and shown reverence. Accompanying *la place* during this initial stage of activity are two female *houn'sih* who serve as flag bearers (the *co-drapeaux,* fully initiated members of the *oum'phor*). The larger body of *houn'sihs* is important because they comprise the ritual chorus that marks off segments of the ritual, including the manifestation of various *loas,* through song and dance.[67] This chorus communicates with the *loas* encouraging them to descend and guiding their actions once they are present. In larger measure, the success of their dancing and singing determines the effectiveness of the sacrifice and other ritual activities.

Also of ritual importance is the "bush priest" *(pret-savanne)*, who begins vodou ceremonies with Catholic prayers and recognition of the saints in order to secure the cooperation of the Christian God and to ensure proper ritual progression.[68] From this figure's functional importance one sees the degree to which Catholicism has blended, albeit unevenly, with vodou. Recognition of Catholicism with vodou through prayers and songs is followed by the "heating up" of the service through songs and recognition of the *loas.* The bush priest and other officials are rounded out by the general body of *serviteurs* (those possessed by *loa* during rituals), devotees who are not open to possession, and curious observers.

For practitioners, the structure and expense of service to the *loa* is essential because it provides for the basic spiritual and physical needs of life; the energy necessary to maintain "balance" is available through communication with and attention to the cosmic forces.[69] When the *loas* are fed during ceremonies they are obligated to provide for their servants. Service to the *loas* does not mean blind obedience. Events are never unquestioned because they are associated with the divine. The will of God does not move events beyond human inquiry; rather, *loas* served properly are called to give an account of events and deeds. Functionality and utility give shape to the relationship between *loas* and *serviteurs.* The best evidence of this exchange occurs through possession—a practitioner "mounted" by a *loa.* During possession, the *loa* manifests and provides information for various persons gathered, reveals their flaws, and suggests alterations in behavior or attitude. In addition, healings take place and social relations are renewed as a *loa* reproaches those who have acted improperly and forces those who have harmed community to make amends. More directly relevant to the "horse" or devotee mounted is the energy or "power" given to surmount obstacles and challenges. This closeness to cosmic energy and power renews a vital sense of self and provides the grounding or revitalization necessary to survive the hardships of Haitian life. Through possession, devotees are reminded of their place in the cosmos and community.[70]

Intermingled with attempts to destroy *vodou* has been an appreciation for its power to orientate, to adapt and persist. The revolution already mentioned is the first example of this. Another prominent example from the recent past is the use of vodou by the Duvalier regime (1957–86) to maintain control over the island populace. Although various Haitian leaders made use of vodou or attempted to destroy it through the country's troubled political history (including the U.S. occupation, 1915–34, and Catholicism's resulting growth), none reached the severity of the Duvalier years. "Papa Doc's" use of Vodou as a political weapon began with his desire to recognize and appreciate the Africanness of Haiti and to reflect this in the Catholic Church and its officials in Haiti. As part of this effort, he replaced many foreign church officials with Haitians, which resulted in more tolerance toward Haitian cultural practices and ideals. Vodou practitioners were no longer harassed by the government. In fact, Papa Doc's government sponsored many ceremonies.

Papa Doc also recognized that the respect accorded vodou priests and priestesses could be used to solidify his control over the island. Their compliance with his desires and dictates could bring about the acquiescence of the larger population. In order to achieve this, Papa Doc gained the allegiance of Vodou's most feared elements—controllers of *baka* and those relying upon Petro—and housed them within his secret military force referred to as the Tontons-Macoutes. In 1986, with the fall of the regime, these *houn'gans* faced the wrath of Haiti's population, and a greater degree of "balanced" Vodou practice was recognized. Even before this many Haitians fled Haiti taking with them their religious traditions; among their destinations were major East Coast cities in the United States. Yet this is not the first instance of political transformation resulting in diasporic movement. The Haitian revolution that ended in 1804 had the same effect, the movement of Haitians to other Caribbean locations and the United States (e.g., New Orleans). With this movement, vodou in its third wave of practice gained additional "New World" devotees. But was this the United States' first exposure to these Vodou-related practices?

THE UNITED STATES AND VOODOO

Most scholars acknowledge strong African religious practices in the Caribbean and South America because of large numbers of slaves and the presence of Catholicism that easily lent itself to syncretism with African deities. Yet if we keep in mind that religious conversion in large numbers came late to the North American colonies, it is insufficient to dismiss the presence of African gods simply because of a less than welcoming environment. In light of hush arbors' (or secret gatherings of slaves) potential for religious reenactment and retention, it is conceivable that the religious orientation elsewhere known as Vodou survived in the United States in theologically complex ways prior to strong Haitian immigration. Perhaps what Haitian immigration sparked was not new practice, but rather the memory of former ways, softened by the years but not forsaken. One need only look at African American religious expression without assuming Christianity as normative to conclude that it would be feasible and fruitful to pursue this theory.[71]

Although one cannot convincingly argue for a voodoo presence as strong as that of African American Christian churches in terms of numbers, open practice, and possibly influence, the words of Jessie Gaston Mulira are important: "The word and the system arrived in North America when the first Africans landed in Jamestown in 1619 as indentured servants. The number of voodoo worshippers increased as more Africans arrived, first as indentured servants and later as slaves directly from Africa or through the West Indies, where African slaves were introduced as early as 1504. With the influx of more Africans, voodoo became entrenched in the North American colonies and later in the United States."[72] Add this statement to the words of Albert Raboteau, who writes:

> Louisiana bought the first slaves from the islands of Martinique, Guadeloupe, and Saint-Dominique as early as 1716, when five hundred were imported, followed by three thousand more during the next year. Slaves from the French West Indies continued to enter Louisiana until after prohibitions hindered import. A decree of the Spanish governor Galvez in 1782 forbade further importation of slaves from the island of Martinique because "these negroes are too much given to voodooism and make the lives of the citizens unsafe." In 1792 slaves from Saint-Dominique were also banned, though some were allowed to enter when their masters were granted asylum at the outbreak of the Haitian revolution. In 1803 the United States acquired Louisiana and the ban on West Indian slaves was lifted.[73]

In spite of the fact that by 1860 more than 90 percent of the slaves in the United States were native-born, how can scholars assume with certainty that clandestine slave meetings served only to nurture black Christian thoughts and practices?[74] It is possible that the system of voodoo did not die or survive only in the form of hoodoo or conjure, but rather that it remained "hidden" until it was again safe to acknowledge participation and to refine practices.[75] The various combinations of African ethnic groups in areas such as South Carolina and Georgia could result in new religious combinations without the eradication of the African gods. As Charles Joyner comments, "Many slaves in the South Carolina and Georgia lowcountry continued to embrace African supernatural beliefs that were not incorporated into African American Christianity but instead persisted in a kind of parallel stream."[76] It is likely that the Christian "God the Father" replaced other representations of the African high God, but this does not mean that lesser deities died nor could they have been completely consumed in the persons of Christ and the Holy Spirit. For example, the abilities and personality traits of the various divinities could be represented in the antics of culture heroes such as High John the Conqueror. This thinking, I believe, is affirmed in the conversation of African Americans in Georgia such as Thomas Smith, who argues that the power used by Moses (whom Theophus Smith calls a conjurer) exists among African Americans in the United States: "Well den, duh descendants ub Africans hab duh sam fig tuh do unnatchul ting. Ise heahd duh story uh duh flyin Africans an I sho belief it happen."[77] Thomas Smith is not alone in believing that Africans in North America had a special connection to cosmic, life-altering forces.

The testimonies of many slaves and former slaves speak to alternative forms of religious expression alive on plantations. For example, Leonard Haynes's relative says the following concerning Mr. Haynes: "My grandfather of three generations came over from the Gold Coast of Africa and was sold to a Mr. Haynes in Georgia. My grandfather was an African priest. This fact made him hostile to Christian preachers and to the religion of the Christians. Hence, he refused to join with the other slaves in their religious gatherings. . . ."[78] Charles Joyner records the words of fugitive slave Charles Ball, words that shed light on the cosmology that priests like Haynes might have preferred to Christian cosmology: "At the time I first went to Carolina, there were a great many African slaves in the country. . . . Many of them believed there were several gods; some of whom were good, and others evil."[79] Because of relative isolation, the Gullah of South Carolina maintained many African religious practices with respect to spirits, rituals, and other elements.[80] Similar practices may also be the point of contention in the following comment on the part of a traveler through Florida (1870): "At one of the Protestant churches, here [St. Augustine, Florida], and subsequently at Jacksonville, we saw shocking mummies, which belonged to the [fetish] worship of savage Central Africa, and not of Christian America."[81]

Additional examples abound. The two-volume collection by Harry Middleton Hyatt, *Hoodoo—Conjuration—Witchcraft—Rootwork*,[82] provides various accounts of ritual altars and the presence of the African gods. Several of these are given here as a further basis for the existence of a strong and complex tradition that relates to voodoo. One of the more notable links between U.S. "non-Christian" practices and voodoo (in the Caribbean) involves the requirements, temperaments, and nature of the deities. For example, Hyatt records a conversation with a "spiritual worker" who provides the following prayer as one used to bring business and to "open de do' ":

> St. Anthony [elsewhere in the text referred to as St. Peter], open dis do'. St. Anthony, please open de do'. An' dear St. Anthony, who lives in Jesus' love, open dis do'. St. Anthony, ah consecrate mahself to yo' an' use yo' as mah patron saint, an' ah ask yo' tuh keep mah do' open. Ah ask yo' tuh send me customers, St. Anthony, an' ah'll always use yo', through Our Lord givin' yo' de power an' strength tuh send me customers an' give yo' de lights on yore [altar']. . . .[83]

Readers will recall that Legba, the keeper of the gates, is in vodou associated with St. Peter. And so the connection between St. Anthony (or St. Peter) and doors (opportunities) is striking.[84] Further, it is commonly understood that these saints have particular days on which they should receive attention and on which it is most profitable to ask for blessings and benefits. In a manner similar to that found in Haiti, it is necessary to "heat up" or enliven the saints in order for them to perform their work. In keeping with this, these saints are also, at times, given strong drink. One informant who referred to St. Raymond but meant St. Peter indicated that the picture of St. Raymond must be given whiskey, beer, or wine before the request is made.[85]

I do not offer the above examples as proof positive that vodou existed in the United States in the exact form found in Haiti. Rather, my argument is that the cosmology and theological systems associated with vodou and commonly considered lost in the United States are maintained beyond the practice of hoodoo.

The use of saints for communal or individual gain does not reduce the practice to simple religio-magical activity, but preserves ritual enactment in keeping with the Haitian concept of mutual exchange with the *loas*—the goods in exchange for services rendered. And like the Haitian *loas,* U.S. saints are vengeful when the items promised in exchange for favors are not provided. Like their Haitian counterparts, the saints are considered capable of good and evil. One informant tells Hyatt the following concerning St. Peter: "Well, you see, I had promised him a quarter. Well, I wasn't able to give him that quarter that certain day, and I left a little bit of fire in my furnace in my room, locked up, and goes out. When I comes back—I didn't see no way in the world that fire could pop out and set nothing afire. All my clothes and one side of the house was in a light blaze."[86] In comparing this with earlier stories about the *loas*, it becomes clear that the African gods are transformed but not lost in the United States. Vodou in Haiti is, I argue, voodoo in the United States.

The cosmological and theological holdovers presented above provided a theological and ritual base to which vodun from Haiti attached itself. With the successful Haitian revolution, many slave owners fled to Cuba, only to be expelled in 1809. Roughly ten thousand slaves then made their way to New Orleans, bringing with them their vodou tradition. Before the mid-nineteenth century, public gatherings for celebration (ritual activity) in Congo Square were banned, but it was much too late in its development for this to kill voodoo. Furthermore, attempts to vilify the tradition and cast it as evil did not prevent its widespread practice. The "worship" of snakes (a eurocentric perversion of devotion to Damballah manifested as a snake) was considered dangerous, and as a result, the continued importation of slaves from the Caribbean was curtailed.[87] The prohibition of certain voodoo dances, however, and the monitoring of activities allowed near Lake Pontchartrain (Bayou St. John) may have hampered some less credible practitioners and scam artists and diluted late-night ceremonies held for the benefit of curiosity seekers, but it did not prevent devout believers from keeping the tradition alive.[88] Reporters' fantastic accounts of "evil work" could not taint actual and clandestine voodoo.

Private voodoo practices maintained components of the vodou cosmology, most notably Damballah, commonly referred to as Li Grand Zombi. The accounts of voodoo activities were sensationalized and myopic, however, focusing on the "snake cult." Yet the appreciation for and devotion to Li Grand Zombi is profound. Often represented by the snake, Li Grand Zombi is intimately associated with the activities of voodoo practitioners—"Queens"—such as Marie Laveau. Robert Tallant provides this account: "The Queen would begin a chant: L'Appé vini, le Gran Zombi, L'Appé vini, pou fe gris-gris! He is coming, the Great Zombi, he is coming, to make gris-gris!"[89]

The presence of other *loas* is evident within New Orleans voodoo. They include the representation of vodou's Legba, known as Papa Limba. One of Robert Tallant's accounts, also noted by Raboteau, indicates the appeal and presence of this *loa*:

> She went outside and here come Marie Laveau wit' a big crowd of people followin' her. . . . All the people wit' her was hollerin' and screamin', 'We is goin' to see Papa Limba! We is goin' to see Papa Limba!' My grandpa go runnin' after my ma then, yellin at her, 'You come on in here Eunice! Don't you know Papa Limba is the devil?' [This miscorrelation was com-

mon among Christians. Because Legba is a trickster he was often mali-
ciously associated with the Christian's devil.] But after that my ma find
out Papa Limba meant St. Peter, and her pa was jest foolin' her.[90]

This association of Legba (Papa Limba) with St. Peter is telling and con-
cretely connects New Orleans practices with Haitian vodun. This, along
with the earlier stories of St. Peter, serve to confirm the continuation of
voodoo in New Orleans. Also present within early New Orleans voodoo are
Blanc Dani (St. Michael), St. Anthony (Vert Agoussou), and Joe Feraille
(Ogun Feraille). Other Catholic saints who are petitioned for assistance are
St. Expedite (for rapid results), St. Mary (to cure illness), and St. Joseph (to
secure work). The presence of some of these "saints" or *loas* is indicated in
the following statement concerning a girl seeking help with love from a
"voodoo-woman":

> In the room were paintings of the various Catholic saints, and an altar
> before which was a saucer containing white sand, quicksilver, and
> molasses, apexed with a blue candle burning for Saint Joseph (Veriquete).
> All the way through, there is this strange mixture of Catholicism and
> voodooism. The "Madam" kneels at the girl's feet and intones the "Hail
> Mary" of the Church, there is a song to *Liba* (voodoo term for St. Peter)
> and another to *Blanc Dani* (St. Michael). The money collected at the
> seance is put in front of the altar with the sign of the cross.[91]

All of the above *loas* are not necessarily present during each voodoo ceremony, although several of them, such as Li Grand Zombi, are typically present. Raboteau observes:

> Each account mentions the presence of a snake representing the god Li
> Grand Zombi; drumming, singing, dancing; possession, which usually
> begins when the priestess comes into contact with the snake god; oracu-
> lar statements by the possessed priestess and priest; possession of the
> devotees; the pouring of rum or other liquors as a libation to the god; the
> spewing of liquor from the mouth of the priest as a form of blessing;
> Catholic syncretistic elements such as candles, an altar, prayers to the
> Virgin. All of these elements are characteristic of the Haitian's Afro-
> Catholic synthesis as well.[92]

VOODOO LEADERS

Much of voodoo's organizational and ritual thrust, including recognition of
the "saints," centered around certain dominant personalities referred to as
kings and queens. The queens dominated the religious landscape, and
women made up the bulk of voodoo practitioners. The first voodoo priest-

Congo Square, New Orleans, where voodoo ceremonies were held, as it currently looks. Photo by the author.

ess or queen in New Orleans was Sanité Dédé, a free black from the Caribbean. It is commonly held that she dominated New Orleans voodoo from 1822 until 1830. Also important during this time was Marie Saloppé. However, collective memory and voodoo lore center on the queen who displaced these two—Marie Laveau. Born in 1794, Marie Laveau ruled for forty years. Trained by Doctor John—a voodoo-hoodoo doctor—and Marie Saloppé, Marie Laveau began to secure the clients of other practitioners by advertising her powers and magical knowledge.[93] Challengers to her authority were swiftly dealt with, and Laveau used her opponents' unfortunate end as evidence of her voodoo powers. In fact, much of the emphasis on magical practices may have been attempts by religious leaders to maintain their authority and control by relying on the sensational and fantastic to elicit fear and loyalty. If this were the case, only devotees would have been exposed to the true voodoo rituals and theology. Also, advertisements by conjurors often indicated that they were trained in voodoo. This suggests an underlying stratum of voodoo practices and theological knowledge that extends beyond the magical lure of popular practice.

The magical experts flourished during the reign of Marie Laveau, but her time as queen also marked the emergence of a more complex pantheon and the maintenance of refined ritual activity outside of the gaze of the curious. According to Jessie Gaston Mulira, voodoo under Marie Laveau points to this complexity as it

> became an interesting mixture of Catholicism and African–West Indian voodoo worship. This mixture clearly illustrates the Africans' survival abilities. Prayers, incense, candles, holy water, and a host of Catholic saints were added to voodoo paraphernalia. St. John the Baptist became the patron saint of voodoo in New Orleans. St. Michael became "Daniel Blanc," St. Anthony "You Sue [Ogu?]," St. Paul "On za tier," and St. Peter "Legba." Some saints not recognized by the Catholic Church were invented for the specific experiences of blacks. For example, St. Marron, or Maroon, became the black patron saint of runaway slaves. . . . Other Catholic saints were accorded new powers—for instance, St. Raymond for favors and St. Rita for children.[94]

Marie Laveau held sway over the New Orleans voodoo community until 1869, when her advanced years brought the loss of her position.[95] Even after her death in 1881, the name of Marie Laveau remained powerful; and in keeping with the African and Haitian practice of translating highly regarded ancestors into gods or goddesses, Marie Laveau began to function as a *loa*. One sees this in the manner in which voodoo devotees make requests of her in exchange for offerings. The markings on the items left at her grave (St. Louis Cemetery Number One) speak to this position. In the words of one devotee:

> pick up a piece of brick chalk . . . make an "X" on the tomb, tap the left foot three times in the "goopher dust" (soil or marble dust from the tomb), knock on the tomb three times with the left hand, flatten the left hand over the "X" mark, silently make the wish, keep the chalk as a charm.[96]

The importance of Marie Laveau also points to the importance of ancestors within voodoo practice. Scholars have frequently mentioned the attention given to the dead. Items valued by the dead were often placed upon graves in order to appease them and to make their transition easy. It is also understood that the spirits of the dead hold great power that can be used for gain or harm. Those trained to work with spirits can make use of this power. One must be careful in dealing with the newly dead because "[T]he spirit newly released from the body is likely to be destructive. This is why a cloth is thrown over the face of a clock in the death chamber and the looking glass is covered over. The clock will never run again, nor will the mirror ever cast any more reflections if they are not covered so that the spirit cannot see them." In addition to being petitioned for "work," spirits of the dead can also correct for communal or moral shortcomings through recognition of the fault and proper action. According to Zora Neale Hurston, "Sometimes the dead are offended by acts of the living and slap the face of the living. When this happens, the head is slapped one-sided and the victim can never straighten his neck. Speak gently to ghosts, and do not abuse the children of the dead."[97] In general, it was understood that the world was also inhabited by the unseen spirits that interact with humans in both positive and negative ways. And so, it was always best to remember them and to provide for their needs. In one account, an informant says that a feast was always concluded with something for the spirits: "Den wen we all finish, we take wut victuals lef an put it in a dish by duh chimley an das fuh duh sperrit tuh hab a las good meal. We cubbuh up duh dish an deah's many a time Ise heah dat sperrit lif um."[98]

It is said that the daughter of Marie Laveau took over as leader of the "voodoos" and reigned for many years in this position. Others in New Orleans have attempted to establish their voodoo careers by claiming descent from Marie Laveau. Zora Neale Hurston states that she encountered two practitioners, Samuel Thompson and Albert Frechard who claimed to be Marie Laveau's grandnephews.[99] After the Marie Laveaus, voodoo underwent a variety of changes resulting from leadership struggles. Yet those who argue that voodoo in New Orleans degenerated into hoodoo prior to the twentieth century without theological and cosmological refinement and complexity are incorrect. On one level, much genuine activity is kept out of the public eye because of hostility toward practitioners. The Catholic saints continue to function as *loas;* altars remain important, and initiation with recognizably vodou-related symbols continue to take place.

Current practice of voodoo extends beyond mere magical practice in part because of the manner in which the "spirits" possess practitioners. Possession is in keeping with Caribbean and West African ritual activity and differs from a Roman Catholic understanding of the saints and the magical use of herbs and charms associated with conjure. Renaldo J. Maduro provides interesting commentary concerning possession by *loa* in San Francisco (1975). His testimony reinforces the possession by gods often associated with voodoo leaders such as Marie Laveau.[100] Although he uses the term *hoodoo,* his own remarks indicate that he is using the term interchangeably with vodou or voodoo.

> While hoodoo adherents recognize a monotheistic universal godhead, a "Great God," they maintain that he manifests himself through spirits, known also as "loas," and through the catholic saints. The number of actual hoodoo spirits appears to be limited and to provide a vast stylistic

repertoire of both "good and bad" characterizations for individual selection. A spirit may at times be identified with a particular saint, demon, animal, or African deity. For example, one of my patients, a fifty-three-year-old woman in treatment for more than three years is periodically possessed by "the devil," a spirit . . . she knows intimately by the name of "Ramon de la Vera." She speaks in his deep masculine voice and receives important "messages" from him, as well as from other characters belonging to her inner world and hoodoo culture.[101]

Possession by the *loa* is often combined with Christian attitudes and symbolic representations. That is to say, "Devotees seek communication with the supernatural world through spirit possession. This state is spoken of as 'receiving the Holy Ghost . . . being filled . . . being mounted . . . being ridden like a horse. . . .' "[102]

A boost to the public perception of voodoo took place in 1945 when the World Order of Congregational Churches recognized voodoo as a 'legitimate' form of religious expression and activity. This served to recognize publicly the numerous voodoo churches throughout Louisiana responsible for maintaining the tradition. Among those who maintained the practice of voodoo as distinct from hoodoo, in the late twentieth century, is Lady Bishop—Jo Ann McShane. Lady Bishop was trained by practitioners from Haiti and West Africa, and because of her training, she considers herself a "mambo." Lady Bishop began her practice in New Orleans because "St. Barbara asked [her] to bring her [St. Barbara] here . . . and New Orleans is the voodoo capital of the United States, even though many wrong practices are perpetuated here." Lady Bishop understands her activities as "an African science tied into the laws of nature, and dealing with spirits and the saints."[103]

One of the most widely recognized New Orleans practitioners of voodoo is Ava Kay Jones.[104] Like Lady Bishop, she was raised Catholic and was trained in Haitian vodun rites (at the Temple of the Cloak of St. Peter) and in Palo Mayumba (a tradition associated with the Congo). For Ava Kay Jones religious practice revolves around dance. She comments:

I have always been interested in my West African heritage. African music and dance intrigue me. In college and even today I am involved in a cosmopolitan dance ensemble, the Voodoo Macumba Dance Ensemble, and we bring the performance side of Voodoo to the public in hopes of having them better understand what Voodoo is all about . . . So you see I walked away from a possible teaching career and a legal career [she has a law degree] to help keep alive the traditions I value from Africa. A tradition that was never completely lost. . . . I don't want to turn my back on my heritage. . . . I had a calling. Some of the calling was cultural, but most of it was based on my early experiences in the positive occult. I now see my role in life as working with the spirits. There are many spirits of course, and they are not far off.[105]

The problem faced by voodoo and its practitioners in the twentieth century has been one of maintaining some sense of ritual roots in the face of mass interests on the part of tourists. That is, how does voodoo maintain itself as a vital and viable religious system in an economy overrun by tourists and seekers of the "exotic"? Although some question the motivation and "legitimacy" of his efforts, Charles Massicot Gandolfo's "New Orleans Historic Voodoo Museum" advertises itself as committed to the preservation of and spreading of popular knowledge concerning the voodoo religion.[106] The cover letter accompanying information packets says the following:

> We have been in operation since 1972 and have built our reputation on diversity and authenticity, both in our Museum displays and in the crafts which we offer for sale in our gift shop. Our staff is made up of authentic Voodoo practitioners who will greet you at the door with a pinch of good-luck herb and escort you on your tour. . . . For our preferred clients, we can organize an unforgettable evening with an authentic Voodoo Ritual, directed by an actual Priest or Priestess.[107]

The displays within the museum include voodoo altars (to Exu, voodoo leaders, ancestors); a cemetery area in recognition of the ancestors; ritual items, charms (including dolls); and other elements (books on voodoo and items from other traditions that have influenced voodoo). In addition to the photos of Marie Laveau and other leaders of New Orleans' voodoo community, there are photos of two of the city's current and prominent figures in New Orleans voodoo—Priestess Miriam Williams and Priest Oswan Chamani (1943–1995), the founders of the Voodoo Spiritual Temple.

THE VOODOO SPIRITUAL TEMPLE

Priest Oswan Chamani, who passed away (March 6, 1995) shortly before I began my research on the Voodoo Spiritual Temple, was born in Belize City, Belize, in Central America. He recollected studying the tradition of "Obeah" under the guidance of several teachers as well as through his own personal readings.[108] Primarily concerned with the healing and enlivening qualities of herbs, Priest Oswan spent much of his time in Belize learning the medicinal properties of various plants. In addition, he studied divination and the language of the drums during his youth.

Priestess Miriam Williams (Chamani), born in Jackson, Mississippi, states that from an early age she was aware of the invisible beings and forces that operate in the world. In the priestess's words:

> From childhood I felt more than I can put in words, I'll say universal presence. I felt the presence that wasn't relating to any physical structure. And I felt close to whatever it was that caused me to get off by myself to pray, comprehend the time of quietness as a child.[109]

Initially, this connection with spiritual energy was manifest within the confines of the Christian church, which Priestess Miriam joined at the age of eleven. She recounts that

> when we were back in service on that night, we were sitting, the minister had given the message and he went in silent prayer, and I remember kneeling and Rev. Jarret, he came and laid his hand on my back and I remember when he put his hand on my back, sort of like spirit of electrifying forces went through me and I was like lifted in a rapture. . . . And so it's from those times, I felt a presence.[110]

This experience was mixed with the reality of hypocrisy within the church setting. Those who professed Christ often treated other humans with little respect and concern, and this negatively affected Priestess Miriam. Priestess Miriam comments that there is a need to be open to the "Spirit," and churches often hamper this openness because attention is focused on the preacher. The spiritual leader, as Priestess Miriam understands the role, should not obstruct devotion to "Spirit" but should facilitate this connection through his or her role as a healer, seer, and so forth. In this capacity, the religious leader serves to help clients and devotees recognize the spiritual energy—"Spirit"—that dwells within each person. In response to this hypocrisy, Priestess Miriam moved in the direction of the teachings of the Spiritual church.[111]

It was not until 1975 that she began sustained training in this area. Having spent years in Mississippi and later in New York, she began developing her spiritual talents while living in Chicago, in the process of moving from her Baptist roots to Spiritual churches. This concern for and training in spiritual realities of the world was combined with a concern for the physical body through training and work as an operating room technician. Linking the physical and the spiritual was and remains of vital importance to Priestess Miriam. According to the priestess, the human soul seeks fulfillment through the acquisition of knowledge gained firsthand: "You can try all you want to and go everywhere you want, read every book, but unless you come back to your door, your keeper, then you have no answers. You can marvel at every person who gained some insight and wrote it . . . and it sounds great. But until you find that within you and express it outward, then you can say freely that you have gained under-standing of life."[112] What results is balance—harmony between the spiritual forces and the physical forces. Priestess Miriam remembers her introduc-tion to spiritual churches this way:

> I started back to the Baptist Church and it didn't fit me. It wasn't the answer and finally one day there was a young lady that was working at the Hospital, that I worked at, she said I know where I will take you. And she took me to this old Spiritual man that had a little church on the Southside of Chicago. And that was when I had my first, what we call reading consultation. And he looked at me and he saw this force within me. He said you can come and work here in my church and you can teach Sunday school or whatever you want to do. . . . I stayed there until I was ready to venture. I felt rounded spiritually and so I stayed with him through 1973, 1974, 1975. Then I met up with a lady that was setting up her church and I helped her. From that I met the lady where I stayed thir-teen years, from 1977–1989.[113]

Her involvement in the Angel Angel All Nation Spiritual Church resulted in ordination as a bishop (1982–89). According to the priestess, her studies included "staying up all night, from midnight until daylight, learning the different rituals, prayers, offerings, and sacrifices."[114] As Hans Baer and oth-ers have highlighted, many spiritual churches incorporate within their rit-ual activity voodoo and other elements.[115] Thus, Priestess Miriam was open to the knowledge of African religions possessed by the man who would become her husband—Priest Oswan Chamani (Richard J. Williams). They met in 1989 and were married in 1990.

Under the leading of the spirit, in the words of Priestess Miriam, she and Priest Oswan moved to New Orleans to begin the building of a center committed to the spreading of proper knowledge concerning voodoo (1990). According to Priest Oswan, voodoo is properly understood as

> the power—who is invisible—that created all things; it also means all vis-ible things created by the invisible power; the reason for this, according to the Voodoo teachings, is that there was nothing, nor no one, in the beginning except the Creating or Creative Power. . . . it must be therefore that all visible manifestations are forms of his [the Creative Power's] own thought. . . . In Voodoo we do not separate the Creation from the Creator, nor do we separate the Creator from the Creation. This is the reason why Voodooists believe there is power in trees, rocks, animals, birds; in the sea

and rivers, thunder and lightning, and more importantly, in themselves. This is the philosophical translation of the word Voodoo. The religious meaning of the word Voodoo [he at times refers to this as "Rada Voodoo" or the Royal Path of the Sun] has to do with the worship of the Creator in his several aspects or forms, that is to say, as the many kinds of energies in the universe and the physical shapes and events they give visible expression to. He being invisible we find it is easier to reach him through the visible things, which after all, are the materializations of himself or his thoughts.[116]

The initial vision for the temple occurred to Priest Chamani in 1983, but it did not begin to take form until meeting Miriam Williams in 1989. According to their printed materials: "The Purpose of the Voodoo Spiritual Temple is to educate the community about Voodoo and to dispel the myths and misconceptions associated with Voodoo since time immemorial." The materials continue outlining the temple's purpose with the following: "The purpose of the Voodoo Spiritual Temple is to train and develop the spiritual and mental powers lying latent or dormant in each and every person or individual."[117] The temple understands itself as working for the health and welfare of persons, not for destructive or negative purposes. To this end, the temple offers opportunities for spiritual, mental, physical, and cultural development. With health as the objective, Priestess Miriam sees no functional distinction between Voodoo, Spiritualism, Santería, Christianity, and so on. At their best, all are attempts to heal the wounded.[118] Priestess Miriam explains the temple's orientation as one of "Afrocentric American Voodoo," which readily blends vodou and other practices based upon the theory that there is one source of energy with various names and manifestations.[119]

For some time after their arrival in 1990, Priestess Miriam and Priest Oswan gave readings at the Marie Laveau Gift Shop and were also associated, as pictures on display at the Voodoo Museum indicate, with the Voodoo Museum. Until March 1994, the Voodoo Spiritual Temple's meetings were held in the home of Priest Oswan and Priestess Miriam. In 1994, the temple moved to its current location at 828 North Rampart. During 1995–96, the Voodoo Spiritual Temple extended its influence through participation in various festivals and media events.[120] A temple and retreat center are currently under consideration in Belize. In addition, Priestess Miriam has refined her knowledge of voodoo through a trip to Haiti and through a mentor relationship with a mambo in New York City who will prepare Priestess Miriam and help her obtain the Asson. In addition, the Voodoo Spiritual Temple has also played host to visitors from the Republic of Benin, including High Priest Daagbo Hounon (September 1995).[121]

The temple is housed in a white structure that once served as slave quarters. These quarters now serve as the priestess's residence, guest housing, the pen for birds used by the temple, and the temple (with large altar room). Upon entering the temple, one first notices a collection of herbs and instruments used in various ceremonies. Above this display is a statue of the Buddha that Priestess Miriam explains as a representation of a power source she respects. Moving beyond this hallway, one enters the altar room where readings and other ritual activities occur.

Exterior of the Voodoo Spiritual Temple, located on Rampart Street on the edge of the French Quarter, across from Congo Square. Photo by the author, May 1996.

In terms of cosmology, the Voodoo Spiritual Temple understands the source of all life and energy as "Spirit." At times, Priestess Miriam appears to equate this energy source with the Christian God, through use of scriptural descriptions of the "Spirit." It is this "Spirit" that in fact makes up the essence of humanity; the physical form of the human is the temporary abode of Spirit. This Spirit, which receives prayer, manifests itself in forces that provide more concrete and consistent assistance. These manifestations are, within the Voodoo Spiritual Temple, referred to as *loa* and *orisha* (a term for deities discussed in chapter 2).[122] The *loas* or *orishas* connected with the temple are: Shango, Oshun/Ezurlie, Ogun, Papa Legba/Eleggua, Marie Laveau, Yemaja, Oya, Obàtálá, Simbi, Guede, Damballah, a Peruvian figure associated with healing, and the twins. (The altars in this temple change periodically; thus it is difficult to determine definitively which *loas* are honored.) Although the *veves* for the *loas* are not consistently found in the temple, the *veve* for Eleggua does appear on the cover of the temple's newsletter. These *loas* or *orishas* usually manifest in the Rada form; however, on some occasions, they do manifest in Petro. In addition to these *orishas/loas*, the temple also recognizes the importance and presence of *loas* who were once ancestors connected to Voodoo in the United States. Among these are Marie Laveau, Dr. John, and Priest Oswan. Priestess Miriam and members of the temple also make mention of Jesus Christ as an important spiritual reality. During my time at the temple, one member was possessed by Christ and in this form began to provide advice to several of us who were gathered for casual conversation. Christ and many of the other spirits are called and manifest in ways that are connected to spiritual seances. Again it appears that this overlap is a result of Priestess Miriam's early training in the spiritual tradition.

The Voodoo Spiritual Temple also places a great deal of emphasis on the ancestors. The ancestors are understood to provide the most intimate link between humans and cosmic reality, and thus they must be remembered and cared for. According to Priestess Miriam, the ancestors operate on both the physical and metaphysical level, and they are eager to communicate with humans if the living are calm and open to contact. Because the temple rests on former slave quarters, Priestess Miriam and several others acknowledge that among the ancestors who make themselves periodically known are former slaves. One in particular, a talk man, appears on occasion and offers advice and guidance.

The temple is composed of Priestess Miriam, the drummers (including Louis Martini, who is also a priest), those who serve the *loas*, and casual clients. In addition to providing readings and other ritual activities for residents of New Orleans and those who travel from elsewhere, Priestess Miriam also serves as a "mother figure" who nurtures and teaches. The priestess explains that many who come to the temple are not actually interested in assistance but in smoke and mirrors, potions and spells. This they receive, but as soon as they are open to deeper spiritual realities, Priestess Miriam is there to provide this information. It is only when people reach this inner level of inquiry, she says, that healing and health can occur. In her work, the Christian Scriptures provide a spiritual resource that is combined with herbs and voodoo ritual activities. In dealing with her various clients, Priestess Miriam understands that human nature is destructive and must be brought in line with cosmic energy. Our deepest needs are often dealt with through

Herbs, candles, and other ritual items used and sold at the temple. Photo by the author, May 1996.

selfless acts of kindness and thoughtfulness toward others. In the words of Priestess Miriam, "Those things we seek aren't always the things we need. It is not always through the elaborate ritual that we receive; we often receive through quiet listening and opening ourselves to Spirit. We must cleanse and free ourselves. We concentrate too much on the physical and ignore at our expense the spiritual."[123]

Priestess Miriam's temple also allows devotees to enter new stages and levels of knowledge, but these are not referred to as initiations. Priestess Miriam emphasizes levels of knowledge acquired over against ritual movements that symbolically represent levels of knowledge. According to the priestess, knowledge is of fundamental importance, and corresponding outward demonstrations are dispensable. Rather, initiations are called levels of consecration, which correspond to levels of praxis, and they result not only from ritual activity but from personal reflection (i.e., prayer keeps the path to Spirit open and maintains high levels of positive energy) and personal contact with Spirit. Elaborate temples and ritual enactments are of little importance if one understands the transforming nature of knowledge acquired naturally and simply.[124] These events contain a great deal of repetitive pronouncements of *loas'* names because through sound (including music) the presence of the deities is manifest. Members of the temple understand that Spirit manifests when and in whomever it desires. Priestess Miriam argues that some are selected at birth by Spirit and thus receive capabilities that with time should be developed. Because of this, ritual knowledge and "experience" are not the only measures of legitimate involvement in ritual activity and possession by the *loa*. Everyone is called to serve Spirit, and so everyone is a potential "horse" for Spirit and its various manifestations. Of more importance than ritual knowledge, it seems, is a willing and open heart because the Spirit provides the necessary information. Sacrifices for particular needs, however, are private. Thus ceremonial activities extend beyond the information for tourists, without exposing all the secrets of voodoo. The result of this attitude is a general openness to all interested in attending ritual activities (Thursdays and Sundays).

Although the Spirit chooses whomever it will, the presence of knowledgeable persons is needed to monitor ritual activity because both good and evil spirits can be present depending on the condition of the person's heart—deceit brings malicious spirits. Those with experience are able to discern the differences in spirits. For devotees, although Spirit moves freely among all, levels of consecration are important because they provide discernment and allow one to protect oneself from spiritual harm through increased understanding of self and the spirit world. Devotees know to appease and cleanse the environment through rum, Florida Water, or prayer, and those who hope to have intimate contact with the spirits must also purify themselves. Although Spirit can use any vessel, it is possible to become so defiled (e.g., hateful or vengeful) that *lwas* will not manifest. Although the practices of the temple appear rather eclectic, it is likely that the continued contact between Priestess Miriam and members of the Haitian vodou community will result in greater "orthodoxy."

Priestess Miriam begins formal consultations and ritual work before nine in the morning, and consultations for the curious and for sin-

One of the altars in the altar room of the Voodoo Spiritual Temple. This altar was established for the *loa* associated with iron. Photo by the author, July 1996.

cere devotees continue well into the evening. It is Priestess Miriam's policy to address the needs of all those gathered before ending the day's activities; the only exception during my visit was with one client whose questions and needs—the ritual activity, conversation, and personal mediation—were addressed over the course of several days. Those who come for the priestess's assistance must be willing to wait; through this exercise in patience, the "healing" process in whatever form necessary is begun. In addition to work with individuals, the Voodoo Spiritual Temple also provides communal activities.

As with the Haitian *oum'phor,* the Voodoo Spiritual Temple's outer courtyard is the focus of much activity and casual conversation; it is the gathering place for some ritual, but also for commonly held social functions. The Thursday night of my first visit involved a ceremony in honor of the *lwas.* The activities actually began earlier during the day, however, as two members of the temple arrived to help the priestess with daily chores. As the day progressed, the two women began to experience trance-like states during which various *lwas,* including Christ and Oshun, spoke to me, providing guidance and warnings. I was also blessed with rum and cigar smoke. With nightfall, chairs were placed outside and drumming began. One of the women, after spraying the courtyard with rum, went into trance under the influence of her *loa*—named Shango. She began moving around the courtyard and eventually blessed those gathered by removing negative energy. This was accomplished by placing each person on her back, one at a time, and spinning the person around. She then proceeded to move her hands over the person in a way that symbolically removed negative influences and forces.

After this period of cleansing, the other woman went into trance and was possessed by one of the Guede *loas.* This was marked by his typical playfulness. At this point, those gathered—a mixture of regulars, myself, and curious tourists who happened to pass by the temple during the activities—were invited to drum and dance in recognition of the *loas'* goodness and presence. The ceremony concluded with words of wisdom from Priestess Miriam that in tone and style resembled prophecy within black Pentecostal churches. The final act was a communal move through the altar room and the cleaning of the courtyard. Much of what took place during this ceremony would not be described in other texts as authentic practice; important for our study, however, is the manner in which Priestess Miriam embraces voodoo and blends it with other practices in ways that make sense of life for her and her community. For the Voodoo Spiritual Temple, questions of orthodoxy in a world marked by contact and conquest are false questions, because all reference points are inadequate to gauge authenticity.

THE *LOAS* AND THE PROBLEM OF EVIL

The vodou/voodoo tradition answers a fundamental theological question: What can we say about God(s) and interaction between the divine and humanity in light of human suffering and moral evil? According to Karen McCarthy Brown, the existence of voodoo is a testimony of Haitian wrestling with this question: "Vodou is the system they have devised to deal with the suffering that is life, a system whose purpose is to minimize pain, avoid disaster, cushion loss, and strengthen survivors and survival instincts."[125] In this religious system it is understood that good and evil are not separate realities or entities. This epistemological schema is born out in the very nature of the *lwas,* the sparks of divinity who have tremendous contact with humanity. Vodou understands that the good and bad (suffering) are intimately connected and are both components of life on earth. Desmangles states, "Although *lwas'* personae appear to oppose one another, they are nevertheless reconciled (or rather transcended) by Bondye's vital force, which not only permeates the universe but fosters the forces of good and evil." Because of this connection between good and evil, as joined in the reality of God, Haitians understand that "poverty becomes a means of salvation; illness, a source of divine power; and earth is suddenly transformed into life itself."[126] Such an understanding of good and evil does not seek to rob suffering of any meaning. Evil and suffering remain pain-filled realities. They are not a result of intrinsic human failure, however, nor do they merit long-term punishment. Rather, suffering and evil can be corrected through balance—through proper relationship with the cosmic forces.

Vodou does not resolve the problem of evil by disassociating body and soul, rejecting the former for the sake of the latter. It emphasizes reliance not upon divine maneuvering but rather on human action intended to correct wrongs through remembering the ancestor, fulfilling spoken commitments to the *loas,* and proper relations between members of the community. Situations in life that seem difficult are pragmatically rectified through these practices and through *lwas* who benefit devotees in exchange for service. The latter is telling; in part, the problem of evil is resolved or dealt with through the *serviteur's* ability to ask the *loa* hard questions concerning the *loa's* conduct and human situations. In essence, the example and characteristics of the *loas* provide strategies for success and highlight useful ways of dealing with tricky situations. Hence, the question does not entail the Christian problematic of finding ways to justify a God that appears to be historically unconcerned and/or inactive. For the *serviteur*, the *lwas* "do not have a supernatural prerogative of arbitrary decision. An event which, to the *serviteur*, does not seem logical is not accepted with good grace as the 'will of god.' . . ."[127] Hence, the moral universe for the *serviteur*, the universe in which questions of evil are addressed, is premised upon the notion that proper service will result in benefit, both internal and existential. In the words of Deren:

> The Haitian does not mean, for example, that health will *result* from a certain ritual action; he means that health will be a *reward* for his performance of it. . . . That action reaffirms first principles—destiny, strength, love, life, death; it recapitulates a man's relationship to his ancestors, his history, as well as his relationship to the contemporary community; it exercises and formalizes his own integrity and personality, tightens his disciplines, confirms his morale. In sum, he emerges with a strengthened and refreshed sense of his relationship to cosmic, social and personal elements. . . . *The miracle is, in a sense, interior. It is the doer who is changed by the ritual, and for him, therefore, the world changes accordingly.*[128]

This line of reasoning, with respect to the problem of evil, is continued in the theological framework offered by the Voodoo Spiritual Temple. According to Priestess Miriam, all life events are of value because they provide us with opportunity for internal growth and existential renewal. Furthermore, our thoughts also influence our physical well-being in that good and positive thoughts promote health and prosperity while negative thoughts harm the body and predispose the thinker to a variety of misfortunes. In the priestess's words, "[We] should not feel ashamed because of our experiences. Don't pity anything in life—to pity can involve picking up those things. Bless people; through blessing people [we may] alter life."[129]

She continues:

> Experiences are necessary because we build on them, we learn from them. There is no "suffering" [intrinsically evil deeds or happenings]; all experiences are useful in that they teach us and help us achieve balance. . . . To label something suffering is to misunderstand the true nature and benefit of all experiences. There are no negative experiences because they all correspond, if we embrace them, to our growth and development.[130]

What can we say about God and God's relationship to the world in light of human suffering? Voodoo answers this question by connecting good and evil in a web of life. Some experiences we would prefer not to have, but in the long run we must learn from them and seek to maintain balance in order to make life as rich as possible.

2

▲▽▲▽▲▽▲▽▲▽▲▽▲▽▲▽▲

ASHE!

Santería, *Orisha*-Voodoo, and Oyotunji African Village

YORÙBÁ RELIGION IN AFRICA

The Yorùbá represent roughly 30 million inhabitants of southwestern Nigeria, Togo, and Benin, and they are one of the largest ethnic groups in Nigeria.[1] The Yorùbá are an urban people who have lived in cities for centuries by means of agriculture and trade. Although the Yorùbá share a common language, their government model is based upon independent city-states.[2] Exercising a strong degree of independence, each city-state developed in keeping with its resources and the strength or weakness of its leadership. Early in its history, Yorùbáland was primarily divided into two dominant regions—the savannah (Oyo) and the forest (Ile-Ifè). By the nineteenth century, the various city-states were grouped into several clusters: Oyo, Egba, Egbado, Ijesha, Ife, Ijebu, Ekiti, Ondo, Akoko.[3] The complexity of Yorùbá society marked by these various clusters of city-states and their developed economic system was well known and noted even by such Western missionaries as R. H. Stone:

> Instead of being lazy, naked savages, living on the spontaneous productions of the earth, they were dressed and were industrious . . . [providing] everything that their physical comfort required. The men are builders, blacksmiths, iron-smelters, carpenters, calabash-carvers, weavers, basket-makers, hat-makers, mat-makers, traders, barbers, tanners, tailors, farmers, and workers in leather . . . they make razors, swords, knives, hoes, billhooks, axes, arrow-heads, stirrups . . . women . . . most diligently follow the pursuits which custom has allotted to them. They spin, weave, trade, cook, and dye cotton fabrics.[4]

Yorùbá origin accounts proclaim them the descendants of Odùdúwà, the first ancestor, who was a child of one of the kings of Mecca named

Lamurudu.[5] According to the accounts, Odùdúwà rejected Islam and embraced "pagan" practices with the hope of drawing others into his idolatry. Odùdúwà's efforts resulted in the conversion of the great mosque into a temple housing his idols. The new temple's priest, Asara, had a son who objected to this idolatry and, when the opportunity arose, he destroyed the idols. As punishment he was ordered burned, but the Islamic forces that had been suppressed fought on his behalf and defeated the idolaters. Odùdúwà left Mecca and headed toward the East with two idols. He traveled for three months until he reached Ile-Ifè, recognized as the holy city, the home of Ifa worship and the "birthplace" of the original Yorùbá deities, or orìsà.[6]

According to several of the origin accounts, Ile-Ifè is the place where the Yorùbá emerged as a distinctive group through Odùdúwà and his children. The children of Odùdúwà who lived in Ile-Ifè became the various tribes making up the Yorùbá. Oranyan was the youngest son and the most widely recognized because of his connection to an important Yorùbá locale. One of the stories reports that Oranyan was determined to fulfill the desire of his family by avenging Odùdúwà's expulsion from Mecca. Gathering the support of his brothers, Oranyan left for Mecca, but the Tapas prevented him from crossing the Niger River. Unable to return to Ile-Ifè without being disgraced, he took the advice of King Borgu and followed the path of a charmed boa constrictor. He was led to the site that became known as the ancient city of Oyo. Oranyan's family grew in this place and established good relations with Ile-Ifè.[7] The eventual dominance of Oyo is easily understood in light of its fertile location and resources that allowed it to trade with an extended area. But in spite of Oyo's political and military dominance for some time, Ile-Ifè (Ifè) maintained spiritual dominance and authority based upon the legendary origin of humanity in Ifè (according to some accounts), and the religious relics (or items of power and memory) housed there. In fact, many of the orìsà or deities worshiped as part of Yorùbá tradition are associated with this sacred city.

In addition to mythic accounts, archaeological discoveries shed light on the population of early Nigeria from whom the Yorùbá may be descended. These archaeological assertions are based upon similarities in pottery methods and styles found, in 1931, among pottery pieces associated with a Nok village. According to this pottery, the Nok culture is a good two thousand years old and reached maturity sometime between the second and third centuries B.C.E. Archaeologists claim that the Nok society was the earliest culture to make use of ironwork in its region of Nigeria. It is also asserted that the Nok are the descendants of many of the groups within Nigeria, and the link includes the Yorùbá, whose artwork, the metal work of Ifè, is in keeping with Nok figurines.[8] Nonetheless, the history of the Yorùbá, when archaeological evidence is combined with myth, legend, and other sources, remains uncertain.

The history of the Yorùbá is intimately tied to the Yorùbá's religious system. Yorùbá religion begins with reference to the high God, Olódùmarè or Olórun, who is responsible for the creation and maintenance of the universe. Olódùmarè's importance is not premised upon direct contact with humanity but upon the Supreme God's maintenance of the world. Because of the Supreme God's responsibility for cosmic order, he can give little attention to human affairs. He is master of the skies, owner of the universe, and the owner of character (olu iwa). Yet, he is manifest in the world through àse (divine energy) and the collection of this energy in the form of the orìsà—the deities who interact with human beings. Although Yorùbá religion notes the power or àse represented by the various gods, it also recognizes that all of creation participates in this energy.[9] Hence, it is inaccurate to claim that the Yorùbá pay no attention to the Supreme God because he is remote and unconcerned when, in fact, the Supreme God is present in the concern demonstrated by the orìsà.

The nature and origin of these deities is complex; several of them were great ancestors who were translated into deities at death, while others directly participate in God's essence and originate as divinities. Undoubtedly Yorùbá religion has borrowed other deities as a result of contact with and conquest of neighbors and enemies. Regardless of their origin, there are hundreds of deities, some of whom are local deities associated with particular villages and homes, and others who are recognized beyond the local level. Following is a brief discussion of some of the "national/international" divinities with limited attention to some of their many attributes and manifestations. (See Figure 3.)[10]

Contact with the orìsàs is essential for human life. For practitioners of Yorùbá religion, this contact reaches its highest point through possession. This intimate link with àse allows for the maintenance of balance in life through the gaining and dispensing of advice, health care, family counsel, and so forth. Contact between humanity and the deities is made possible through the workings of Èsù (Eshu-Elégbá), the keeper of the gates associated with crossroads and the messenger of Olódùmarè.[11] His position as messenger makes him extremely important, and his role as the divine trickster makes him potentially dangerous. With the movement of Christianity across Nigeria, missionaries often associated him with Satan; but the Yorùbá regarded this deity, like the others, as capable of both good and harm. And both of these possibilities can be harnessed by humans through proper sacrifice and general attention to the likes and dislikes of Eshu-Elégbá.

Ifá (Òrúnmìlà) is central within Yorùbá religion and within human affairs in general. This is because Ifá is the god of divination, the one who knows the future and can thereby guide conduct. With such ability and authority, Òrúnmìlà harnesses the knowledge of the ancestors and the power of the *orìsà*. Figures of religious authority—*Babalawos*, or fathers of secrets—seek assistance from this divinity using several different ritual tools, including a divination board, cowrie shells (*awoeyo*), palm-nuts, kola nuts (*obi*), or the *opele* chain made of *opele* nuts.[12] When these divination tools are used properly, Ifá provides sacred sayings (*odus*) that correspond to particular conditions and necessary solutions. It should be understood that the *babalawo* ranks highest in the religious leadership hierarchy. Having trained for a long period of time (ten to sixteen years in some cases), the *babalawo's* authority stems from the attainment and use of the religion's secrets and the knowledge of divination by which humanity is linked to the past, present, and future. It is worth noting one example of this practice. The person stops by a *babalawo* who openly practices religion in the marketplace and

> kneels before the Ifa tools and whispers her fears to a coin. This is the fee of the *orisha* Eshu, a mischievous trickster-*orisha* whose good will is necessary for the proper transmission of the message to Olódùmarè. If Eshu is satisfied, the *babalawo* will be permitted to keep the coin as part of his professional fee for his consultation. The *babalawo* now begins the process of determining the precise spiritual situation of the querent mother. Taking sixteen consecrated palm nuts in his left hand, he rapidly draws the bulk of them away with his right. He is trained in this maneuver to leave behind only one or two nuts remaining in his left hand. He does this eight times at each point leaving one or two nuts behind. The woman and the *babalawo* believe that it is purely a random process that determines whether one or two nuts remain on each occasion—random, but not chance. For, in the will of Olódùmarè, there is no such thing as chance. . . . As each of the eight passes is made, the *babalawo* draws a corresponding figure in a special sawdust on a carved tray called opon.[13]

The information provided relates to sacred *odus* or a set of stories or poems that provide information concerning the person's dilemma and life situations. There are sixteen possible situations and sixteen variations, resulting in a total of 256 possible *odus*.[14]

Concerned with the hidden benefit of natural elements is Osanyin, who is the deity of herbal treatments and medicines. Within his domain are the plants and herbs that house *àse* and are usable in a variety of beneficial ways. These elements are also vital in the initiation process undergone by those who practice the religion. Hence, without Osanyin physical and spiritual health suffer. In terms of appearance, he does not have the beauty associated with other deities. He is "deformed," having only one eye, one leg, and one arm. According to Yorùbá tradition, Osanyin suffered this deformity because he attempted to dominate the herbs and plants that promoted health.[15]

Whereas Osanyin lacks physical prowess and strength, Ògún, the god of war and iron—is strong and a supreme warrior.[16] He is associated with machetes and other iron and steel instruments of production and destruction. In more recent times, his symbolic representation was extended to include trains, guns, and other things made of his metal. Associated with this deity is Oshoosi, the god of the hunt and archery. Like his companion and brother Ògún, Oshoosi is strong and well formed. He is honored by those who are concerned with hunting and similar activities that require the skill and patience of one who knows the forest. Another divinity associated with the earth is Oba-'lu'aiye (Sòpòná), the deity who controls the ground or earth. He is similar to Eshu in that he metes out justice and punishment, in this case through smallpox and other diseases. Because of his ability to inflict mortal illness, he is feared and respected.

One deity is noted for her role as the divine loving mother and as potentially deadly to those whose actions demand retribution—Yemoja, the goddess associated with salt water. Also associated with water, specifically with rivers or sweet water, is the deity Òsun. Because of her sensual nature and her connection with matters of the heart, Yorùbán religion links her romantically with several deities, including Ifá. Òsun's warlike abilities with the sword add to her complexity and connect her with Ògún, in whom love and war are combined. Òsun's connection with Oya, in turn, involves Sàngó, who has had an intimate relationship with both. Oya was one of his wives. The potential for aggressive and vengeful activity also link these two goddesses as does Oya's association with water—the Niger River. In fact, Oya's fierceness is present in her appearance; she is often described as a "fierce, bearded Amazon who is absolutely indispensable to her husband in every way. . . . Her face is so terrible that none dare behold it, her wrath so devastating that it must be absolutely avoided." In terms of natural forces, Oya is associated with the whirlwind—fierce weather—that destroys the landscape with its energy.[17] The complexity and apparent contradictions inherent in Yorùbá religion and life in general are present here as well because Oya can also be a beautiful woman in a traditional sense. In fact, it was this manifestation of Oya that attracted Sàngô.

One of the most widely recognized gods is Sàngô, the god of thunder and the third king of Oyo.[18] There are two accounts of his translation to the realm of the orìsàs I will rehearse here. The first entails his experimentation with a plant leaf that had the ability to produce lightning. While toying with this leaf, Sàngô accidentally set the roof of his palace on fire, killing his family. In despair, he left the city and committed suicide by hanging. Having caused destruction by misusing God's power of lightning, Sàngô's lot involved becoming lightning itself. ". . . in the lightning bolt Shàngó (Sàngô) met himself. He became an eternal moral presence, rumbling in the clouds, outraged by impure human acts, targeting the homes of adulterers, liars, and thieves for destruction."[19] In addition to this fierce and destructive character, Sàngô is also noted as a premiere dancer and lover. In another account, Sàngô as king of Oyo was counseled by his wife, Oya, to solidify and guarantee his political authority by causing friction between two courtiers who rebelled against his tyrannical reign. The hope was that one would kill the other and the remaining soldier would be much easier to influence and control. The outcome was not in keeping with the plan, however. Sàngô was forced out of his kingdom by the survivor and, due to his shame, he hanged himself. Those loyal to him argue that the king was translated to heaven.[20]

Although the gods and goddesses described above are of central importance, the orìsà closest to the Supreme God in authority is Orìsà-nlá (or Obàtálá). He was the first of the gods, and, in some accounts, he participated directly in the nature and substance of the Supreme God. This god is responsible for the creation of humanity, a task assigned to him by the Supreme God. "He is the sculptor-divinity who has been given the prerogative to create as he chooses, so that he makes man of shapely or deformed features. The hunchback, the cripple, the albino, are regarded to be special marks of his prerogative, either signifying his displeasure at the break of some tabu, or to show that he could do as he likes."[21] Because of his wisdom and connection to the Supreme God, this deity is associated, with high ethical and moral standards and with purity of deed and thought. As part of this wisdom, he also knows the history and the ontological essence of each god and goddess. In this capacity he is often depicted as a very old man clothed in the purest of white garments. According to one mythical account, he is also responsible for the creation of the earth.[22] Other accounts claim that he became drunk on palm wine after receiving instructions to create the earth. After waiting for his return, the Supreme God sent Odùdúwà to find out why Obàtálá had not completed the task. Odùdúwà found him drunk and, taking the supplies given Obàtálá, he did the work of creation. As a reward for his efforts, the Supreme God made Odùdúwà senior deity.

To Odùdúwà is attributed fundamental and timeless significance for the Yorùbá sense of ontology and communal epistemology. Furthermore, stories of his life raise important questions concerning Yorùbá theological anthropology—that is, where and how do contemporary humans and their ancestors fit into the cosmic order?[23]

The multiplicity of deities indicates the importance of the ancestors as well as the dispersement of divine energy throughout the cosmos. All ancestors, or *Egúngún,* derive their importance not only from their association with "elite" figures but also from their position between divinities and humanity.[24] Here they are able to help or harm their descendants depending upon the respect or disrespect shown them by those still in the realm of the living. The ancestors also may be "reborn" in their descendants as revealed by the emergence of a similar personality and physical appearance. This "reincarnation," so to speak, is attested to by an oracle identifying a child's *orí* (duplicate on the spiritual plain, ancestor manifest in the "head," related to "destiny" and the soul). This interaction with the family also provides the basis for the Yorùbá moral code and proper ethical conduct. A valuable link such as this is maintained with great care through ancestor veneration, in the form of the cult of the ancestors (*Egúngún* cult) and the ancestral shrine. Although the ancestors are concerned with humanity and can exercise some "influence" over developments in the human realm, their ability to contact descendants through dreams, visions, divination, and so forth, and their freedom from earthly constraints do not put them on the ontological level of the divinities. Only the divinities are "of the heavens."[25]

Understood correctly, the human is body and spirit (*èmí*). The latter component is present during physical life and absents itself upon death. Just as the Hebrew Bible speaks of God giving humans the breath of life, so does Spirit, as understood by the Yorùbá, entail breath from the Supreme God.[26] Besides these two components, Yorùbá also believe that the emotional substance of the human is located in the "heart," or the *Okàn*. The Yorùbá also often speak of a personality-soul named the *orí*. Although the term literally refers to the physical head, the Yorùbá also regard it as sym-

---

Figure 3. Yorùbá Divinities: Names and Functions

Name	Function
Olódùmarè	Supreme God who created/controls the world
Orìsà-nlá	God of wisdom who created humanity
Eshu-Elégbá	Trickster and messenger of Olódùmarè and other orìsà
Ògûn	God of iron tools and war
Oshoosi	God of the forest and hunting
Ifá	God of divination (associated with destiny)
Oba-'lu'aiye	God of disease (smallpox)
Osanyin	God of herbs and herbal medicine
Sàngô	God of thunder/lightning and sexual prowess
Oya	Goddess of the whirlwind and battle
Yemojá	Goddess of water/motherhood
Òsun	Goddess of water/sensuality

Adapted from Robert Farris Thompson, *Flash of the Spirit: African and Afro-American Art and Philosophy* (New York: Random House, 1983); George Brandon, *Santería from Africa to the New World* (Bloomington: Indiana University Press, 1993); E. Bólájí Ìdòwú, *Olódùmarè: God in Yorùbá Belief* (New York: Wazobia, 1994).

---

bolic of the inner "head," the guiding element. This soul is often associated with the concept of a guardian angel, and it receives offerings. Such attention is given not only to an individual's personal soul but also to that of his or her parents. It is this *orí* that selects the destiny the individual will seek to fulfill on earth; and the person's ability to fulfill this destiny directly depends upon his or her relationship to cosmic forces and the ancestors.[27]

Morality (*Ìwà*) and moral conduct are premised upon and inseparable from proper attention to one's religious obligations, a recognition of the "exchange" among the various levels of the cosmic order. Moral codes apply most strongly among those who are connected to the same divinities and ancestors. Morality is characterized by a profound optimism, humanism (i.e., a generic interest in human life and human possibilities), and attention to character.[28] To be human is to be open to life and sensitive to the obligations that go along with the destiny one has selected.[29]

The Yorùbá believe that the outcome of an individual life is preordained, but that the individual has influence over it. That is, the human soul selects its destiny before birth and proceeds to fulfill this destiny while on earth. The soul forgets its selected destiny once the individual is born, but it strives to fulfill it often with the help of divination. One can also have one's destiny hampered not only through one's own character flaws and improper actions, but also through evil agents who seek to do damage. All of this is balanced through a combining of "predestination" (i.e., the pre-born individual's selection of a destiny), human accountability, and external malicious forces. After this life, whether destiny is fulfilled or not, the deceased must face the Supreme God and justify his or her actions, receive judgment, and await the attention of his or her descendants.

Human activity does not always result in what is best. The slave trade with Europeans can be understood as a notable example of this. Granted, slavery had existed for centuries in Yorùbáland and elsewhere as a means of paying debt and as the result of war.[30] But this "trade" pales in comparison to the slave trade fostered in the 1500s by Portuguese and other Europeans in response to the "New World" labor demand. Few are unaware of the trauma, angst, and ontological hardship experienced by enslaved Africans. And although one might expect such hardship to result in the demise of culture (e.g., religious systems), this was not the case. Yorùbá deities, for example, made the journey across the ocean and made Cuba their home. The strength of these divinities and their cults is not only a matter of history and mythic importance; these cults also mark an important source of identity that could not be easily detected nor taken by slave traders.

A psychological component to these traditions is embedded in devotees in ways that extend beyond set ritual structures and enactments. This component allowed for a flexibility necessary on new and hostile terrain. Primary symbols survive; only their outer levels of meaning developed in response to contextual concerns are altered. Combined with natural fluidity and ritual flexibility (e.g., the ability to incorporate divinities and rituals of other groups), the psychological component (connected to the essential nature of àse or àshe) allowed for the growth of Yorùbá religion throughout the Americas.

YORÙBÁ RELIGION IN CUBA: SANTERÍA

Columbus, looking for India, stumbled across the populated Caribbean. He was inspired by a sense of progress and exploration fueled by the scientific and technological advances (e.g., navigational equipment) of the fifteenth century.[31] These advances made possible a combination of aggressive economic agendas with a sense of limitless potential, all covered with a thin religious veneer, that would enrich Europe and forever change the Americas. In 1492, Spaniards caught sight of the Caribbean and recognized it as overflowing with potential: flora and fauna, possibly rich metal resources such as gold, and a strategic location. That year marked Columbus's encounter with Cuba.

By 1508, stories of possible wealth through gold were reaching Spain, sent to the crown via Hispaniola (Haiti). Interest in wealth meant establishing a governor on the island—Diego Velázquez. In 1511, he established the first permanent settlement, and conquest was under way. Although the indigenous population resisted, Spaniards ultimately took control of the island and began their economic campaign. Velázquez attempted to avoid the widespread killing of unwilling Indian laborers by securing their cooperation with the help of Bartolomé de las Casas.[32] Efforts to secure cooperation largely entailed offering Christianity in exchange for labor. Economic concerns took precedence, however, and many Spaniards failed to provide fair treatment and religious instruction. The pool of Indian laborers continued to dwindle, and religious leaders such as de las Casas continued to object to the poor treatment of the Indians. Although a similar argument to end African slavery was made by some, the crown did not feel the same obligations, because Africans were purchased, in legal trade, from the Portuguese.[33] And regardless of moral responsibilities, labor was necessary because economic goals could not be sacrificed. A source of this labor could be secured from Africa and the slave trade. It was initially the policy to avoid the importing of "raw" Africans in favor of Christianized Africans brought from Spain. This policy, however, was not practical, because it failed to respond adequately to labor needs and thus was rejected by 1510.[34] So, "by 1544 Cuba had a population of less than 7,000, composed of 660 Spaniards [mainly officers, soldiers and clergy], some 5,000 Indians and 800 black slaves."[35] Although the slave trade officially ended in the early 1800s, some argue that slaves were still brought to the island as late as 1870.[36]

Africans were brought to this colony in increasingly larger numbers primarily to keep pace with the sugar industry. Although it is difficult to know the exact number of slaves in Cuba because slave owners often miscounted, for example, to avoid high taxes, by 1755 there were over 28,000 slaves, and by 1841 there were over 400,000.[37] Some estimate that the slave population reached numbers as high as 700,000 or 1,000,000.[38] When combined with free blacks and mulattos, this accounts for a substantial population. At times, this large population created fear of rebellion within the Spanish population. In an ironic twist, the slave revolt in Haiti (Saint-Dominique) spread stories of torture and death but also increased the demand for Cuban sugar, which maintained the need for a sizable slave population.[39] Although Cuba faced its own revolts engineered by bands of escaped slaves and free blacks (*cimarrones*) who attacked and took refuge in the less accessible regions of the mountains, the nature of slave labor often defused this rebellion by spreading out the labor force across plantations and within cities.[40]

Regardless of potential dangers and difficulties in regulating slavery on the island, slaves were needed, and the crown, local authorities, and the church worked to guarantee stability through legal regulations. The church's concern for regulating life in Cuba took the form of religious and theological instruction involving the central elements of the Catholic faith and sacramental preparation: baptism, confirmation, matrimony, extreme unction, the eucharist, penance, and holy orders.[41] In addition, special attention—cult-like in nature—given to saints was also promoted in Cuba. This saint veneration gave rise to stories of miraculous occurrences, and saints who performed these miracles were honored through feasts.

Because of the training and technical knowledge necessary for the sacraments to be performed in keeping with their transformative potential, church officials maintained tight control over them. The veneration of the saints did not require the same level of expertise, however, and nonclergy were able to exercise control over the cult of the saints and the tales of wonder that accompanied these practices. Although the church was not at ease with these "folk" ways, it was not realistic to believe that they could be effectively ended because the church did not have access to the inner life of the "masses" in a way that allowed it to monitor relationships with the saints.[42] According to Fernando Ortiz, those who study the Catholic Church's reaction to Protestantism gain insight into the Catholic Church's attitude toward practice and ritual, which required a peace with "folk" ways:

> the change from an intellectual to an emotional outlook, the decline of the spirit of criticism and the reaction against Protestantism led to excessive importance being attached to rites, images, devotions, relics, indulgences and of other attributes of an external, formal religion.[43]

Even with the inability to monitor popular practices, the centrality of the Catholic Church as a basis for social control in Spain was maintained by the State as a tool for controlling the diverse population of the West Indies. In Spain, as in other European countries, the church functioned as the arbiter of moral and ethical standards as well as intellectual growth. Hence, it was assumed that the church would play a major role in developing the structures and standards of life in the Americas. As a result, the Catholic Church exercised a strong presence in Cuba primarily as a proselytizing force. It was, in fact, representatives of the Roman Catholic Church more than other officials who exercised direct contact with slaves and slave owners.[44]

Attention initially given to Spaniards and Indians in the Americas was turned to African slaves through the official regulations concerning the required introduction to the Christian gospel. The law stated:

> We order and command to all those persons who have Slaves, Negroes and Mulattoes, that they send them to the Church or Monastery at the hour which the Prelate has designated, and there the Christian Doctrine be taught to them; and the Arch-bishops and Bishops of our Indies have very particular care for their conversion and indoctrination, in order that they live Christianly. . . .[45]

This commitment to the religious education of slaves was spotty due to such factors as economic growth and the question of whether slaves were capable of understanding the gospel of Christ. Yet there was another factor that, in time, became major.

Church instruction, as important as it was said to be, had to take into consideration labor concerns of slave owners and the stated need for social outlets that would prevent discontent (and rebellion) on the part of Africans. One such outlet was the *cabildos,* or clubs where Africans met for entertainment and conversation. On one level, these clubs allowed for an outlet that reduced the push toward rebellion and, on another, they allowed for the preservation of cultural memory based upon maintenance of particular *nacións* or African "national" identities. Some in the church, being familiar with similar arrangements for blacks in Spain, ignored these clubs. Others such as Bishop Pedro Agustin Morel de Santa Cruz sought gradually to bring these clubs into the Christian fold. In his words:

> Not being satisfied with similar scruples, I attempted a gentle method of going by turns to each of the cabildos, to administer the sacrament of confirmation, and praying the Holy Rosary with those of that organization (gremio), before an Image of Our Lady which I carried with me. Concluding this act, I left the image in their houses, charging them to continue with their worship and devotion.[46]

At times, the church was convinced that the strength and "superiority" of the Christian gospel would manifest itself and slaves would forsake their old ways often manifest in the clubs. At other times, the church was not so certain of this gradual transformation. Hence, the church's position with respect to these clubs vacillated between opposition and reluctant tolerance. Catholicism, as Bishop Pedro Agustin Morel de Santa Cruz intended, gradually moved into these clubs through the occasional presence of priests and the association of a particular saint with each house.[47]

Contact between these saints and their devotees became a vital component of the religious life cultivated through prayer, candles, and other forms of devotion.[48] Here the initial linking of Africa *orìsà* and Catholic saints is perceptible. The Yorùbá *orìsàs* (orishas) were masked by Catholic saints who exhibited similar characteristics and functions.[49] Resulting from this syncretism was a "New World" religious tradition—*Santería* (way of the saints, often referred to as *Regla de Ocha* to distinguish it from Palo gods and ancestor veneration[50])—centered in urban areas such as Havana and Mantanzas. Syncretism did not simply involve the Catholic Church and Yorùbá religion. Rather, what is known as Santería also borrowed from other African practices in Cuba as well as what remained of indigenous influence.[51] The Catholic Church's inconsistent policies with respect to this new religious tradition enhanced its development through the continual building of nation-based societies or *cabildos,* while, on the other hand, the church's occasional concern resulted in efforts to negate Santería's existence through legislation and the restriction of African and mulatto gatherings. Nonetheless, this New World Yorùbá tradition adapted to its environment. In the "New World," the worship of *orishas* could not find expression in regional communities of which each held to a particular divinity. Instead, priests had to strive for the maintenance of a whole system, and so detailed knowledge of more than one divinity grew in importance. Additionally, information concerning the *orishas* could not be restricted to members of one's bloodline. Religious ties had to move beyond genealogical ties to ritual information. The "Lucumi," as the Yorùbá frequently called themselves, sought to maintain important connections with the forces that monitor and shape the world. In order to survive, this religious development had to occur with a great deal of secrecy, and it needed to make use of Catholic elements in order to avoid suspicion.

Each club or society paid devotion to a variety of *orishas* while giving primary allegiance to one particular divinity (e.g., El Cabildo Africano Lucumi—Santa Barbara or Shangó). In the words of George Brandon:

In the urban areas worship took place in church cabildos, in the independent cabildos (i.e., those not physically located in church buildings), and in the homes of devotees. At the autonomous cabildos and in the homes of free blacks it was possible to have permanent shrines and altars, even if they had to be hidden. The cabildo and the home took the place of the temple and became known alternately as the *ile ocha* (Yorùbá, house of the orisha) or *casa templo* (house temple). When permitted, the great religious processions, the comparasas, were the major public venues for Lucumi worshipers, but temporary wayside shrines could be put up in parks and near large trees, and the cathedrals also figure in the practice of Lucumi religion.[52]

Initiation in the cult of a particular saint (*orisha*) was based upon a series of rituals marking the believer as a devotee to a particular divinity, with obligations and advantages arising therefrom.[53] Regardless of currently available accounts and videos, the substance of these rites continues to remain relatively secret. Only certain elements are divulged to the outsider, because knowledge must accompany the various levels of religious conversation in order to avoid people being harmed by information they are too religiously immature to process.

As clubs in the late nineteenth century were disbanded, Santería moved into private homes without connection to strict national standing.[54] These houses (Ilé) are headed by those with the most knowledge concerning the ways of the divinities, ritual and liturgical structures, and the nature of cosmic energy. Lines of authority and allegiance are clearly defined and respected. Each house abides by its own understanding of the religion and is responsible for its economic survival and ritual structure. As a consequence, there can be variation from house to house. Nonetheless, there are strong similarities concerning basic and fundamental points of theological importance. The *babalawo* is the religious leader with the greatest level of ritual and theological knowledge due to his connection with the god of divination. In Cuba, these *babalawos* are men, but this is not necessarily the case in Nigeria. A priest (*babalorisha* or *babalocha*) has a great deal of direct and daily interaction with those within the religion due to his initiation into the mysteries of the tradition. His studies are acknowledged by his title, which means "father of the saint." This role is also held by women (*iyalorisha* or *iyalocha*), who are "mothers of the saint."[55]

During an initiation ceremony (*kariocha* ceremony), those who become priests and priestesses become the child of the divinity who "rules the head." This is the divinity to whom primary allegiance is given. However, a variety of divinities actually receive attention from each religious leader and his or her house (his or her "children" in the religion and others of various degrees of involvement).

Not all believers are initiated into the priesthood. It is a complex and great responsibility, and there are clear distinctions

> between . . . faithful attendees and the true *santera* or *santero* [initiated woman and man] who has "made the saint." This is a ceremonial passage into a lifelong commitment to a particular *orisha* wherein the initiate is reborn *en santo,* in the spirit. The discipline and expense necessary to be qualified for the ceremony, together with the seriousness of the pact of service to a patron orisha ensure that only a fraction of *ilé* members will be *santeras* or *santeros.*[56]

The *orishas* in Cuba select their devotees, although it is not uncommon for religious devotion to develop genealogically. More commonly, however, those selected have attributes or traits identifiable with a particular divinity, which make the person the divinity's child (or *omo*). When a divinity's desire for a particular person is manifest, initiation—the instilling of the divinity in the head of the person—necessarily follows.[57] Once initiated, the person must observe the taboos associated with that particular divinity. Because the characteristics of the divinities who make the middle passage remain rather consistent with those characteristics discussed earlier, they are given limited attention here.

As in Yorùbáland, Cuban believers recognize Olódùmarè as the source of all existence. Olódùmarè receives very little primary attention, because he has established "ministers" or messengers who care for the daily concerns of the world. The fact that the divinities participate and live through Olódùmarè's *ashé* unites them in what might be labeled a "family." The most important of these are the seven powers or the seven dominant divinities, of which the most important is Obàtálá. He is associated with wisdom, and his children tend to be very "cerebral." He represents purity, as depicted by his white clothing. Like the other divinities, Obàtálá can manifest in a variety of forms, male or female, young or old.

Eleggua is also important because of his roles as Olódùmarè's primary messenger and the trickster god. He is addressed first in all cases, because if he does not open the gates of heaven, the *orishas* cannot communicate with humans and humans cannot communicate with the divinities. Eleggua is usually represented by a mound with eyes, mouth, and nose of shells. He can also be represented by a coconut or a large sea shell. Eleggua is connected to Ochosi and Ògûn. These three represent the warriors that are often the first point of contact between interested believers and the *orishas*. Association with other deities follows this initial step. It is possible, however, to receive Eleggua first and later receive the other warriors. Those who receive this divinity are responsible for his care, which entails strengthening him with blood and making offerings of candy, cigar smoke, and rum. If the devotee fails, the divinity can produce calamity until the offense is rectified. Ultimately the other warriors are received (*Guerreros* initiation) because they can provide protection from enemies. Receiving the warriors is also necessary for those who want eventually to "make saint" (become *santero* or *santera*). Ògún, the god associated with iron and war, is usually represented by a pot with iron implements in it. The final warrior, Ochosi, is the hunter represented by the bow and arrow cast in iron.[58]

Ògún and Ochosi are not the only divinities who are known for their warrior skills. Oya, known by the rainbow, is also a capable warrior. Her abilities in this regard are marked by her connection with battle and the whirlwind. She is also the wife of Shango, who is one of the more widely recognized deities, found throughout the Caribbean and South America. As in Nigeria, he is associated with thunder and lightning and is a culture hero, having been a king of Oyo. Shango is also known for his dancing ability and virility.

Yemaya is associated with the ocean and is considered the great mother. Also connected with the ocean is Olokun, who represents the deeper layers of the ocean. Oshún is the goddess of rivers and affairs of the heart. She is also the patron saint of Cuba. Orula or Ifa is associated with divination and the outlining of human destiny. Also present in Cuba, but of lesser importance, are Babaluaye (god of smallpox and other diseases) and Osanyin (god of plants). There are numerous other deities who do not receive the level of attention given to these *orishas*.

Respect for the ancestors was maintained, although the devotion shown them was greatly scaled back. Members of a house venerated their ancestors as well as the ancestors associated with the house through other members, including the *padrino* or *madrina* (leader of the house). Hence, one's ancestors are not strictly biologically determined.

Humans hold the same station in the cosmic order, although some of the complexity with respect to the human constitution is lost. Even so, humans are still regarded as complex entities composed of more than just physical form. As in Yorùbá religion in Nigeria, the physical form is a later manifestation of the person. The first presence is the *ori* mentioned earlier in this chapter. Its nature and function do not significantly vary from that in Yorùbá religion. Balance in life and community are achieved when *ashé*, the energy represented in the divinities, flows through individuals (hence the community). This must entail proper relationship with the *orishas,* ancestors, other humans, and the earth. Yet the regard for cosmic energy through a sensitivity to the earth, which the Yorùbá knew in Yorùbáland, could not be maintained in their new home. Life in Cuba with little more than economic (e.g., labor) connection to the earth reduced the importance of earth cults; the ancestors were no longer connected with the earth as they had been in Yorùbáland. Ancestors were remembered on the level of individuals paying respect, not on the level of communal remembrance and shrine-based reenactment. It was acknowledged, however, that believers should first strengthen their relationship with the ancestors before attempting to foster a connection with the *orishas.*

Restructuring also occurred as religious community moved away from family lines toward race lines—black slaves and white owners—resulted in the need to blend the various cults into one overarching practice. These changes in the family-based tradition also stemmed from marriages between Lucumi and non-Lucumi.[59]

This cosmological structure comes to life within the celebrations of the various Santería houses. Some houses observe Catholic rituals that include prayers and ritual movements reminiscent of the Catholic mass. Others have effectively removed the Catholic worship elements and instead focus on the essence of the gods as found in sacred stones and representative colors. The Catholic saints did not possess the believers in these settings; it was the African *orishas* who possessed their horses.[60]

Those who are committed to the religion on a deeper level can be identified by the necklace of colored beads (*collar de mazo, elekes*) associated with particular *orishas.* The *elekes* are usually presented by females already initiated during a very involved ceremony described by Canizares:

> To prepare the collares, each necklace is ritually washed in an herbal infusion consisting of water and the sacred herbs of each of the orishas represented. The string used in the collares must be cotton or some other absorbent material, . . . for sacrificial blood must be absorbed through the thread, to charge the necklace with ashé. The color pattern of each necklace indicates which orisha is being represented. . . . The actual ceremony in which a person receives the collares . . . is very involved; the collares recipient is ritually bathed and must shed his or her old clothes for new white ones. [There are prayers and incantations that accompany this.] . . . The first necklace to be conferred is usually, but not always, that of Eleggua, who as the Lord of the Gate opens each Santeria ceremony. . . . A few ilés give Obatalá's . . . first, since Obatalá is the greatest

Figure 4. Some Santería Divinities: Names, Functions, and Colors

Yorùbá Name	Santería Name /Saint	Function/Color
Olódùmarè	Olódùmarè (Olofi)/Christ	Aspect of Supreme God who controls the world
Orisa-nla/Obàtálá	Obàtálá/Virgin of Mercy*	Elder *orisha* connected with wisdom and morality/white
Eshu-Elégbá	Eleggua/Child of Atoche	Messenger of Olódùmarè, keeper of the gates/black, red
Ogún	Ògûn/St. Peter	Associated with iron tools and war/green, black
Oschoosi	Oshosi/St. Norbert	Associated with the forest and hunting/blue, orange
Orunmila/Ifá	Orunmila/St. Francis Assisi	Controller of divination/green or yellow
Obaluaiye	Babaluaye/Lazarus	Associated with disease (smallpox)/black or light blue
Osanyin	Osanyin/St. Joseph	Controller of herbs and herbal medicine/green
Sángó	Shango/St. Barbara	God of thunder and battle/ red and white
Oyá	Oya/Virgin of La Candelaria	Associated with whirlwinds and cemeteries/maroon, red, or brown
Yemojá	Yemaya/Virgin of Regla	Associated with ocean and motherhood/blue, white
Olókun	Olokun/Virgin of Regla	Associated with lower levels of the ocean/blue, white
Oshún	Oshun/Virgin of Cardiad del Cobre	Associated with water and sensuality/yellow

* Joseph Murphy indicates Mercedes. Adapted from Joseph Murphy, *Santeria: African Spirits in America* (Boston: Beacon Press, 1988, 1993), and George Brandon, *Santería from Africa to the New World*.

of all orishas. The number of collares given at the ceremony varies slightly, and santeros may keep on adding necklaces as needed. Most of the time, however, the first five necklaces conferred are Eleggua, Obatalá, Yemayá, Shangó, and Oshún. Other orishas commonly represented are Ogún and Babalú Ayé.[61]

Those who receive the necklaces are associated with the religion, but they are not *santeros* or *santeras*. In Cuba, to become the latter means being selected by an *orisha*. Once selected and able financially to afford the initiation, the three-year period of initiation begins. (The length of time varies from location to location.) The final stage of this complex process is described thus:

> The culmination of the ceremony, which is also called *asiento* or *hacer santo* ("making saint"), is a three-day fast during which the neophyte is presented to the community as a new brother or sister. In Cuba, it was usually at this time that the orisha that had been "seated" first possessed the neophyte. Actual orisha possession, obligatory in Cuban Santeria, is becoming rarer in America, possibly because consecrated *batá* drums, which have to be played for the orishas to possess the neophyte, are also very rare. After initiation, both males and females are known by the feminine name *iyabó* (in Yorùbá, *iyawó*), which literally means "bride" but is understood in Santeria to mean "novice." During the one-year novitiate that follows, [they] must wear white and observe numerous taboos, some of which they must continue to respect for the rest of their lives. [This information is attained through divination, referred to as the *itá*.] . . . During their first year . . . santeros also learn the technical and practical aspects of their new status as fully initiated priests or priestesses.[62]

For *santeros* there are additional levels of expertise. For example, those trained with the cowrie shell divination are called *italeros,* and those who have been trained to use the knife during a sacrifice *(pinando)* perform other tasks. Women cannot perform this aspect of ritual activity until after menopause.

If divination demands it, *santeros* can be initiated into the cult of Ifá and thereby become *babalaos (babalawos)*. Although this initiation was considered the most secret of all, it was described in print in 1975. The account is worth quoting at length:

> The initiation process fills a week, during which the initiate has no contact with the outside world. He spends this time in the company of the babalaos from the surrounding area who have come together to initiate and welcome a new member to their fraternity. These babalaos lead the initiate through ritual cleansings, force him to endure specific punish-

ments, and teach him secrets of divination, including the *oddus* of the Book of Ifá. The emphasis of the week's activities is on the initiate renouncing his former self, accepting the responsibility of his new position, and taking his place with his fellow babalaos. . . . Communication is almost exclusively in Lucumí—and partially in a veiled Lucumí that eavesdropping outsiders cannot understand. . . . Some of the individual rites emphasize the babalaos' identification with the legendary first sixteen kings of Yorùbá. One of these is the "receiving of Orula," probably the most important part of the seven-day ceremony, which takes place on the first day. The initiate has been shaved, painted, and crowned with a headdress of coconut shell, beads, and red parrot feathers. One of the senior babalaos . . . paints the names or symbols of the sixteen kings on a long block of cedar that is laid before the initiate, and the five senior babalaos then paint their symbols on the block to show that they witnessed the event.[63]

After this, treated palm-nuts are given to the initiate, who must clean them with his mouth by eating the material covering the nuts. After this, the initiate promises not to touch his head without the permission of Orula.[64]

Many are familiar with Santería because of the religion's most public activity, the *bembé* or drum dance. Through drumming, when permitted, Africans were able to continue to communicate with divine forces through the language of the *batá* drums. This music as divine language remained vital even within the restrictive environment of Cuba's slave system. And the words of the drums were an important part of celebrations for the *orishas*. General dance is often followed by dance and drumming geared toward persuading the *orishas* to possess their children. Once the divinities descend, those present receive messages, advice, and healing.[65] One of the more private but highly publicized elements of this religion is sacrifice (ebó). As one *santero* informed me, some things are only accomplished through blood. Although not all sacrifices involve blood, blood-offerings are the most powerful because of the concentration of *ashé* in blood. The importance of sacrifice and blood is understood everywhere the religion is observed.

Santería, even when periodically persecuted, has continued to grow and to incorporate an ever-increasing cross-section of Cuban society. Although forced to maintain a strong secretive tone, this religion developed in ways that further strained its relationship with the Catholic Church and brought it into contact with emerging traditions such as *Espiritismo* (a form of spiritism). The Afro-Cubanism documented by Fernando Ortiz focused contemporary attention on the religion and generated a sense of pride that revitalized African roots, including religious roots.[66]

This religion had a unique home in Cuba until the revolution of 1959, at which time practitioners who fled Castro's government transplanted the religion to locations such as Puerto Rico and the United States. Others who had not openly embraced the tradition in Cuba found it a source of security, resources, and balance once transplanted to U.S. soil.[67]

ORISHA **WORSHIP IN THE UNITED STATES**

Without doubt, the twentieth century witnessed a large movement of believers to North America, but it would be wrong to assume that religious practices resembling Santería did not exist in the United States before the late twentieth century. Although the United States is more influenced by Congo-Angolan populations of slaves than by the Yorùbá and Dahomey, I contend that substantial "retention" provided fertile ground for the development of traditions such as Santería within African American communities.

It was noted in chapter 1 that by the late nineteenth century the vast majority of slaves in the United States had been born in the States. There were African-born slaves, of course, but as of 1776 this number only represented about 20 percent of the slave population. Yet it was possible for African religion—particularly deities who had been associated with natural forces—to survive in vital and vibrant ways.[68] In fact, the historical record demonstrates the persistence of religious beliefs and practices associated with Yorùbá tradition. For example, Raboteau writes that "hints in the historical record suggest that some slaves in Virginia in the 1830s thought of Christian conversion and baptism as similar to the initiation rituals of spirit possession. Henry Brown, a former slave from Virginia, remarked that when his sister 'became anxious to have her soul converted' she 'shaved the hair from her head, as many of the slaves thought they could not be converted without doing this.' . . . Shaving the head of the initiate, according to African custom, prepared the individual for possession by his or her patron god." This certainly shows some consistency in terms of ritual reenactment with the African traditions brought to the New World, including those of Yorùbá, Dahomey, Congo, Angola, and so on.[69]

Hyatt's *Hoodoo—Conjuration—Witchcraft—Rootwork* contains other examples applicable here. Regarding the Mother of Perpetual Help, Hyatt's informant told him: "And the Mother of Perpetual Help, she opens the way, she gives you bread when you got children like I have—she opens the way for you to have success. Well, you give her a blue candle—that's for children. And you pray twice a day to her. . . . And whatever you promise her when you get your wish, why you give her that."[70] The reader will notice strong similarities between this saint as recognized in the United States and the Santería divinity, Yemaja. The color blue is the color of both, and the association with children—the divine mother—is consistent. In addition, in both Santería and U.S. practices, saints are, at times, given strong drink. This certainly is consistent with the representation of *orishas* for whom cigars and drink are important. One of Hyatt's informants had this to say about approaching St. Anthony with drink and cigars:

An' Yo' put 'im [St. Peter] ovah de do'
If Yo' ain't got but a nickel
Try tuh git a nickel's wuth of beer
an' when Yo' gittin' up in de mawnin'
an' Yo' want a good time in yore house
an' some fellahs come in an' give yo' money
Yo' jes' throw beer on 'im [St. Peter]
jes' throw plenty beer on 'im an' light a white light
an' ah bet chew St. Peter gon'a open dat do'
Yo' git St. Anthony, yeah, a brown candle . . .
Yo' git a cigar. . . .
Yo' git 'bout a little whiskey glass of whiskey see
'cause St. Anthony he's a Saint he laks cigahs
an' he wus a good-time man . . .
an' yo' wake up de nex' mawnin' an' Yo' see
de glass dry an' de cigah half smoked.[71]

Elements of the cosmology and theology associated with Santería are noticeably maintained. The movement of Santería to other areas of the Caribbean and the United States served to *strengthen* appreciation for African-based religious practices, an appreciation forged through centuries of retention. Many have minimized the importance of such findings by arguing that African deities could not significantly survive in the United States because of the dominance of Protestantism. Such scholars contend that these gods are best able to survive in Catholic countries because of the saint cults and accompanying ritual practices that resemble African attitudes toward the *orìsàs*. I think, however, that Erika Bourguigeon's argument is useful for its refutation of this assumed direct relationship between Catholicism's presence and the presence of African derived religions:

. . . an explanation for the presence or absence of Afro-Christian spirit cults cannot simply be found by asking what the dominant form of Christianity in a given area is. It is true that these cults have incorporated into their liturgy and ritual certain elements of Catholic practice, and the

Africans could not have done so without having been taught rudiments of the Catholic religion. But this fact in itself is not enough, it seems, to explain the existence of the cults. It merely provides a necessary element for their development. Some Catholic countries such as Cuba. . . . have Afro-Catholic cults. Others such as Martinique . . . do not have them.[72]

The presence of *botánicas* on the streets of many urban areas such as New York, Boston, West St. Paul, and Los Angeles point to the existence of Santería in these locations.[73] These are shops for practitioners of this religion. Careful observers may see Shango's wooden axe or Ògún's blacksmith's tools and tools of war on the shelves of these shops. The *botánicas* I have entered in Manhattan, Boston, and elsewhere are full of these items as well as of lithographs of the various saints, the *eleke,* statues, herbs, and so on. The fact that these shops are typically located in Spanish-speaking communities indicates that Cuban and Puerto Rican practitioners form the core of the Santería community. Joseph Murphy reports that Oba Ifa Morote (Francisco Mora) brought Santería to New York in 1946, when he came from Havana where he had become a *babalao* in 1944. With time, his knowledge and the interest of those living in New York resulted in the development of a house *(ile).* His reputation grew and he produced over six thousand "godchildren" (those he brought into the religion), who represent a committed group that provides for the house's needs based upon a sense of faith and family.[74] According to Steven Gregory:

> The relationship between godparent and godchild lies at the core of the social organization of Santería. Symbolically, it connotes the bonds existing between parents and children, and the living and their ancestors, and the Orisha and mankind. Practitioners of Santería conceive this relationship to be reciprocal. The godparent directs the spiritual development of the godchild and provides an array of supportive assistance. In return, the godchild contributes labor and resources in support of the ritual and secular activities of the house.[75]

Such was the relationship between Mora and his godchildren. Mora asserts that he was commissioned by the *Asociación de San Francisco* (a group of *Babalawos*) to bring the tradition to the United States. It is possible, however, that there were some practitioners here prior to this, but not with the influence that Mora would exert.[76]

Although Cubans began making their way to North America in the nineteenth century (perhaps informing early North American religious practices in some ways), it was not until the demand of the 1950s that the ritual substance of the tradition found strong expression on U.S. soil, as more than fifty thousand Cubans moved to the United States before 1970. Those moving during this period, whether or not they followed the *orishas* in Cuba, found the *orishas* a stabilizing force in the United States, which was then troubled by human rights struggles.

During these earlier years ritual focus was still on Cuba, where many went to receive initiation when this was possible (Puerto Rico when Cuba was not a possibility). Many contended that proper Santería initiation ceremonies could only be held in Cuba because of materials such as sacred stones that were not present in the United States. Others argued that the location was unimportant; otherwise the tradition would not have survived in the New World.[77] It is said, however, that *babalao* Carlos Ojeda of Miami possessed important ritual items taken from Cuba. This combined with the presence of consecrated *batá* drums, made initiations and ceremonies possible.

Levels of involvement correspond to levels of knowledge and training, beginning with the receiving of beads, then receiving of the warriors, and ending with initiation into the priesthood. Those who receive the beads are referred to as *alejo* and are protected by the godparents' saint. They are then able to move to receiving the warriors and perhaps the priesthood. One's position within the house is based upon years initiated rather than chronological age. These houses, for the most part, are within the living space of the priest or priestess; various rooms serve the ritual and theological needs of the community.

Marta Moreno Vega argues that before 1960 there were only twenty-five persons in New York City who followed the way of the saints. But although small in numbers, their work was enhanced by the presence of two traditional drummers from Cuba living in New York City, Julito Callazo and Francisco Aguabella. Other musicians also entered the world of Santería that was developing in New York City. In addition to Cuban participants, there was a growing number of Puerto Ricans.[78] And although some African Americans participated at this point, Chief Medahochi K. O. Zannu argues that African Americans who might have been interested assumed that these *ile* were Spanish clubs and that the activities were limited to Spanish speakers because Spanish was the dominant language.[79]

It is commonly held that many African Americans in the twentieth century first became acquainted with the superficial aspects of Santería through the music of figures such as Mongo Santamaria, Ray Barretto, and Tito Puente, and through dance.[80] George Brandon claims that the first devotee to be initiated in the United States was Julia Franco (1962); the initiation was done by Cuban-born priestess Mercedes Noble. Yet Brandon and others recognize that the first African American priestess, Margie Baynes Quiniones, was initiated in New York in 1961 by Cuban priestess Leonore Dolme.[81] She subsequently developed a house that consisted of twenty-one priests.

As of 1986, there were as many as ten thousand African American practitioners in New York City alone. Some African Americans, after initiation and proper training, began establishing their own *iles* (houses) with their own godchildren, while others remained in "multiethnic" houses. Murphy's description of one encounter in the house of Oba Ifa Morote on the day of Ifa's (Orunmila's) feast sheds light on African American involvement in Santería:

> As I move back from these senior priestesses, I fall into conversation with Olatutu, a black American man in his fifties. As the priestesses radiate strength and worldly wisdom, Olatutu is small and gentle and only newly initiated into the way of the *orishas*. But his story is that of many other seekers who find themselves in Padrino's *ile*. Olatutu is a self-taught scholar of the mystical traditions of the world. He has found in santería a grand synthesis of his reading in Egyptology and his participation in Moorish Science and Masonry. For him, the *orishas* are the purest expression of the primordial African wisdom that gave birth not only to Egypt and Ethiopia but to human life itself in the Rift Valley.[82]

Steven Gregory also provides useful information concerning the involvement of African Americans in Santería, based upon field work done in the Bronx, New York. One *ile,* referred to as "Fernando's house," had, in 1972, roughly twenty-five African American members, most of whom were in their twenties and thirties and had moved into the tradition through the influence of friends and acquaintances. Although this tradition has its deepest roots in the black African practices of the Yorùbá, some African American members of "Fernando's house" claim that racism on the part of Hispanic members often prevents them from progressing in the tradition.[83] As one of the first African American members of the house noted, many objected to his early involvement at the house; and he attributed this animosity to racial prejudice. His initial discomfort was increased through the heavy use of Spanish as the house's language. He overcame these difficulties, however, and his reputation and responsibilities have grown. In addition, he has also begun producing godchildren of his own.[84] Despite these difficulties the number of African Americans continues to grow.

In addition to joining Cuban and Puerto Rican houses, African Americans established a good number of houses that reflect the "unique" needs and concerns of African Americans. One such house, "Peter's and Katherine's house," was studied by Mary Curry during the completion of her dissertation. It was understood as an important house in the African American sections of New York City and is a fairly good size house, with Peter numbering his godchildren at roughly two hundred (with beads). There are at least nineteen priests within the house who have godchildren of their own. According to Curry, Peter was initiated in 1973 and began producing godchildren three years later, while Katherine was initiated in 1974 and began producing godchildren in 1977. As with all houses, growth results from the reputation of the padrino or madrina and his or her knowledge. Those who have needs they believe the padrino or madrina can meet begin to attend, first casually.

Mary Curry asserts that notable ritual differences between African American houses, like Peter's and Katherine's, and other Santería houses do not exist. Nonetheless, there are differences in that nationalistic tendencies and race-based issues inform theology and ritual activities. One sign of this is the tendency of African Americans to call the tradition "Yorùbá religion" instead of using the term *Santería*. For nationalistically-minded African Americans, their own term provides a much wanted and much stronger link to an "African past" and allows for attention to race-based issues. In some African American houses the religion is practiced without any attention to spiritist influences present in Cuban and Puerto Rican houses, and without attention to Christian (Catholic) influences also present elsewhere.[85] In many of these cases there is a concern with ritual and theological orthodoxy using Nigerian practice as the standard. These are, for the most part, conceptual differences undoubtedly fueled by the Black Power Movement, Civil Rights movement, and an overarching rethinking of African American identity.[86] Concerning this, early African American priests made an effort to think through the *odus* and the *orishas* and there find significance for black life.[87] For example,

> It was these same . . . priests . . . who also thought about Olokun . . . The great *Orisha* of the sea. They reasoned that Olokun was the *Orisha* of the dark and unknowable *bottom* of the sea, that mysterious harbinger of the secrets of creation and in whose murky but stabilizing wetness is the actual support of all of life. They saw the bottom of the sea as being in principle the same as the layer of fluid that supports the human brain at its bottom. . . . "Ancestral memory," as we have since come to call it, is a [sic] ability that refers back to the Middle Passage itself and recalls the many millions of Africans who in defiance of the *thought* of "slavery" dove or rebelled and were thrown into the sea—ultimately to form a spiritual

collective that could forever be sympathetic to children of their comrades who did survive the journey. The assumption is that that body of souls forms a kind of *collective unconsciousness* in the psyche of Black Americans in general and is totally essential to Orisha Worship in the New World. That collective unconscious is seen as a manifestation of *Olokun*.[88]

Unlike the majority of other priests, many African American priests have organized themselves into societies. As of 1991, the following societies were active: the Society of the Children of Obàtálá, the Society of the Children of Yemaya, the Society of the Children of Oshun, and the Society of the Children of Oya.[89]

Julia Franco, the first African American initiated in the United States, was not the first African American to make the tradition her own. In fact, the first African American to seek religious selfhood through this religion was Walter Eugene King (b. 1928), a priest of Obàtálá, in 1959 in Mantanza, Cuba.

King recounts that as a member of the Baptist Church, baptized at age twelve, he had an interest in African dance, which he pursued at the Detroit Urban League. This sparked an interest in African studies, which ultimately resulted in his break with Christianity at the age of sixteen.[90] This interest in African philosophy and nationalism was not simply a result of external stimulation, but also of his family's orientation. King's father had moved to Detroit from Georgia in 1912 and became involved in the Moorish Science Temple (see chapter 3) and the Garvey movement. Yet, in addition to the exposure to alternate religious systems provided by his father, King recounts that his reading of Somerset Maugham's *The Razor's Edge* and Mbono Ajiki's *My Africa* moved him in the direction of Eastern traditions and African religion.[91]

At age twenty, King danced with the Katherine Dunham dance troupe for two months in late 1950. Shortly after this he married and became entrenched in the culturally eclectic world of Greenwich Village.[92] With his wife he developed a coffee house and, with those who frequented the shop, he developed an organization called the Order of Dambala Hwedo. This was a nationalist group practicing Akan and Dahomean religion.[93] Under the leadership of Fritz Vincent, the group was small but interested in deepening its understanding of African religion. But the group began to move in a direction with which Nana Oseijeman (King's new name) was not comfortable. It was a movement away from pure commitment to establishing African religion and society. According to Carl Hunt, "[The group] did not want to worship more than one god, though they would salute such deities as Damballa, Ògûn and Shango. They argued that black Americans could not understand and would not accept more than one god. Nana Oseijeman disagreed because blacks understood and accepted Christian emphasis [on the Trinity]."[94]

Nana Oseijeman's progress from casual training to his interest in the priesthood was, in part, motivated by what he understood as a need for leadership within the black nationalist movement. But he was only interested in a religious priesthood that would leave him free to speak to the unique ontological and epistemological concerns of African Americans in ways Christian clergy did not.[95] Having done initial readings in voodoo and other African religious traditions, he was convinced that priesthood in the Yorùbá religion and the espousing of its importance to African Americans would provide the type of nationalist movement and vision African Americans needed. With time, he became convinced that he should train for priesthood in the cult of Obàtálá in Mantanzas, Cuba. At first Nana Oseijeman resisted the idea of initiation because as a black nationalist he did not like the idea of incorporating Catholic saints into an African religion. Finally, convinced that it is an African religion with a necessary Catholic covering, he decided to seek initiation. This initiation took place on August 26, 1959, in Mantanzas, under the guidance of a *santero* named Sonagba.[96] Initiated (to the deity Aganju) with him was Christopher Oliana, whose parents owned a *botánica* in New York and who thus was familiar with the rituals and theology of Santería.

King describes the process this way:

[W]hen we got there [Mantanzas] they took us into a room, as I recall, and they then began to divine. They wanted to do their own. . . . They read me as Obàtálá. . . . It took a week then to buy all kinds of stuff that we needed, to purchase the animals and other live stock and to get us psychologically prepared. . . . I understood absolutely nothing because I was waiting for them to ordain me some kind of way but with words. But they got everything together. . . . So they did then my entire initiation without interruptions. . . . Then we [he and Chris] stayed in the room for six days. We had to perform and everything like that . . . . I wanted everything to be African. They had some type of Spanish clothes they wanted us to wear. I didn't want to wear those, not on a daily basis. So I [wrapped] my sheet around me the way the Akan people do. . . . The only part that I didn't really find African there was, one final day when we had to visit a church. We had to get some holy water. . . .[97]

THE SHANGO TEMPLE

Upon his return to the United States, Nana Oseijeman, as King was now called, was removed from the Order of Dambala Hwuedo. And after another name change, to Adefunmi, he developed the Shango Temple in 1959 on East 125th Street. The charter members of Shango Temple were Adefunmi, Oliana, Clarence Robbins, Henry Maxwell, Royal Brown, Bonsu, and Mama Keke. During this period, his efforts to organize cultural events resulted in his recognition as an important cultural nationalist. He also developed and incorporated the African Theological Archministry Inc., in 1960, and an African market in 1961 that sold cloth and other goods as well as books written by Adefunmi, such as *The Yorùbá State, Tribal Origins of the Afro-Americans,* and *The Gods of Africa.*[98]

Adefunmi held nationalist leanings that would eventually result in a split with Christopher Oliana, who rejected a removal of Catholic influences on the tradition. Adefunmi remained convinced that a more authentic form of religious expression, one that was Yorùbá in nature and action, was possible and desirable. His goal was to acquaint African Americans with their heritage and provide them with a strong sense of community through mutual respect and kindness, by introducing them to Yorùbá culture as a means of ending their "cultural amnesia." According to Adefunmi:

> African and Western cultures were fundamentally opposed. The purpose of Western culture is to perfect the physical world. Africans want to perfect the spiritual environment. Our achievement is "human technology." Here in America we have been briefly conquered by European culture, but we are Africans nonetheless. The Italians have their festivals. The Chinese have their New Year. . . . We're just "Negroes." What does that mean? Afro-Americans are suffering from cultural amnesia. They don't know which nation they belong to.[99]

The temple responds to two major needs. For black nationalists, it provides a sense of cultural identity and a unified community. The use of dashikis and other indications of an African connection sparked the interest of nationalists who wanted to add a religious dimension to their agenda. And for others it provided a response to pressing personal issues by taking into consideration their explicitly articulated spiritual questions. Adefunmi and the members of the temple were committed to regenerating African American cultural life. He renamed Harlem "New Oyo," in order to highlight the regeneration of Yorùbá culture exemplified by the temple.[100]

Tension naturally developed between the Santería community and the Shango Temple because the temple openly expressed the more delicate elements of the tradition.[101] As Stephen Clapp records, African American devotees associated with Adefunmi advertised their beliefs by placing a sign outside of the temple and parading through Harlem wearing African attire while carrying statues of the orìsàs. In addition, they openly performed ceremonies during the World's Fair and on film in "Only One New York." Furthermore, the temple organized such high-profile events as the Afro-American Day, which attracted roughly six hundred people wearing African attire.[102] The alterations advocated by the temple extended beyond this level of display in that the traditional secrecy observed with respect to ceremonies and knowledge was questioned by African American participants, who proselytized openly and aggressively. African Americans were clearly doing away with traditional protocol and religious sensibilities. Also notable among these alterations was the removal of Christian influences. Adefunmi believed that the maintenance of the Catholic cover, which was no longer necessary, compromised the purity of practice.

Many within the larger Santería community believed that misunderstandings concerning animal sacrifice and a general assumption that Santería lacked values (i.e. Christian values) already made Santería dangerously vulnerable to attack from self-righteous and fear-driven officials and community leaders. Thus, African Americans who openly altered the religion to meet their nationalistic goals might bring even more pressure from the authorities. Many practitioners of Santería acted upon their concerns by questioning the authenticity of the temple's ceremonies and thereby distancing the temple from the larger religious community. For example, it was argued that the drums used were not consecrated and, as a result, the participants were not actually possessed by the orishas.[103] In addition, restrictions were placed upon Adefunmi's function as a priest. In this way, his activities were monitored because he had to work with Puerto Rican and Cuban priests in order to gain a better knowledge of the rituals and to perform important ceremonies such as initiation. This allowed Santería houses to keep practitioners away from Adefunmi by claiming that his knowledge was too limited and that he preserved a sense of racism that should be offensive to true devotees. Nonetheless, clients came from cities such as Philadelphia, Chicago, and Washington for consultations with him, primarily over money concerns.[104] According to Hunt, a common ritual solution to this problem involved the following: "the person [burns] orange leaves and peels together with brown sugar. Another remedy for money problems . . . is for a person to mix some parsley with honey, cinnamon and grains of dried corn and leave it in a high place."[105]

By 1964, the division between the temple and the larger Santería community was irreconcilable.[106] Again, *santeros* objected to his overt ritualism and nationalism and Adefunmi rejected their Catholic-Yorùbá synthesis. Those involved in Santería were not the only ones to question the feasibility of "purifying" the tradition. Others questioned the ability of Adefunmi and his group to fully understand and connect with the actual culture of Nigeria, a culture that had itself undergone alterations.[107]

Adefunmi was not alone in his quest for "authentic" Yorùbá culture. John Mason and Edward Gary also refer to a return to precolonial Yorùbá tradition. Although many argue against the potential of such an endeavor, Mason and Gary maintain a vision of a "Yorùbá Reversionism," a tradition free of Catholic and slave-trade connotations. This process permits the preservation of an oral tradition that is slowly disappearing and fosters a "re-Africanizing" of the religion in a way that allows blacks in the diaspora to maintain an epistemological and cultural connection with their African heritage. Finally, Gary contends, this process provides otherwise inaccessible educational resources to interested persons.[108]

In response to the larger Santería community, Adefunmi and the members of the temple, eventually renamed the Yorùbá Temple, asserted that the religious is political and the political is religious; it is impossible to separate the two. As part of this reenvisioning, it was necessary to redefine various terms, including religion itself. Baba Oseijeman understood it as encompassing "the ethnic heritage of a particular people." As such, it entails their collective and complete history and philosophical outlook as a response to their environment. In short, it is an "ethnic celebration" inseparable from what it means to be alive. Understood in this way, each community possesses its own tradition, and it is dangerous to embrace that of another group. To do this, according to Baba Oseijeman, is equivalent to cultural suicide.[109] Very early in his practice of this tradition, Adefunmi indicated a strong connection between the self and the community's religious practices. He argued that religious practice is actually "worship of one's own personality" with the goal of controlling the forces that influence one's being. In this way the tradition provided ground rules and models for living properly in the world. Acceptance of these rules is first marked by the receiving of a new name symbolizing one's move toward the essential self.[110] The religion was idolatrous, but this idolatry allowed for the reconstitution of self-identity and self-worth based upon a close connection to cosmic forces and energies. This tradition provided African Americans with a connection to Africa that is deeper than rhetoric and mere aesthetic appeal; it is spiritual, a connection to energies that can never be understood strictly in light of material appearances.[111]

The name given to the practices of the Yorùbá Temple, Orisa-Vodu, reflects the theological and ritual break with the larger Santería community noted above. Chief Adenibi Edubi Ifamyiwa Ajamu, an early leader in this movement, explains that the temple's cultural practices, as of 1966, were dominated by the Yorùbá reality. There was also, however, a Dahomean and Congolese influence. According to Chief Ajamu, there is no conflict in incorporating these various cultural elements. The task of building a cultural complex that speaks directly to the needs of African Americans (a mixture of various African cultural groups) requires the blending of various cultural realities.

Although the temple's language was strongly racial, it took time for restrictions on white participation in the religion to be fully enforced. And so, during the first phase, the 1960s, white Americans were free to attend some of the functions. The collection of elders, the Ogboni council, decided that white Americans can attend all but the Night of Oshun, which is a secret rite.[112] According to Baba Oseijeman, "There is no room for racism in our religion. . . . If the religion is valid for blacks, it applies to whites as well. We teach that when an Afro-American has self-respect, he has no need to fear or hate the white man."[113] Stephen Clapp offers an account of his visit to a Friday evening meeting called the *Bembé*:

> On the second floor landing was a door painted in triangles of red, yellow and blue. Beyond a small hallway a dozen or so people sat on folding chairs and low stools along two walls. A team of drummers was ranged along another wall. At the base of the fourth wall a waist-high altar had been fitted out with statues and squat, flickering candles. The walls themselves were decorated with drawings of the five-footed fowl whom Obatala sent to mix earth and water in the Yorùbá myth of Creation. There were paintings of carved columns and inscriptions in an alphabet that Adefunmi had concocted from symbols used in the phonetic alphabet. . . . The bembe began with the "cleaning" of the temple with incense. The priests went around the circumference of the room with incense and water in order to seal off those inside from negative forces. Next Adefunmi petitioned the Yorùbá ancestors for permission to hold the ceremony. Through divination he determined whether quarrels in the room were likely to break up the ceremony. . . . Adefunmi called upon Elegba, the spirit guardian of the door, to protect the room. Permission to hold the bembe was asked of Obatala, patron god of the temple. When this was secured, those present were invited to salute the statue of the god that dominated the altar. Men prostrated themselves on the floor. Women lay at full length on one hip and one elbow. Adefunmi then blessed the drum-

mers, asking the orishas to allow the drummers' rhythms to reach them without mistake. The heart of the service was a series of dances, with accompanying chants and drumming, that honored the twelve major orishas in the Yorùbá pantheon. . . . The first gods honored were the male orishas—Ògûn, Oshosi, Obatala, Shango, Babalu-aiye, Agunju and Irenle. Those were followed by dances honoring Yemoja, the mother of the gods, Oshun, Ibeji and Oya, the female orishas. The cycle closed with another invocation to Elegba, the messenger. Throughout the bembe various onlookers rose and danced along with the priests. . . . Frequently dancers went into trances of possession.[114]

The average day within the life of a temple member was less dramatic than these celebrations might indicate. According to Adefunmi, a typical day began with the presentation of water to the *orishas*. Other ritual activities might include a reading by Adefunmi.[115] For the average person the tradition enabled material gain and social status. For those with a stronger interest in the religion, the first step in becoming a member involved gaining a new African name, which, as noted above, marked the awareness of one's African self and the necessary break with the cultural perspective of white America. If interest remained strong after this point, the person was given the opportunity to purchase proper African clothing. The next stage was the receiving of *ileki (eleke)*, or the beads. After receiving these initial beads, the person received the warriors—Elégbá, Ògûn and Oshosi.

The work of the temple was not without problems and internal strife, as the questionable intent of some "clients" might suggest. For example, conflict over Adefunmi's marriage to a white American and his decision to take a second wife from within the temple resulted in the secession of many members. Other problems surfaced, which ultimately resulted in the closing of the temple except for necessary rituals. Adefunmi, along with a few families who participated in the temple, gave some thought to moving out of New York since it was hopelessly devoted to the ways and worldview of white Americans.

ORISHA-**VODU AND OYOTUNJI AFRICAN VILLAGE**

Until 1969 the temple's essential self was defined within the context of New York City. Chief Adenibi Edubi Ifamuyiwa Ajamu, foreign minister of Oyotunji Village, asserts that the 1960s were the appointed time for reintroducing African Americans to their cultural legacy through the Yorùbá religion. The 1970s, by contrast, marked the time for institutionalizing this Yorùbá way of life by gathering together those committed to the lifestyle and settling in a place outside of New York City.[116] Movement away from

New York City in the second phase of growth was vital because a physical connection to earth is vital. This connection to nature allows for a better understanding of one's ancestors' relationship with the cosmic energies. Hence, this tradition could not reach its zenith among the buildings and concrete of New York City.

After several false starts, including a failed teaching position for Adefunmi in Bricks, North Carolina, and other uncertainties (some wanted to go to Nigeria or the Caribbean), the Village was undertaken in Savannah, Georgia. It was eventually moved to Paiges Point, South Carolina, and then to Brays Island. It finally moved to its current location in Sheldon, South Carolina, in 1970. The initial population was composed of Oseijeman Adefunmi I, one of his wives (Majile Olafemi and her two children), and a few other families.

In 1979, when Carl Hunt published one of the first studies of Oyotunji Village, the Village consisted of 125 people and ten acres. Since then the number of residents has fluctuated between 125 and 260, with many "citizens" (those initiated by the Village) living outside of the Village. The basic unit within the Village is the family based upon one's ancestors, husband, wife (wives), and children.

During its early years, membership in the Village was easily obtained. For most, it was simply a matter of arriving and requesting permission to establish a home. The reasons for wanting to do so ranged from discontentment with city dwelling to a solid desire for an African-based existence.[117] Early in the Village's history, to become a permanent resident required that one live there for six consecutive months. In addition, an oath to the village, its leadership, and laws was taken. Following all of this was the reading to determine the orìsà that rules the applicant's head. Chief Ajamu has indicated that these rules have been altered in order to address the current circumstances of African Americans and the needs of the Village. In some instances, the initial interest was not carried through to the development of the land given. Currently those interested in establishing themselves must have sufficient resources to develop the land, granted by the Ogboni Society of elders, within an acceptable period of time.[118]

Land is important because for most of the residents it is the first time they have had this type of connection with nature. The rules that governed residency during the early phase of the Village's existence were:

1. All villagers must wear African attire at all times.
2. All men must work on the dokpwe, community projects. District dokpwes are scheduled by the King each week.

3. All persons living in Oyotunji must receive tribal marks within three months. The marks demonstrate to the ancestors that those in the village are a different people, a unique community.[119]

An issue that surfaced early for the residents of Oyotunji Village involved the suspicion of white neighbors and the fear expressed by many African Americans whose perceptions of the Villagers' practices were only partially based upon fact and overwhelmingly guided by stereotypical depictions of African traditions as "evil" and "dangerous." This was addressed in two ways. First, Village residents attempted to gain a better knowledge of their cultural heritage through the Yorùbá Royal Academy.[120] In addition, these concerns were addressed through the establishment of a Foreign Minister (Chief Ajamu), who is responsible for fostering relations between the Village and the larger South Carolina community, and between the Village and "Yorùbá" around the country. Chief Ajamu does this, in part, through speaking engagements and assistance with the ceremonial needs of other communities. With time, the African Americans within the larger community recognized commonalities in practice and began consulting with priests in the Village for divination and root work.[121]

After the move to the South, a complete break with Santería occurred, marked by the conducting of initiations. Omowale, a person interested in the Village, came to visit from Gary, Indiana, and persuaded Baba to initiate him. Omowale argued that African Americans, like other groups, must develop the tradition in a way that fits their context and meets their needs. This must include developing ways of bringing people into the higher levels of the religion.[122] The replacing of the old self with a new perspective and relationship with the world should reflect the particular circumstances of African American identity. Baba agreed and made preparations to initiate the first group, which included Omowale, Akanke, and Akinyele. Hunt records the ceremony:

> The first part of the initiation took place at night at the river near Paiges Point [their current home]. As they left the house to make their way to the river, a terrible storm broke out and everyone was frightened but Baba. . . . [He convinced them to go on.] Akinyele had to strip naked, and all his clothing was thrown into the water. Baba then washed and prayed over him and performed the remainder of the ritual by the river. After that part of the ritual was completed, Akinyele was dressed in clean white clothes and they returned to the house to complete the initiation. . . . [By 1971, the time required for initiation had increased from seven days to three months.] The three stayed isolated in a room with only a mat for

seven days. That was the length of time Baba had learned from the Cubans that new initiates had to be confined in a Temple room. After that time, they were allowed to emerge and go about their business.

With time the initiation into the priesthood entailed the following:

During the three-month period while the person is in the temple his head is shaved and many incisions are made. [Similar cuts are made at the joints as well.] A ball of organic matter of herbs and other ingredients are rubbed into the scalp so that it can go into the cuts . . . and that gives them their *Ashe*. . . . After the three-month confine-

Gate leading into Oyotunji African Village. Photo by the author.

ment the *Iyawo* leaves the temple. If he is not a resident of Oyotunji he can leave the Village with the gods he has received. [The person] returns to the Village after a year and brings his gods back for the chief priest to reopen and make another sacrifice of a goat and some birds. Once that is done the [person] becomes *Aworo*, which means a working priest.[123]

[With initiation completed, the new priest becomes] at once a trinity of entities: (1) an olorisha (the owner of Orisha powers), (2) an omo-orisha (an Orisha's baby or God-child), and (3) an Iyawo-orisha (a "bride" of the God or Goddess). After this series of sacred rites—actually the most sacred moments of [one's] entire life—[one] will be informed by the presiding Oriate (Chief priest) of the vows, the obligations and the responsibilities which [one] as a new priest or priestess must now have toward our Ancestors, our Orisha and our people. It is now time for the Olorisha to baptize [the new priest] in the blood of the animals purchased for sacrifice to the orisha. They will also prepare shrines [for the new priest to use].[124]

A major component of this process is the revealing of the "road" or path that the new priest or priestess must follow throughout the remainder of

H.R.H. Oba Ofuntola Oseijeman Adelabu Adefunmi I in the Royal Palace in Oyotunji Village during an interview. Photo by the author.

his or her life. (If life is revealed to include hardship for the new initiate, sacrifice can be made in an effort to alter this path.) After this work is done, the new priest or priestess remains in the Village for an additional period of time during which an elder priest or priestess is responsible for their further development. The major thrust of this additional work involves destruction of old attitudes and ways, which allows a new behavior and new characteristics to take hold and provide guidance for life. In this way, new priests and priestesses become psychologically in tune with the power and energy given to them. Those initiated into the priesthood at Oyotunji take a sacred oath to teach only Yorùbá culture to those of African descent. Those who come seeking initiation must "prove" their African ancestry in some convincing way. In addition, the ancestors, who are asked to keep those not of African descent from asking for initiation, provide a safeguard against giving the tradition to those for whom it is not intended.

The ultimate independence of the Village from those who challenged its existence came when Adefunmi ("Crown gave me") received the recognition of Nigerian leaders. Having had an opportunity to travel to Nigeria in August 1972, Adefunmi was initiated into Ifa's priesthood in Abeokuta, Nigeria, by the *Oluwa* of Ijeun in 1982. (He had been made *Alase* [King] of Oyotunji in October 1972.) This occurred because His Divine Royal Majesty King Okunade Si Juwade Olobuse III, the *Ooni* of the ancient Yorùbá city of Ile-Ifé,

ordered the Ife chiefs to perform coronation rites on Him! Thus, Oba
Ofuntola Oseijeman Adelabu Adefunmi I became the first of a line of new
world Yorùbá Kings consecrated at and to the Ooni of Ife. He was presented with a special ceremonial sword of state incised with the name of
His Liefe Lord of Ooni of Ife. It is his emblem and license to speak in the
name of the King of Ife. . . . His coat of arms is the rampant golden leopard clasping an ankh in one claw and a sword in the other. Leopards are
a traditional emblem of African Royalty. The beast is subscribed with the
challenge: "In time, the field belongs to the leopard."[125]

According to Oba Adefunmi I, Yorùbá religion at its core contains the
wisdom of the Egyptians as well as the astrophysical knowledge housed in
other regions of Africa. As a result of the slave trade, this wisdom was
brought to the Americas and enacted in a variety of ways—*Candomblé* in
Brazil; Santería in Cuba, vodou in Haiti, and most recently, *Orisha*-Vodu in
the United States.[126] In terms of theological foundations, the religious system of Oyotunji Village (Oyotunji means "Oyo rises again") is based upon
an understanding of: (1) a High God; (2) *orìsàs;* (3) ancestors; (4) humans
and other life forms.

Olódùmarè is considered the creator of the universe (the self-born
Father) and Olorun, a manifestation of the Supreme Being, is the literal presence of *ashé* (God Omnipotent). Olódùmarè/Olorun does not have a priest
or cult; worship and devotion are directed instead to the *orìsàs* who are
active in daily life. According to materials provided by Chief Medahochi I.
O. Zannu (one of the first priests initiated by Oba Adefunmi I), "Olorun is
not directly involved in human affairs, because the spiritual force emanating
from Him is of such potency that it would shatter our human bodies; just
as, were the sun to come down nearer the earth a few million miles, the
result would be, not more light and heat and life, but so much of it that it
becomes destructive, and death ensues. Hence Olorun keeps his distance,
for our safety, but it is his life, his everything, that we use."[127] Olódùmarè is
addressed only in cases of extreme need. The recognition of energy as the
fundamental source of existence, according to Oba Adefunmi I, renders
Yorùbá religion advanced physics rather than "faith."

According to Oyotunji's theology, there are between four hundred and
one thousand *orìsàs* (combining Dahomean and Yorùbá divinities), not all
of whom are represented at Oyotunji Village.[128] The first of those represented is Obàtálá (Orisanla), the Village's patron. Obàtálá is the patron of
the Village because Oba Adefunmi was initiated into the mysteries of
Obàtálá in 1959. Obàtálá is associated with wisdom, the intellect, and the
formation of humans. At the present time, the shrine for Obàtálá is housed

in a portion of the Ogboni Society building because a fire destroyed the shrine and other structures.

For the most part, the *orishas* recognized at Oyotunji Village have the same association with natural forces observed in Santería. The variations that exist are ones that African Americans in Santería have made. For example, Olokun is considered the patron of all those of African descent. In some respects this is a reflection of Olokun's association with the lower levels of the ocean, where many Africans found freedom from slavery. Also, the water with which Olokun is connected is also considered representative of the middle passage and hence of those of African descent.

Ògún is the God of iron and warfare and is closely associated with Elégbá and Ososi (*orìsà* of the hunt). In the Village there are elements for Ososi (or Oshosi) in the shrine for Ògún and both are also represented in the shrine for Elégbá. As stated earlier, Elégbá is the *orìsà* associated with

gates and is the messenger of Olódùmarè. Those wishing to make contact with other *orìsàs* must approach Elégbá first and encourage him to "open the gate" so that the others might manifest. Sàngó is the *orìsà* associated with thunder and lightning and is the patron of warriors. Yemoja, the *orìsà* associated with the upper levels of the ocean, is the mother of many of the *orìsà* and patroness of child nurturing, community, and communal respect and love. Oshun is connected with love and sensuality. Oya, Sàngó's wife, is associated with hurricanes and is the guardian of cemeteries. The *orìsà* who owns divination, Orunmila or Ifa, is also worshiped at Oyotunji Village.

This shrine to Elégbá is located close to the main entrance to the Village. Note Sàngó's double-edged axe on the post. Several of the shrines incorporate the ritual items of more than one deity. Currently the shrine to Ògún also houses the implements belonging to Oshoosi. Photo by the author.

To the right of Olokun is a statue of Malcolm X. Photo by the author.

Orunmila is the prophet of the Supreme Being, who conveys the will and messages of God and the orìsàs (including one's personal orìsà—Ori) through divination. Orunmila can help those who seek divination, because Orunmila was present when each human (omo eniyan) selected his or her destiny before coming to earth. Also important within the village are Erinle and Ibeji. Worship of these deities is conducted outside of the elaborately arranged and decorated shrine.

The orìsàs are associated with particular planets and thus regarded as neutral energy forces. Obàtálá is Jupiter; Ògún is Mars; Sàngó is Uranus; Oya is Pluto; Yemoja is the moon; Elégbá is Mercury; Oshun is Venus; Olokun is Neptune; Ifa is the sun; Oshosi is the constellation Sagittarius; Babaluaiye is Saturn.[129] The energy produced by the planets is stimulated when animal blood from a sacrifice is mixed with the metal, stone, or other items upon which the sacrifice is made. Through the proper "feeding" of the orisha's symbolic representations (housed in pots) this flow of energy is maintained to the believer's benefit.[130] According to Chief Ajamu, each "race" is ruled by a particular planetary force. For African Americans, this force is Olokun, or Neptune. This planet moves through each sign of the zodiac, staying in each one for fourteen years. Based upon this one can "scientifically" outline the historical development of the African American communities: "When you look at what happened when Neptune was in Scorpio, this was a time of violence and turbulence. I guess it was the 1960s, the Civil

Rights Movement, the Black Power Movement. . . . They have the nature of the Scorpion."[131]

Members of the Village conduct themselves in accordance with a calendar of major events for the year; this is combined with the reading of the week conducted by Oba Adefunmi I. The calendar receives only minor alterations from year to year. For 1995 the calendar was as follows:

- Reading of the Year (January 1). The priests consult the Ifa Oracle to reveal the future of the United States and the world.
- Olokun Festival (February 25–26)
- Yorùbá New Year (March 20th). Recognition of Yorùbá Culture's 10,037th year.
- Eshu [Elégbá], Ògûn, Oshosi Festival (March 24–26), including the annual Akinkonju Men's Rites.
- Oshun Festival (April 28–May 3)
- Egúngún Festival (May 26–June 5), including the king's sacrifice to his ancestors.
- Yemoja-Egbe Moremi Feast (June 24–25), including the Women's Society's Rites of Passage.
- Ifa Festival and Yorùbá National Cultural Convention (July 1–4), including the development of plans by which to keep the tradition moving forward.
- Shango Festival (July 22–23)
- Obàtálá Festival (August 26–28)
- King's Day (October 6–8). Celebration in honor of the king's birthday.
- Oya Festival (October 28–29)
- Hwedo Festival (October 31). Celebration for the "unknown" African dead.
- Babaluaiye Festival (December 21–31)

The status of an individual's relationship to the orisàs is assessed through divination by one of the village priests. When conducted by a babalawo, the chain containing eight pieces of coconut shell (with markings) is thrown six times. The resulting pattern relates to a particular Odu—sacred prose. From this Odu the babalawo can assess the nature of one's problem and the task(s) necessary to correct the imbalance. For example, Chief Ajamu, the Village's foreign minister, provided divination for me during my trip to Oyotunji. The following Odu was presented. It indicated that I had selected the destiny (before coming to earth) of a priest to Ifa—a babalawo. Upon coming to earth, however, I had lost sight of my destiny and had entered (later to leave) Christian ministry. The Odu indicated that balance would result only from

---

Figure 5. Partial List of *Orisas* **of Oyotunji Village and** *Orishas* **of Santeria**

Santería	Oyotunji Village
Olofi (Aspect of Olódùmarè, Jesus)—No shrines	Olódùmarè (God)—No shrines
Obàtálá (Virgin of Mercy)—Father of Orisha	Obàtálá—Creator of humans
Shango (St. Barbara)—God of thunder	Sàngó (Shango)—God of thunder
Oya (Virgin of La Candelaria)—Whirlwinds	Oya—Guardian of cemeteries, god of whirlwinds
Oshun (Virgin of Caridad del Cobre)—Patron of love	Osun (Oshun)—Patroness of love and fresh water
Yemaya (Virgin of Regla)—Mother of the Orisha	Yemoja—Mother of *Orishas,* water goddess
Eleggua (Holy Child of Atoche)—God's messenger	Elégbá (Eshu)—Messenger of Olódùmarè
Babaluaiye (Lazarus)—Patron of the sick	Babaluaiye—No shrine in the Village
Ògûn (St. Peter)—God of iron and warfare	Ògûn—God of iron and warfare
Ibeji (Cosmas and Damian)—Twin deities	Erinlè/Ìbejì—Twins
Orunmila (St. Francis of Assisi)—Owner of Ifa	Orunmila (Ifa)—Owner of Ifa
Olokun—Lower levels of the ocean	Olokun—Lower levels of the ocean

Adapted from George Brandon, *Santería from Africa to the New World;* Joseph Murphy, *Santeria: African Spirits in America;* and interviews conducted by the author.

---

my acknowledgment of my destiny by being initiated first to Obàtálá and then to Ifa. Some might question this process; however, what is important here is the correlation between the *Odu,* ancient story, it's interpretation, and act of resolution. This process guides the believer and is, for him or her, a reliable source of balance. This form of divination, *opele,* is used for common concerns, while the *ikin* is used for more urgent and serious concerns.

Figure 6. Colors for the *Orisas*

Obàtálá	White
Sàngó	Red, white
Oya	Reddish brown
Oshun	Red, amber, yellow
Yemoja	Blue, crystal
Elégbá	Red, white, black
Ògûn	Red, green, black, white
Erinlè/Ìbejì	Green, blue/red, blue
Orunmila (Ifa)	Green, yellow
Ososi	Green, blue

There are noticeable distinctions between Santería and *Orisha*-Vodu. In the latter, ancestor worship is highlighted through the *Egúngún* society, and the composite of the soul is given additional complexity.[132] It is understood that many problems experienced by African Americans result from their not worshiping their ancestors and thereby not allowing their ancestors to find rest. Hence, African American ancestors must be given a welcome to the land of their descendants—the United States. Early in the Village's history, those consulting a priest would be told to do the following in order to recognize the significance of their ancestors:

> Write down the names of all the deceased people in their families on a card . . . and place it on an altar. Along with those items they should place some cigars, some candles for light, and from four to nine glasses of water so that their spirits can have the power of water which represents a river that all dead spirits must cross over. The person must then kneel before the altar and call out the names of each person three times. This should be done once every two weeks for the rest of the worshipper's life.[133]

Those who seek initiation into a priesthood must first receive initiation into the *Egúngún* Society—the society for the worship of the ancestors.[134] The rites of passage taught by the ancestors are administered to young men and women in order to keep alive their sense of identity and history. Each boy and girl begins the day with this pledge:

I am compelled by a spiritual force I cannot resist to swear my eternal allegiance to the king and the flag of the Yorùbá nation. I also solemnly swear
to do everything in my power and use every means conceivable . . . for
the welfare of my people and the preservation of the culture and tradition
of my ancestors. So let it be, oh ye gods of Afrika. . . . Then these initiates, as they progress, are also to recite that Afrika is great . . . or Yorùbá
is great, and must come before all else! Yorùbá is . . . "the beginning and
the end."[135]

The Village holds that the human is composed of nine souls: Universal
Soul, Human Soul, Sexual Soul, Racial Soul, *Orisha* Soul, National Soul,
Ancestral Soul, Historical Soul, and Guardian Soul. The first, Universal
Soul, controls the connection between humans and all else. The second
allows for the energy-based connection to all other humans, and the next
narrows the human connection to those of one's sex. This is further nar-
rowed by the fourth soul, which accounts for one's connection to one's race.
The *Orisha* soul connects the individual to certain talents and characteristics that will mark him or her throughout life. The national soul connects
a person to his or her nation, and the ancestral soul connects the individual to family. A connection to one's immediate generation is provided by the
historical soul. The final soul provides protection as individuals attempt to
fulfill their destiny.[136]

The imbalance experienced by African Americans is, in part, a result of
their not having addressed the needs of several of these souls, namely, the
Racial Soul and the Historical Soul. They have been taught by society to
devote their energy to the development of the individual soul. This does
not allow for a balanced healthy existence. Chief Ajamu claims that the
African American constitution is 60 percent influenced by White American
ideals and standards and 40 percent under the healing influence of an
African psychological, moral, and theological perspective. The goal is to
have the latter neutralize the harmful possibilities of the former. Initiation
helps the individual to find and fulfill his or her destiny (*Ayanmo*) by helping the person travel the road that is in keeping with his or her character.
It helps the individual find and live out the goals and challenges (destiny)
accepted before coming to this world.

ORISHA-**VODU AND THE PROBLEM OF EVIL**

Unlike Christian theology, Yorùbá theological understanding of the human
does not contain a notion of "original sin" or permanent stain. Humans are

regarded as connected through family, ancestors, devotion to the divinities, and participation in the life force referred to as *àshe*. The problems and tribulations associated with human life are not a consequence of a distorted and problematic nature but result from disrespect of the fine balance of cosmic life and the reverence this should promote. In keeping with this concern for the circulation of cosmic energy, the Yorùbá also highlight proper character as a reflection of Olorun that humans should attempt always to emulate. Failure to do so, combined with improper regard for cosmic energy, can bring about various misfortunes.[137] This sense of suffering as a result of imbalance and the consequences of this imbalance is also held within Santería. In fact, it is Santería's core response to the problem of evil.

In terms of *Orisha*-Vodu, many became involved in the early work of Adefunmi because Yorùbá religion provides a more satisfying response to moral evil. As one member of the early New York Temple explained:

> Yorùbá religion is far more explanatory. . . . If you have so many people in the world, how can they all worship one god? Christianity can't explain why there are fights or prostitutes or bitter people. You find Babalus around the doctors and albinos. Sexy people are ruled by Oshun. You find fiery people under Shango—also rich people. Cops are Ògún people.[138]

The existence of planetary influences in the form of the *orishas,* when considered in the context of the above statement, sheds light on the problem of evil. Because of their concentrated energy and power, the planets affect human life. Yet these energies are not always in harmony. In Oba Adefunmi's words:

> [E]very human being is composed of various energies, when these energies connect [in a positive way], then you are feeling good. When you feel good [in] some particular part of your body, those planetary energies square . . . then . . . the energy in you, the same energy in you is going to have a square. It's going to have an opposition and you are going to not feel quite so happy. So now that would explain for us the way that . . . there is so called evil. Because there are a lot of things that human beings don't like and they would have to be classified as negative to human being[s] or negative to that individual's mind or his eye.[139]

It is believed that African Americans encounter hardship because they have come under the influence of the wrong planetary force. They have embraced Ògún, the aggressive god of war—the god associated with whites—and this results, for example, in black-on-black crime. African Americans should remain under the influence of Olokun, whose deep and cooling influence allows for the lifestyle necessary for the ontological survival of black Americans. As one of the residents of the Village noted, when problems arise, Olokun allows us to remain deep, with deep thoughts, and avoid the madness.

Even in light of the above, the *orìsàs* are neutral energy forces affecting our lives. They are ambivalent toward our individual needs; their activities affect life but without moral or ethical imperatives. Hence, they are amoral forces that we can tap into as a means of resolving difficulties. Because of their neutrality toward human life, the energy they represent can be used for good or ill.

> [T]hey don't have any human characters or human feelings. They are energy sources. As energy sources they don't have to do any thinking. They don't have to do any loving, or petting. . . . And they don't have to apologize or listen to you in prayer. Humans made all that up in their own mind because they couldn't conceive that these forces are parent forces of this cosmos and they don't have any relationship. They don't do anything for human beings. . . . So, we deal with Shango not because He's benevolent or gentle or generous. We deal with Shango because He's a dynamic energy.[140]

Understood this way, the dilemma of moral evil also stems from humanity's desire to anthropomorphize energy in ways that give this energy (the gods) a subjective connection to humanity. We deceive ourselves when we think that the order of the cosmos is based upon a concern for our welfare. Hence, our respect for and devotion to the gods is necessary because they are forces indispensable to us. Devotion is not a consequence of compassion expressed for us. That is,

> human beings just happen to have [adapted] to these various energies. Certain levels of cold, certain levels of heat, water, fire and so forth, these are the forces we worship. These forces we cannot live without. These are forces you have to deal with whether you believe in them or not.[141]

Why do we attribute characteristics to these energies? According to Oba Adefunmi, these characteristics, anthropomorphic as they are, are used because these energy forces stimulate certain reactions in the human body. Hence, we make use of our limited context, feelings, and language to understand ageless energies that exist beyond our context and beyond our control. They are worshiped simply because they exist and manifest in the natural world in ways we can understand: storms and harvest, illness and health, love and war, and so forth. Divination and sacrifice, as developed by the ancestors, allow us to "neutralize" these natural or cosmic forces by properly naming them and by redirecting energy.[142] Problems emerge when we fail to maintain this connection with natural forces. When a community forgets or neglects these forces and loses sensitivity to their movement, the entire community is adversely affected. This means that individuals who on their own may continue to be mindful of these energies suffer because of the community forgetfulness. Hence, the suffering of individuals points to larger issues of imbalance and "cultural amnesia."

The traditional question of theodicy makes no sense in this context: If God is as we describe, why do we suffer? For Oyotunji residents, God and the *orìsàs* are not concerned with this. Why should they be? They are energy. In the words of the Oba:

> Olorun is a Universal Energy permeating everything. . . . Everything has life, everything has energy. But this particular force has no anthropomorphic characteristics! It has no human feelings, it has no likes nor dislikes, it has no favorite people, it has no cursed people. . . . Rather it is a passive energy, dictating no laws, nor rules, nor morality. Indeed, there is no force in heaven which dictates a morality.[143]

Our moral sense derives from the teachings of our ancestors (about the *orìsàs*), their stories and lives. In the words of Oba Adefunmi I: "What's good for our people, what's bad for our people and what you should do and what you shouldn't do and how you should treat this person [comes from the moral sense established by the ancestors]."[144] What is evil for one person or group is not so for another. One begins to see the importance of the ancestors for the maintenance of this way of life. As Oba Adefunmi observes, "Above all else they are the most powerful source for our resurrection and in time our hegemony. So, that is why we have the motto at Oyotunji, 'Eluju di ipe di eluju ekun,' 'In time the field belongs to the leopard.' "[145] When the ancestors are neglected, when they are forced to wander the spirit world without food and water (sacrifice), we become psychologically disconnected and open to a variety of problems (moral evil). Evil is an imbalance in energy that we as humans foster and that we, as human agents, correct through the *ashé* made available by our ancestors and *orìsàs* and through sacrifice (*ebos, Etutu* or *Ipese*—respectively: to the *orìsàs,* to the ancestors, and to the energies controlled by Elégbá).

Finally, Oba Adefunmi provides another example that directly takes into consideration the plight of Africans and African Americans. He contends that decline or suffering is a natural component of the cosmic and historical cycles. Accordingly,

In the case of Africa, why did Africa suffer? It's because in nature every-thing has a birth date, and a period of decline, a period of birth. So the African people, their history you must remember was written, was classi-fied, was recorded throughout all of what is known as pre-history. . . . For us it was all historic. . . . African civilization had already existed for such an eternity that it was beginning to decline and to weaken and to become impotent. [This] is the way that we would explain what was going on at the time that the White people came to power and Africa began to decline and West Africans finally were pressed into slavery. But it wasn't that we did anything evil; it was simply that nothing can last forever.[146]

Suffering, therefore, is not pedagogical in nature. It is not a result of the gods needing to teach African Americans a lesson in order to strengthen and refine them. On the contrary: "We didn't do anything evil that we had to be punished about. We just weakened, collapsed and died as everything [does]."[147] If we pay attention to the natural environment, we learn lessons concerning the natural course of development and decline. It is only evil when viewed in the context of one group's interests. When viewed with respect to universal energy, forces, and cycles, it is not evil. It just is.

3

▲▼▲▼▲▼▲▼▲▼▲▼▲▼▲▼▲

THE GREAT MAHDI HAS COME!
Islam, Nation of Islam, and the Minneapolis Study Group

MECCA, MEDINA, AND ISLAM

As Alfred Guillaume has noted, much of the history of Arab society during the time of the Prophet Muhammad is known only through study of the Qur'ān and the Muslim writers who wrote about the pre-Islam Arabic world. Economic life within Arabic society before and during the time of the Prophet Muhammad was characterized by trade routes and raiding by nomads.[1] These trade routes were matched by a religious landscape marked by animistic leanings toward a variety of nature based gods, male and female, and lesser spirits who interact with humans for good or ill.[2] This religious worldview would change, however, with the divine revelation given to an unlikely character.

"Recite!" This was the charge given to the Prophet Muhammad (born in 570 C.E.) that marked his calling as a prophet of surrender to one God. Muhammad was raised by his grandfather and uncle (Abu Talib) because his mother died when he was still young. His early years were marked by a violent vision that is recounted by his foster mother (Halima): "His brother came running to us saying, 'Two men in white garments seized my Qurayshite brother, knocked him down, split his belly open, and are stirring it up!' We went to him and found him standing erect, his countenance pale and wan."[3] Encounters with this spiritual calling continued until Muhammad, by now a trader married to a wealthy widow named Khadija, surrendered. Accounts of his calling indicate that Muhammad was often given to praying alone, away from others. During one of these periods of prayer, an angel appeared and three times commanded Muhammad to recite or record the words of God:

> Recite in the name of thy Lord who created
> Man from blood coagulated.
> Recite! Thy Lord is wondrous kind
> Who by the pen has taught mankind
> Things they knew not (being blind).[4]

Muhammad could not forget these words after recovering from the experience, but he feared—perhaps remembering his earlier experience, that people would think him possessed. He was not lunatic, as Meccans would discover, but had been given a divine message for humanity. The revelations often involved strong physical reaction and emotional stress. With time, however, the Prophet received the word of God without the same level of intensity, although there was always some degree of physical and psychological exertion that differentiated the coming of God's word from the personal reflections of the Prophet. As Muhammad became more certain of his divine call, the revelations increased, and with time their form changed from the short remarks concerning judgment of evildoers to longer statements of an "argumentative and hortatory" nature.[5]

Despite initial hesitancy, with time some—mainly slaves and those of little means—recognized the power of this message and subsequently surrendered to Allah (God). Initially, to avoid the problems that monotheism could encounter in this polytheistic society, submission to God was done secretly until "the tiny community's habit of daily prayer became known to the Meccans. Initially Muhammad and those with him were mocked. Eventually the Meccans took steps to put an end to the movement that threatened the venerated sanctuary of the gods and wealth many Meccans drew from the annual pilgrimages to the Ka'ba [sacred site in Mecca]."[6] Attempts were made to lessen Muhammad's appeal and maintain the financially lucrative "pagan" practices through false accusations of sorcery and affiliation with "foreigners." In spite of this slander, and with the protection of his converted uncle Abu Talib, Muhammad spread his message of Islam and the oneness of God—Allah.[7] Some in Mecca accepted the message, and some from Medina who had come to Mecca as part of the pagan pilgrimage converted and successfully worked as missionaries in Medina. Muhammad's teachings were less offensive to those in Medina because this place was familiar with monotheism through its contact with Judaism. Hence,

> Muhammad followed the path taken by Christian preaching six centuries earlier when he addressed his message to those who had been prepared for monotheism by Jewish teaching. Indeed, he went further: by denying

the divinity of Jesus he brought peace to Arabian Christian lands which had suffered bitterly from Christological disputes. But the price was the unconditional surrender of the essence of Christianity.[8]

When conditions in Mecca became too troubled and oppressive for Muhammad and his followers, he moved to Medina in 622 and broke ties with Mecca and its people (the *Hijra* or *Hijrah*).[9] Muhammad's goal was to develop a religious community capable of sustaining itself and effectively spreading its message. In essence, the message provided by the Prophet consisted of two primary points: (1) there is one God; and (2) the divine word that provided for proper human conduct had been revealed to the Prophet. This revelation and the Prophet's actions drew believers away from old animistic practices and required undivided devotion.[10] As the Qur'ān indicates: "Believe in God and His Apostle and the book which He has sent down to His Apostle and the book which He sent down formerly. He who disbelieves in God and His angels, His books, and His apostles, and the Last Day, has strayed from the truth."[11]

Continued friction between Muslims in Medina and the Meccans, fueled by Muhammad's desire to see the holy city of Mecca surrender to God, was inevitable. It was sustained because Muhammad was able to convince Muslims to undertake battle against family and friends in Mecca through the concept of the fight against nonbelievers as holy obligation (*jihād*), a requirement for the further development of God's will on earth. Muhammad made it clear: there could be no compromise with idolatry and infidelity.

Muhammad, after some reluctance, was admitted to Mecca for pilgrimage based upon a truce that had been drawn between Muhammad and the Meccans. In 630 the truce was broken by an attack on a tribe under Muslim protection, and Muhammad marched on Mecca. Abu Sufyan surrendered and accepted Islam. Muhammad removed the images and idols from the Holy City and established the Ka'ba as the center of Islamic faith. As a result of this victory, Muhammad was recognized as the prophet of God. Christians and Jews became referred to as *mushrik* (polytheists) along with the "heathen." The surahs, or sections of the Qur'ān, referring to this do not clearly indicate whether this simply means that they are *mushrik* if they fail to obey their own scriptures or if they fail to accept Islam. Whichever is the case, the victory of Islam resulted in a strained relationship between Christianity, Judaism, and Islam. Many members of the Jewish community, for example, rejected Muhammad's teachings primarily because he claimed Jesus was a prophet of God. It is at this point that

Muhammad began to pray facing Mecca rather than Jerusalem. Muslims were to fight the nonbelievers, including Jews and Christians, because "it became a ruling precept in Islam that all areas of non-Islam were areas whose conquest the true Muslim was enjoined to seek until the inhabitants either submitted or were reduced to subject status, the second alternative [subject status] obtaining only in respect of the tolerated minorities, 'the people of the Book' [Jews and Christians]."[12] From Mecca the influence of Muhammad and the divine message spread outward.

This "nation" of Islam continued to be instructed through the divine revelations received by Muhammad in dreams and ecstatic experiences and solidified in the Qur'ān. The production of this Holy Book continued throughout the life of the Prophet. Concerning the recording of the Qur'ān, many claimed that the Prophet was illiterate and, thus, others must have written down the divine revelations. According to Guillaume, however:

> In one passage of the Qur'an it seems to be implied that Muhammad could not read till late in life (though it is possible that the statement refers to the Jewish and Christian scriptures) and it definitely states that he did not himself write down the Qur'an; but someone else must have done, for the passage goes on to say that the Qur'an is read to the Meccans. The latter had accused the prophet of writing down old fables and stories told him by foreigners. However, an early tradition says that he himself wrote on the day that the treaty was made at Hudaybiya, and it is not at all likely that the prophet was content to rely on his associates to read a letter or, in his early days, a bill of lading.[13]

It is from the Qur'ān Muslims draw Islamic theology complete with cosmological structure. And unlike the cosmological structures of the traditions discussed in previous chapters, Islam's structure is clear and lacking in "gray" areas. "There is no God but Allah and Muhammad is His prophet." This is the central faith stance of Islam—the oneness of God and the importance of prophets who brought the word of God to humanity, from Abraham to the final revelation given to Muhammad. This line of sacred writings reaches its fullness with the Qur'ān.[14]

The God that draws humanity unto Godself is compassionate and all-knowing, merciful and just. God is transcendent yet as close to us as our bodies. Muslims are to put their trust in Allah because Allah controls the world and our welfare is in God's hand. God can use the angels (or *jinn*) to fulfill the divine will. (The evil *jinn* are led by Iblis or Satan.) Those who disobey God will suffer at the final judgment and be removed to hell. Only the righteous—those who submit to God (Muslims)—will gain heaven or paradise. It is understood that religion—Islam—entails more than periodic practice. For the Muslim it is a way of life, a way of being in the world centered on righteousness and just dealings.

Muslims are required to perform certain tasks as part of proper relationship to God: prayer (Salāt), obligatory almsgiving (Zakāt),[15] fasting (Saum) during Ramadan, the confession or witness of faith (Shahādah), and pilgrimage (the Hajj, if economically feasible). For details on the practical application of these requirements, Muslims may turn to tradition—the Prophet's practices or tradition (sunna) and the Prophet's customs (hadīth). Of course, the Holy Qur'ān is regarded as the final authority. In terms of prayer, the Qur'ān speaks of three prayers facing the holy city of Mecca (by facing the mihrab, the niche at the eastern end of the mosque designating the direction of Mecca), but Islamic tradition requires five prayers per day: sunset (Salāt al-'Isha'), night (Salāt al-maghrib), dawn (Salāt al-Fajr), noon (Salāt al-Zuhr), afternoon (Salāt al-'Asr).[16] Muslims are also free to add to these prayers their own moments of prayer referred to as Du'a'. Muslims are called to prayer by these words: "God is most great. I testify that there is no God but Allah. I testify that Muhammad is God's Apostle. Come to prayer, come to security. God is most great." The following comes after the general call to prayer:

> [The Muslim] stands and says inaudibly that [he or she] intends to recite so many rak'as or bowings. Then opening his hands and touching the lobes of his ears with his thumbs he says 'Allahu Akbar,' and then proceeds to recite the prayers that go with the bowings. Lowering his hands and folding them, the left hand within the right, he recites the Fatiha, the first chapter of the Qur'an.[17]

The Fatiha contains the following pronouncement:

> Praise belongs to God, Lord of the Worlds,
> The Compassionate, the Merciful,
> King of the Day of Judgment,
> 'Tis Thee we worship and Thee we ask for help.
> Guide us on the straight path,
> The path of those whom Thou hast favoured,
> Not the path of those who incur Thine anger nor of those who go astray.[18]

This is followed by other portions of the Qur'ān and the following movement:

> He then bows from the hips with hands on knees, saying, "(I extol) the perfection of my Lord the Great," assumes an upright position with the words 'Allahu Akbar' (which are used at most stages), then, sinking gently to his knees, he places his hands on the ground and his nose and face

also to the ground. . . . He then rises to his knees, sitting on his heels, and performs a second prostration, using the same words. The prayers of *rak'a* are then completed.[19]

Proper proceedings and unity in actions are guarded through the presence of a leader known as the *Imam.*

Within the mosque proper—the location for communal prayer—there are no painted representations of God; this is forbidden as an act of idolatry. Artistically rendered verses from the Qur'ān, for example, replace these elements. In addition, there is the *mihrab* described above and a lectern holding the Holy Qur'ān. There are also fountains used to wash hands, nostrils, and so forth, before prayer.

Beyond prayer, Muslims are also required to provide alms—obligatory (*zakāt*) and voluntary (*sadaqāt*). This money is used to provide for the poor, widows, and, in some instances, military ventures that advance Islam.[20] Within this requirement is Islam's sense of social accountability and responsibility for creating a society in which the needs of all are met. It is understood that Muslims' personal property is really the property of the community and must ultimately be used for the welfare of the community.

In addition, Muslims are required to fast (*saum*). This fast, during the holy month of Ramadan, lasts from the rising to the setting of the sun, for all except those who must travel (they complete the fast at a later date) and for those whose health does not allow for the strain of fasting. At the end of the month, the fast is broken by the 'Id al-Fitr feast.[21] Ramadān was a holy component of Arab culture prior to Islam, but it is with the emergence of Islam and its ordinances that fasting became a matter of discipline based in part on the fasting observed by Jews and Christians. According to the revelation received by the Prophet, the fast was to occur during the month of Ramadān as opposed to the traditional Day of Atonement fast. This change was, undoubtedly, a religious response to the shortcomings of the Jews and Christians encountered by Muhammad and Islam. Furthermore, this change also correlated the fast with the period of the Qur'ān's revelation.

If and when financially capable, Muslims are also required to undertake the pilgrimage (*hajj*) to Mecca and the Prophet's tomb in Medina once in their lifetime. During this pilgrimage, which is to take place in the rotating month of *Dhu-al-Hijjah,*

> [t]he pilgrims circumambulate the Ka'ba seven times, then run between the two small hills of Safa and Marwa hard by, and gather together at the hill of 'Arafat twelve miles away; on the way back they sacrifice sheep and camels at Mina, where the ceremonial stoning of the devil takes place.

> One of the most important acts in the pilgrim ceremonial is the kissing of the black stone set in a wall of the Ka'ba.[22]

With the above completed, the pilgrimage ends, but the activities do not. The pilgrims then

> sacrifice a sheep, a goat, and a camel and have their head shaved. They return to Mecca where again they do a *Ka'bah* circuit and bathe in the water of the holy well of ZamZam, or sprinkle themselves with it. There follows on the eleventh, twelfth, and thirteenth days of the month the so-called *tashriq,* "relaxation and pleasure." The consecrated state is terminated though stone-throwing ceremonies continue. Before leaving Mecca pilgrims briefly resume the *ihram* [consecration] for a farewell visit to the Great Mosque.[23]

While undertaking the above, all pilgrims, regardless of their socioeconomic status, are dressed in two plain sheets. This symbolizes their consecration *(ihram)* for the journey. Also as part of this process those in this state do not observe traditional hygiene requirements such as shaving and washing. They only observe the ablutions required during various phases of the pilgrimage.

The final pillar of Islam entails the confession of faith *(Shahādah):* "I bear witness that there is no God save Allah and Muhammad is His prophet." This confession grounds the faith and speaks in unmistakable terms about the lordship of Allah and the nonexistence of any other god. The Meccans that Muhammad initially encountered knew of Allah, but they did not recognize Allah, who had ninety-nine beautiful names, as the only god. Their idolatry and concern with lesser spirits *(jinns* and demons) was offensive to the Prophet and was not in keeping with the truth of God's existence. This idolatry is the worst possible sin. The breaking of the idols and Muhammad's role in the taking of Mecca as the messenger of God is implicitly proclaimed in the *Shahādah.* What it means to be a Muslim is defined by this proclamation; hence, in very real ways it shapes character and a Muslim's behavior.[24] In terms of conduct codes beyond what has been suggested, Muslims are also to avoid pork and alcohol. This is combined with restrictions on personal conduct and appearance.

The need to standardize interpretation of the Muslim's duties emerged over time. And by the period A.H. 204, it was believed by many that sacred law *(shari'a),* the guiding force of conduct, should be based upon the Qur'ān, the *sunna* (practice of the Prophet), the community *(ijma)* or consensus, and analogy *(qiyas).* Working in this way, believers were able to monitor their practice through the division of action into five categories: (1) obligatory; (2)

recommended but not obligatory; (3) indifferent; (4) disapproved but not forbidden; (5) prohibited.[25] Muslims agree on basic elements of the faith but differ concerning finer points that break the religion into various groups such as *sunnis* (the larger body of Muslims worldwide) and *shi'ites*.

> In theory, the Shi'ite conception of the supreme authority in law is utterly different from that of the Sunnis, though in practice the difference does not amount to very much. They reject the four schools and the doctrine of ijma' because their Hidden Imam has the sole right of determining what the believer shall do and believe. Therefore their duly accredited doctors can still exercise the power of ijtihad or personal opinion. This power the Sunnis lost a thousand years ago or more. Where differences between Sunni and Shi'i law occur, often they are not so much specifically Shi'i tenets as survivals of primitive Islamic custom.[26]

The development of various sects, most of which are currently defunct, was to be expected once a charismatic and influential leader such as Muhammad was no longer physically present. As the prophet of God, Muhammad was able to provide guidance and balance for the community in a way that subsequent caliphs (heads of the community who provide guidance through the sacred law or *shari'a*) could not. Yet, even after the death of the Prophet, caliphs (subsequent leaders of the Believing community) were able to maintain the tradition against rebellion, and Islam continued to grow and spread its beliefs and influence. For example, efforts by Abu Bakr who followed Muhammad as leader of the community fought against those who believed that their allegiance to Islam died with Muhammad. What resulted was the movement of Islam outside its native home, with areas of conquest including portions of the African continent such as Egypt: "a small force of less than 10,000 men captured in A.D. 640 the whole of Lower Egypt with the exceptions of the fortified town of Babylon near Cairo, and of Alexandria, which fell a year or two later."[27]

ISLAM IN WEST AFRICA

Some of Muhammad's followers moved from hostile territory into Abyssinia or Ethiopia and began to spread his teachings. In this way, Islam entered from Arabia and within a short period of time after Muhammad's death had a stronghold in all of Northern Africa (641–798 C.E.). By the ninth century (C.E.), Islam had spread through much of the eastern portion of Africa by means of Arab and Berber traders and nomads moving across the continent. Their interest in trade combined with an understanding of *jihād* might help explain the eventual infiltration of Islam into centers of leadership and learning as traders made way for teachers (establishing Islamic schools) more directly concerned with the development of Islam in Africa.[28] According to Michael Gomez,

> Islam had penetrated the savanna south of the Sahara Desert by the beginning of the ninth century as a consequence of Berber and Arba commercial activity. Some subsaharan African (or "sudanese") merchants living in the *sahel* ("shore" or transition zone between the desert and the savanna) and the savanna began to convert, so that Islam became associated with trade, especially long-distance networks of exchange.[29]

From the western portion of the North, Islam spread through the central region to West Africa. The organizing of Islamic groups such as the Sanhaja Berbers by Abu Bakr resulted in successful holy war against nonbelievers, and this contributed to the further spread of Islam.[30] Many African leaders accepted, with modification, the religious tradition in order to advance themselves and their families; others sincerely embraced the religion of Islam. By the twelfth century C.E., much of Ghana had embraced Islam, and the Muslims of Mali, for example, had a thriving Islamic educational process, with Timbuktu as a renowned center of learning. Islamic culture developed and thrived in the western portion of Africa. Islamic influence would continue to increase during the nineteenth and twentieth centuries because of its association with anticolonial feelings.[31] In terms of cultural considerations, Muslims moving from the Middle East recognized that Islam needed to adapt to the existing religious sensibilities of Africans in order to entrench itself. Hence, Islam was influenced by indigenous African traditional religions.[32] Ethnic groups maintained the beliefs of indigenous practices and often combined these elements with Islam in a way that promoted health and well-being.

Records indicate that many of the slaves transported to the Americas, including the North American British colonies, were Muslims.[33] Although there is debate over the correct figures, Allen Austin asserts:

> Taking into consideration available figures related to Africans sent from ports serving hinterland areas from which Muslims might have been taken, figures on arrivals from the Senegambia—the source for the most sought-after slaves, especially by American slavers working fast between the end of the Revolutionary War and January 1, 1808, when the trade was supposed to be legally ended . . . I boldly estimate that between 5 and 10 percent of all slaves from ports between Senegal and the Bight of Benin, from which half of all Africans were sent to North America, were

Muslims. If the total number of arrivals was eleven million . . . then there may have been about forty thousand African Muslims in the colonial and pre–Civil War territory making up the United States before 1860.[34]

ISLAM IN THE UNITED STATES

The first African Muslims to reach the Americas came with Spanish explorers. Some of these Muslims were free adventurers intrigued by the wealth and experience the New World offered; others were servants.[35] In both cases, their presence was felt in Spanish Florida and French Louisiana. In addition to those who made the early voyage, a notable percentage of slaves brought to North America were African Muslims, some of whom were Islamic nobles, who came from Senegambia (Senegal River to the Casamance River, and from the Atlantic coast to the Niger valleys). In the words of C. Eric Lincoln:

> The Africans were here with Islam before the founding of the republic, and although the free expression of their religion was prohibited and suppressed during three centuries of servitude, the fire of the faith was never quite snuffed out. It survived in legends and tales, in memories and anecdotes, in unexplained urgencies challenging the terrible aridity of consciousness bracketing the endless centuries of servitude.[36]

Between 1740 and the beginning of the Revolutionary War, South Carolina brought in roughly fifty thousand African slaves. And, in this context, religious possibilities abounded because slaves were valued for their familiarity with rice planting and strength alone. Muslim names such as "Bullaly" (Bilali) and "Mamado" (Mamadu) found on runaway advertisements, birth records, death notices, and church documents point to Islam as one of these possibilities.[37] Furthermore, "several small populations, Free Moors of the Carolinas, Malungeons in Tennessee, Delaware Moors, and Virginia Maroons, have insisted upon Muslim beginnings from colonial times."[38] These Muslims are present, complete with their belief structures, for those who are willing to look beyond the sights and sounds of antebellum Christian churches.

Unfortunately, an economy of religion (as well as other factors such as hostility toward Muslims in Europe) may have resulted in negative propaganda concerning "non-Christian" practices and the subsequent overlooking of Islamic beliefs in the official religious records of the United States. For example, "one effect of such propaganda and suppression was an early disassociation between antebellum African Americans and Muslims. . . .

leading black abolitionists Henry Highland Garnet and Martin R. Delany prided themselves on having Mandingo grandparents, but neither publically expressed any Muslim influence."[39] In fairness, most in the United States were unequipped to interpret the various religious practices they witnessed among slaves; they were limited by their Christian categories and language, which did not easily incorporate the "foreign." The manner in which one slave who escaped but was recaptured had his religious perspective deciphered illustrates this point:

> The great places of general meeting were the court-houses, and as a court was being held in Kent County at the time of Job's arrest some of the gentlemen attending the sessions, hearing of the strange Negro, . . . had Job brought into the tavern. They tried to question him, by word and sign, but all they could make out from "Allah" and "Mohammad" occurring in some lines that he wrote down and read to them, and from his refusing a glass of wine, was that he was a Mohammedan.[40]

In this instance, Job Ben Solomon's ability to write (including the Qur'ān from memory) and reason marked him, according to these men, as a Muslim without denying his Africanness. This was not always the case. In some instances, slaves who were literate and of "high" moral standing were considered Arabs not Africans. Records concerning Islam in African slave communities could have been lost as a result of this system of classification.

Job Ben Solomon is not the only Muslim found in historical records. Allan Austin discusses several of the better-known Islamic slaves, one of whom is Bilali from Guinea. Living on Sapelo Island, in Georgia, Bilali, who had been an Imam in Africa, composed an Arabic manual for Muslims in his community. Although information concerning Bilali was kept relatively quiet, his descendants years later provided helpful information to WPA workers. Katie Brown, Bilali's great-granddaughter, recalled that Bilali prayed on a rug, saying something that resembled "God is one, great" and "Mohammad is his prophet." His wife, Phoebe, prayed with Bilali and made honey and rice cakes (ceremonial *saraka* cakes to end the fasting of Ramadān). His descendants testified that Bilali and his wife preserved the Islamic prayer tradition:

> Bilali an he wife Phoebe pray on duh bead. Dey wuz bery puhticluh bout duh time dey pray an dey bery regluh bou duh hour. Wen duh sun come up, wen it straight obuh head an wen it set, das duh time dey pray. Dey bow tuh duh sun and hab a lill mat tuh kneel on. Duh beads is on a long string. Bilali he pull bead an he say, "Belali, Hakabara, Mahamadu." Phoebe she say, "Ameen, Ameen."[41]

It appears that some of Bilali's descendants maintained Islamic practices, although the lack of an Imam would have allowed the practices to be colored by local traditions. Austin reports that as late as World War II a significant number of Muslims were remembered on St. Simon's and Sapelo Islands, Georgia.[42]

The autobiographical text, in Arabic, of Umar ibn Said of Fayetteville, North Carolina, indicates that he came to the United States as a believer in Islam. His memory was preserved in the naming of a Quranic school in Fayetteville.[43] Accounts by investigators such as Joseph LeConte and Charles Colcock Jones also point to the presence of other slaves who were Muslim.[44] I think Michael Gomez is correct in saying that

> taken together, the testimonies of Ben Sullivan, Cornelia Bailey, and Katie Brown provide the contours of Muslim life in early Georgia—prayer mats, prayer beads, veiling, head coverings, Qur'ans, dietary laws, and ritualized, daily prayer characterized the lifestyle. The composite picture is consistent with a serious pursuit of Islam.[45]

These activities were often altered but not lost as Muslim slaves combined Christian and Islamic beliefs, for example by associating the Christian God with Allah and Jesus with Muhammad.

Regardless of syncretistic moves, memories of Islamic faith remained vivid at least through the early twentieth century and possibly informed Islamic groups that emerged during the mid-twentieth century,[46] so that it is possible that twentieth-century Islamic groups are drawing from a theological and ritual openness generated by past practices and cultural memories. Moses Jeremiah Wilson maintains that this connection between current Islamic groups and memories of the pre-twentieth-century practices preserved by those on the move during the Great Migration is worth exploration:

> Why is it that these holy men were able to compete so successfully with the Christian churches in attracting converts? Did they bring followers with them from the South, or people predisposed to accept Islam? Is it possible that some forms of Islam had survived in the South, along with obeah and voodoo ritual?[47]

Islam made inroads into African American communities when it was able to present itself convincingly as a viable alternative to African American churches during what Gayraud Wilmore calls the period of de-radicalization.[48] Noble Drew Ali's Moorish Science Temple is an early and prime example of this Islamic consciousness. Other early communities include the Ahmadiyyah Movement in Islam (1921), and the First Muslim Mosque of Pittsburgh (1928).[49]

Timothy Drew (Noble Drew Ali) was born in 1886 in North Carolina and spent some time in New Jersey before cofounding the Canaanite Temple with Dr. Suliman in 1913. Internal conflict resulted in a split between Suliman and Drew Ali. Those who sided with Drew Ali left the temple and established the Moorish-American Science Temple in Chicago in 1925. At its peak the Moorish-American Science network of temples may have had a membership as high as thirty thousand in cities such as Pittsburgh, Philadelphia, Harlem, and Detroit by 1925. These temples were organized under the Moorish Divine and National Movement of North America, Inc., officially registered as a religious corporation in 1928.[50]

Noble Drew Ali, like many during the early twentieth century, was disillusioned with Christianity's inability to meet the needs of African Americans. Islam was embraced as the "natural" religion of Africa's descendants and was the only religious tradition capable of transforming black communities.[51] Noble Drew Ali's understanding, developed during his many travels, of Islam's importance involved a rethinking of African American identity buttressed by epistemological shifts resulting from secret information. He was said to have shared this information with African Americans following a request from the king of Morocco and the president of the United States, although the latter doubted that African Americans would embrace Islam.[52] According to Drew Ali's *Holy Koran of the Moorish Science Temple:*

> the lessons of this pamphlet are not for sale, but for the sake of human-
> ity. As I am a prophet and the servant is worthy of his hire, you can receive
> this pamphlet at expense. The reason these lessons have not been known
> is because the Moslems of India, Egypt and Palestine had these secrets
> and kept them back from the outside world, and when the time came
> appointed by Allah they loosened the keys and freed these secrets, and for
> the first time in ages have these secrets been delivered in the hands of the
> Moslems of America.[53]

The basic principles of this Islamic faith are as follows:

> Islam is a very simple faith. It requires man to recognize his duty toward
> God (Allah) his Creator, his fellow creatures, it teaches the supreme duty
> of living at peace with one's surroundings. . . . The name means Peace.
> The goal of a man's life according to Islam is peace with everything. . . .
> The cardinal doctrine of Islam is unity of the Father (Allah). We believe
> in One God. Allah is all God, all mercy, and all power, he is perfect and
> holy, all wisdom, all knowledge, all truth. . . . He is free from all defects,
> holy, transcendent. He is personal to us in so far as we can see His attrib-
> utes working for us and in us but He is nevertheless impersonal, He is

infinite, perfect and holy . . . nor do we believe that God is a helpless, inactive, inert force. . . . This unity of Allah is the first and foremost pillar of Islam and every other belief hangs upon it.[54]

This understanding of Allah was accompanied by respect for both the Prophet Muhammad (and Drew Ali as Allah's holy prophet) and the Qur'ān as well as the temple's own writings. This did not equate with an embrace of "orthodox" Islam. Therefore, members of this community were not made familiar with formal prayers (although they prayed three times each day), fasting, and the pilgrimage. Instead, they were taught principles of community building and the merits of financial contributions to the furtherance of this goal.

The name given to the religion was "Islamism." Its flag has a red background and a five-pointed star, each point representing a virtue: love, truth, peace, freedom, and justice.[55] Drew Ali claimed that African Americans were by origin "Asiatics" of Moorish descent who are now Moorish Americans because of their centuries of life in the Americas. The Moorish American's connection to Morocco should be recognizable by the name embraced ("El" or "Bey" in place of their given surname), the African-style clothing worn, and their "Nationality and Identification Cards" certifying allegiance to the Prophets and Allah, as Muslims and "Asiatics." This emphasis on national identity is considered the basis of social transformation.

> [Drew Ali] contended that the name is all-meaningful, for by stripping him of his Asiatic name and calling him Negro, black, colored, or Ethiopian, the European robbed the Moor of his power, his authority, his God, and every other worthwhile possession. Christianity, he said, is for the European (white), and Islam is for the Asiatics (olive-skinned persons).[56]

This rediscovered identity and religious orientation was combined with economic efforts through businesses that allowed Moorish Americans a degree of independence from white Americans.

Drew Ali's success was carefully watched and eventually challenged by Claude Green in 1929. Drew Ali's problems would begin when Green was found dead in his office on March 15, 1929. Being considered the logical suspect, Drew Ali was arrested for the crime. While in prison, he wrote a letter that reveals a great deal concerning his role and the nature of his Islamic perspective:

> I, your prophet, do hereby and now write you a letter as a warning and appeal to your good judgment for the present and the future. Though I am now in custody for you and the cause, it is all right and it is well for all who

still believe in me and my father, God. . . . Hold on and keep faith, and great shall be your reward. Remember my laws and love ye one another.[57]

Noble Drew Ali was found dead shortly after his release from jail.[58]

Some have claimed that Drew Ali's work was continued by a mysterious figure who went by many names, including W. D. Fard.[59] Some stated that Fard (at times spelled *Farad*) himself claimed to be the reincarnation of Drew Ali, while others disagreed.[60] Although there are some similarities in doctrine between the Moorish Science Temple and Fard's Nation of Islam, key figures in the Nation of Islam have continually denied that W. D. Fard (Master Wallace Farad Muhammad) and Elijah Muhammad were ever members of Noble Drew Ali's movement.[61] Members of the Nation argue that the teachings of Marcus Garvey and Noble Drew Ali simply point to the coming of another—Master Fard Muhammad.[62]

THE NATION OF ISLAM

On July 4, 1930, a man appeared in Paradise Valley, Detroit's black community selling fine silks and other items; but more important he provided information that captivated and intrigued his audience.[63] The work of this man, Mr. Fard, had been revealed to him earlier in a vision during which he pushed several major business leaders of the U.S.A. into hell.[64]

Illusive with respect to his own background, Master Fard Muhammad or W. D. Fard informed his audience that he had come from the East to the "wilderness" of the United States to bring African Americans, his "uncle," into the Truth of their greatness—Islam.[65] When asked who he was, various accounts affirm that he usually remarked: "I am W. D. Fard, . . . and I came from the Holy City of Mecca. More about myself I will not tell you yet, for the time has not yet come. I am your brother. You have not yet seen me in my royal robes."[66] (This mysteriousness was reenforced through frequent coloring of his hair and "tricks" such as picking up a pile of hair using only one hair of his own.[67]) Denke Majied (Mrs. Lawrence Adams) describes Master Fard Muhammad and his early work in these terms:

> He told us that the silks he carried were the same kind that our people used in their home country and that he had come from there. So we all asked him to tell us about our own country. If we asked him to eat with us, he would eat whatever we had on the table, but after the meal he began to talk: "Now don't eat this food. It is poison for you. The people in your country do not eat it. . . . If you would live just like the people in your home country, you would never be sick any more." So we all wanted him to tell us more about ourselves and about our home country and about how we could be free from rheumatism, aches and pains.[68]

Despite Master Fard's statements and the assertions of his followers, law enforcement authorities would eventually argue that Fard was a con man who had possibly studied in both England and the United States (at the University of Southern California) before spending time in prison:

> To the FBI . . . he was also number 56062, an ex-con who had spent three years in San Quentin Prison in California—1926 to 1929—for selling narcotics. To the California Bureau of Identification and Investigation, he was number 1797294. To the Michigan state police, he was number 98076. To Los Angeles police, he was 16448F. . . . whenever Fard was arrested, and wherever he was booked, he identified himself as a *white* man. His standard story was that he had been born in 1891 in New Zealand to a Polynesian mother and an Englishman who arrived in New Zealand on a schooner. Occasionally, he claimed he was born in Portland, Oregon, and that his parents, Zared and Beatrice Ford, had both been born in Hawaii. . . . In either case, he appears to have spent some time in Portland, possibly arriving there from New Zealand in 1913 around the age of twenty-two. In 1918, he headed to Los Angeles, where he opened a café called Walley's Restaurant under the name of either Willie D. Ford or Wallace D. Ford.[69]

With time the identity of Master Fard became clear. Members of his movement began to understand that he was from the Koreish tribe of the Prophet Muhammad, of a black father (Alphonse Shabazz, one of the god-scientists for this age discussed later) and a white mother (a Muslim by some accounts) who was chosen so that her son would be able to move in white society in ways that would benefit those he would guide. According to his followers, Master Fard Muhammad's birth was foretold in the Christian scriptures, the Book of Revelation (18:1): "After this I saw another angel coming down from heaven, having great authority; and the earth was made bright with his splendor."

Master Fard Muhammad preached using the Bible because African Americans were comfortable with it as a source of truth. But once his message attracted their attention he began critiquing the Bible and its stories and thereby moved into his own teachings based upon the Qur'ān, Jehovah's Witness teachings, and Freemasonry. In short, Master Fard's teaching provided a methodology and set of norms by which African Americans could work through racism without sacrificing self. As Master Fard's audience grew, homes could no longer accommodate the crowds. A hall, referred to as the Temple, was rented for meetings during which Fard would speak his wisdom about the "trickology" white people used to keep blacks or "Asiatics" ignorant of their glorious past and future greatness as the chosen people of Allah (God). The importance of information provided by Fard is reinforced by the layer of secrecy surrounding his writings, which he alone was capable of understanding and deciphering. Master Fard also provided knowledge and reprimands concerning moral and ethical conduct (e.g., hard work, honest dealings, commitment to family) in keeping with the history and future status of the Lost-Found Nation (African Americans) still dwelling in the wilderness of the United States.[70] The information was powerful and fostered radical change in its receivers, who were identified in part by a surrender of the slave master's name and the taking of an original name given by Master Fard. Receiving a new name was supplemented by a new allegiance to Mecca as the "Asiatics'" true place of citizenship. Those who became involved with the Nation had to prepare themselves for rigid discipline and order. In keeping with Booker T. Washington's sense of self-help and industry, Muslims were expected to work hard and spend money wisely. Muslims under the leadership of Master Fard were to be responsible, maintaining a rather conservative appearance.[71]

According to some sources, Master Fard attracted roughly eight thousand believers and established a strong organizational base in a matter of four years. The primary institutional structure was the Temple, followed by the University of Islam, which trained African Americans in the proper ways of life; the Muslim Girls' Training and General Civilization Class used to teach women basic domestic skills in keeping with Master Fard's teachings; and the Fruit of Islam, which provided discipline and protection for Muslims. As the Temple and organization grew, Fard moved further away from the forefront and gave hand-picked figures more authority—the Minister of Islam and many assistant ministers. The last of the Ministers of Islam during the time of Master Fard was an unlikely character named Elijah Poole.[72]

Poole was born in 1897 in Sandersville, Georgia, to a tenant farmer and his wife. Moving from job to job, Elijah married Clara Evans in 1919 and moved, in 1923, with his wife and children to Detroit in search of economic opportunity. After struggling with economic hardship and alcohol as a way of escaping various problems, Elijah heard about W. D. Fard, the man whose powerful message transformed lives through radical reconstruction of individual and collective identity. This message spoke to Elijah Poole. Claude Clegg states:

> Informal sermonizing and theological debates became a pastime for Elijah, which helped him to maintain his hunger for the ministry and deal with

the frustration and apparent meaninglessness of life in Detroit. During one of their [Elijah's and his brother Billie's] many theological sessions . . . the Poole brothers were joined by their father . . . who mentioned an interesting encounter he had had with one of his friends, a Brother Abdul Muhammad [who spoke] . . . to William about a Mr. W. D. Fard . . . who had taught him about Islam and bestowed upon him his new 'original' name. . . . [Elijah proclaimed], "I like to hear that man! . . . That is good what Abdul Mohammed told you."[73]

Elijah, like others before him, was attracted to the message of African American potential for self-determination, self-help, righteousness, and salvation. This transforming potential was attractive to a man who had experienced the hardships of life uniquely reserved for African Americans. He would later point to these experiences as the binding tie between himself and the members of the Nation of Islam because he had "walked the streets with them, suffered in the hell of North America, was humiliated in the South by the devils. . . ."[74] At that point, upon first hearing Master Fard, Elijah Poole knew there was something special about that man. He recognized the divine nature of Fard very early on:

Elijah candidly stated, "You are that one we read in the Bible that he would come in the last day under the name Jesus. . . . You are that one?" Caught off guard, Fard paused and looked deep into Elijah's eyes with a "very serious" gaze. He then smiled and whispered into Elijah's ear, "Yes, I am the One, but who knows that but yourself, and be quiet."[75]

Poole, who had changed his name to Elijah Karriem, became a part of the Nation of Islam. Elijah Karriem, eventually called Elijah Muhammad, quickly introduced his wife, Clare, and children to the Nation's teachings.

Elijah Karriem's efforts and potential were recognized by Master Fard, who one evening gave Clare a message for her husband: he had Fard's permission to preach the message. In the words of Fard: "You tell him that he can go ahead . . . and start teaching [Islam], and I will back [him] up."[76] Elijah was delighted with this call to minister, because he had, for some time, considered entering Christian ministry. In time, he, a man with little formal education, became Master Fard's second in command, the "Supreme Minister." A promotion of this magnitude for a man with such little formal education and mastery of verbal communication did not go unnoticed.[77]

Trouble with law enforcement resulted in Master Fard's arrest and removal from Detroit to Chicago, where Temple No. 2 had been developed a few years prior to this trouble. In 1934 Fard disappeared altogether, leaving Elijah Muhammad in charge of the movement.[78] This was not by any means a smooth transition. With Master Fard's departure, several figures sought control of the temple and its resources. A split occurred between those who understood Master Fard to be God incarnate and those who did not abide by this thinking. Elijah Muhammad was forced to leave Detroit and associate with those in Chicago ("Temple People") who, like Elijah Muhammad, regarded Master Fard as God incarnate (Allah). Elijah Muhammad continued the message of his teacher, leading the Nation of Islam toward its mission of resurrecting the "so-called Negro" by moving this group toward self-understanding and the embracing of their true religion (Islam). Elijah Muhammad's problems, both in Detroit and Chicago, extended beyond internal questions of rightful leadership. Elijah Muhammad also had to deal with law enforcement agents who took advantage of opportunities to disrupt the organization because of its separate educational program (University of Islam) and "voodoo" activities. Encounters with law enforcement over the educational apparatus used by the Nation and Elijah's political critique (e.g., of U.S. war efforts) resulted in his serving jail time.

The early years in the Chicago Temple were difficult. At one point Elijah Muhammad was required to relocate to Milwaukee (Temple No. 3) and areas further east for seven years until his physical safety in Chicago was less uncertain. During his time away, however, Messenger Muhammad continued to build the Nation, opening temples in Washington, D.C., and other large cities. He survived internal rivals and slowing his nationalist rhetoric, sparked growth for the movement. Much of this growth, particularly during the 1950s and early 1960s, was due to the vision and actions of Malcolm X as well as the media's infatuation with him.[79] Even problems in terms of orthodoxy were addressed through the pilgrimage, undertaken in time by both Messenger Muhammad and Malcolm X.[80] By the 1960s the Nation's publications were doing well and the Messenger was heard on more than one hundred radio stations each week. The Nation of Islam claimed that its growth was logical because its existence and its leadership were ordained by God. According to Messenger Muhammad:

> Some of the well-read scholars among the Orthodox Muslims are grieved to hear from America that I call myself a Messenger of Allah, though not one of them has been able to do the work that I have done in resurrecting my people in America. They could not do it. It was not for them to do what I am doing (the resurrecting of the dead). Their own Holy Qur'an teaches them that Allah teaches a Messenger from every people that he intends to warn or destroy.[81]

The divinely ordained nature of the Messenger's work left little room for questioning his decisions and insights. As the "Spiritual Head of the Muslims in the West," the Messenger also picked the ministers who exercised national responsibilities. The national officers included the Supreme Captain of the Fruit of Islam (who is the captain at the major mosque in Chicago), the Captain for the women (the Muslim Girls' Training and General Civilization Class), and the National Secretary. Under his leadership, the Nation of Islam also managed several large businesses including bakeries, restaurants, and a line of hygiene products, all under the umbrella of the Three Year Economic Development Program.[82] The Honorable Elijah Muhammad considered the establishment of black businesses, referred to as "communalism," to be a requirement of proper identity.

On the local level, each temple was composed of the following, all of whom are directly appointed or approved by the Messenger: (1) the minister, who communicates the Honorable Elijah Muhammad's message and teachings in the mosque and in the school if there is one; (2) captains of the Fruit of Islam and the Muslim Girls' Training and General Civilization Class; (3) first, second, and third lieutenants who take orders from the captains; (4) secretary; (5) treasurers, one for general funds, the other for funds for those in need; (6) investigators (one man and one woman) who monitor the welfare of members; (7) junior captains who are responsible for the activities geared toward the children. Only those who have completely submitted to the teachings of the Honorable Elijah Muhammad can serve as officers within a mosque because only they are members of the Fruit of Islam and the Muslim Girls' Training and General Civilization Class.

The growth of the Nation as an organization came through personal contact, prison ministry, aggressive recruitment referred to as "fishing for the dead," and public events that drew heavily from the ranks of discontented Christians. This process entailed addressing the contradictions of life in the United States and placing the blame for these contradictions squarely on the shoulders of white Americans—the "Devils" and their religion.

> The colonization of the dark people in the rest of the world was done by Christian powers. The number one problem that most people face in the world today is how to get freedom from Christians. Wherever you find nonwhite people today they are trying to get back their freedom from people who represent themselves as Christians, and if you ask these [subject] people their picture of a Christian, they will tell you "a white man—a Slave-master."[83]

The Nation also contended that

> [t]he black Christian preacher is the white's most effective tool for keep-
> ing the so-called Negroes pacified and controlled, for black preachers tell
> convincing lies against nature as well as against God. Throughout nature
> God has made provision for every creature to protect itself against its ene-
> mies, but black preachers have taught their people to stand still and turn
> the other cheek. They urge black men to fight on foreign battlefields to
> save the whites from their enemies, but once home again, they must no
> longer be men. Instead, they must patiently present themselves to be
> murdered by those they have saved.[84]

Having established this, members of the Nation then appealed to the desire
for a personal and collective identity that sustained self-worth and ability
and that recognized the specialness of African American life and history.[85]
This appeal to blackness—ontological, epistemological, cultural, historical—culminated in the logical necessity of the Nation and its teachings for
the "Lost-Found Nation" of Asiatic blacks in America. Those who recognized this and sought membership in the Nation were required to copy and
send to Chicago the following letter.

> Dear Savior Allah, Our Deliverer:
>   I have attended the Teachings of Islam, two or three times, as taught by
> one of your ministers, I believe in it. I bear witness that there is no God but
> Thee. And, that Muhammad is Thy Servant and Apostle. I desire to reclaim
> my Own. Please give me my Original name. My slave name is as follows.[86]

After a perfect copy of the above letter was received, one similar to the following was issued. The actual content of the letter was determined by the
situation of the convert.[87] The following was sent to a convert who found
Islam during a temple meeting:

> In the Name of Almighty Allah, the Beneficent, the Most Merciful, Sole
> Master of the Day of Judgment; and in the Name of His Divine Messenger,
> The Most Honorable Elijah Muhammad
>
>   Dear _____
>   The Nation of Islam is very happy over your return to your Own
> Holy Nation. We desire to inform you that you are no longer a slave, but
> Free, Independent, Asiatic Muslim with Allah, and a billion of brothers
> and sisters on your side as Friends [sic]. Please report to the office of the
> Temple, Sunday for instructions and lessons.
>   May Allah bless you.[88]

Since many converts came out of the prison system, the letter prisoners
received from Chicago spoke to their particular situation:

As-Salaam-Alaikum:

In the Name of Allah, the Beneficent, the Merciful; Master of the Day of Judgement.

Dear Brother:

Your letter of _____ has been received and I was very happy to hear from you. I am happy to know that you desire to join onto your own Holy Nation of Islam.

We have recorded your name in the "Book of Life," as a Believer. The following are the five fundamental Principles of Islam:

(1) A belief in the One God Whose proper Name is Allah.

(2) Believe in His Prophets.

(3) Believe in His Scriptures.

(4) Believe in the Resurrection.

(5) Believe in the Judgment Day.

Enclosed is one of our small Muslim Daily Prayer Books. Learn the prayers by heart and pray five times daily facing the East. When you are free, you will be able to attend the Temple of Islam and be qualified as a Believer.

May the peace and blessings of Allah be upon you.

As-Salaam-Alaikum: (peace be unto you)

Your brother

Elijah Muhammad

Messenger of Allah[89]

Many did not receive a new name to replace their "slave name" for a significant period of time. Others never received a new name and therefore used their first name and "X" (or 2X if there was another with the same first name). In either case, the new name was representative of a new identity as a Muslim and as the "image" of Allah. Accordingly,

> God offers you His own name. Every attribute of His name means something glorious, worthy, and something of divine. Not one of His names can be interpreted other than something of divine, but you have the name of the devil: Johnson, Williamson, Culpepper, Hog, Bird, Fish and what not [sic]. These are nothing but common devil names.[90]

New members are then given proper instructions to memorize, related to topics such as the "Actual Facts" and the "Lost-Found Moslem Lessons," and tasks within the temple to perform. Learning the required lessons is not taken lightly, as examinations are given that must be passed in order to advance and to have knowledge necessary to undo the work of the "Caucasian world." Part of the lessons revolves around mathematics and the significance of numbers. The University of Islam, the school system of the Nation of Islam, provides knowledge and training for children.[91] Because of the discipline and the seriousness with which education is treated, even those outside of the Nation of Islam seek to enroll their children and avoid the problems associated with city-run public schools.[92] The Messenger argues that education is essential, but too often it only serves the interests of whites. He believes that the "Lost-Found Nation" must educate itself, separating its children for fifteen to sixteen years. During this time they gain invaluable information concerning the sciences, history, and their identity.[93]

Knowledge is combined with care for the physical body, based upon proper hygiene and diet. Muslims are permitted one meal per day, which should consist of recommend foods such as navy beans, cabbage, carrots, lettuce, and certain fish. Forbidden items include alcohol, pork, collard greens, and black-eyed peas, which harm the body and prevent proper exercise of the brain. Muslims must exercise regularly, get medical check-ups, and spend time outdoors. Much of what is necessary for proper life is presented in *How to Eat to Live* and in the writings of Elijah Muhammad found in each issue of *The Final Call*.[94]

In addition to work assignments, dietary laws, and other obligations, Muslims are also bound by a moral code that requires love and respect for all Muslims and forbids fornication, gambling, and other activities that destroy unity and positive identity. Muslims are identifiable also because of a strict dress code that is most obvious with women, who are required to cover all including arms, legs, and head. Men are to also have a neat appearance and wear conservative attire. Muslims uphold these laws and regulations out of a respect for the Messenger, the community, and their personal accountability to both. The laws and regulations correspond to the objectives printed on the Nation's flag—"freedom, justice, and equality for you and I."[95] The rules of conduct can be summarized as follows.

1. Recognize the necessity for unity and group operation activities.
2. Pool resources, physically as well as financially.
3. Stop wanton criticism of everything that is black-owned and black operated.
4. Keep in mind—jealousy destroys from within.
5. Observe the operations of the white man. He is successful. He makes no excuses for his failures. He works hard—in a collective manner. You should do the same. [Without embracing his evil deeds and without buying into his white supremacy notions.][96]

Knowledge and physical health (a result of proper living) cultivate the proper frame of mind for worship. Although space does not allow for a full

Figure 7. The Muslims' Program

This is a copy of the Muslims' program as it appears in each issue of the Nation's newspaper. It articulates, in a concise manner, the ideological underpinnings of the Nation and its objectives. Reprinted by permission.

THE MUSLIM PROGRAM

What the Muslims Want

This is the question asked most frequently by both the whites and the Blacks. The answers to this question I shall state as simply as possible.

1. We want freedom. We want a full and complete freedom.

2. We want justice. Equal justice under the law. We want justice applied equally to all, regardless of creed or class or color.

3. We want equality of opportunity. We want equal membership in society with the best in civilized society.

4. We want our people in America whose parents or grandparents were descendants from slaves, to be allowed to establish a separate state or territory of their own—either on this continent or elsewhere. We believe that our former slave masters are obligated to provide such land and that the area must be fertile and minerally rich. We believe that our former slave masters are obligated to maintain and supply our needs in this separate territory for the next 20 to 25 years—until we are able to produce and supply our own needs.

Since we cannot get along with them in peace and equality, after giving them 400 years of our sweat and blood and receiving in return some of the worst treatment human beings have ever experienced, we believe our contributions to this land and the suffering forced upon us by white America, justifies our demand for complete separation in a state or territory of our own.

5. We want freedom for all Believers of Islam now held in federal prisons. We want freedom for

all Black men and women now under death sentence in innumerable prisons in the North as well as the South.

We want every Black man and woman to have the freedom to accept or reject being separated from the slave master's children and establish a land of their own.

We know that the above plan for the solution of the Black and white conflict is the best and only answer to the problem between two people.

6. We want an immediate end to the police brutality and mob attacks against the so-called Negro throughout the United States.

We believe that the Federal government should intercede to see that Black men and women tried in white courts receive justice in accordance with the laws of the land—or allow us to build a new nation for ourselves, dedicated to justice, freedom and liberty.

7. As long as we are not allowed to establish a state or territory of our own, we demand not only equal justice under the laws of the United States, but equal employment opportunities—NOW!

We do not believe that after 400 years of free or nearly free labor, sweat and blood, which has helped America become rich and powerful, that so many thousands of Black people should have to subsist on relief, charity or live in poor houses.

8. We want the government of the United States to exempt our people from ALL taxation as long as we are deprived of equal justice under the laws of the land.

9. We want equal education—but separate schools up to 16 for boys and 18 for girls on the

The Most Honorable Elijah Muhammad

condition that the girls be sent to women's colleges and universities. We want all Black children educated, taught and trained by their own teachers.

Under such schooling system we believe we will make a better nation of people. The United States government should provide, free, all necessary text books and equipment, schools and college buildings. The Muslim teachers shall be left free to teach and train their people in the way of righteousness, decency and self respect.

10. We believe that intermarriage or race mixing should be prohibited. We want the religion of Islam taught without hindrance or suppression.

These are some of the things that we, the Muslims, want for our people in North America.

What the Muslims Believe

1. WE BELIEVE In the One God Whose proper Name is Allah.

2. WE BELIEVE in the Holy Qur'an and in the Scriptures of all the Prophets of God.

3. WE BELIEVE in the truth of the Bible, but we believe that it has been tampered with and must be reinterpreted so that mankind will not be snared by the falsehoods that have been added to it.

4. WE BELIEVE in Allah's Prophets and the Scriptures they brought to the people.

5. WE BELIEVE in the resurrection of the dead—not in physical resurrection—but in mental resurrection. We believe that the so-called Negroes are most in need of mental resurrection, therefore, they will be resurrected first.

Furthermore, we believe we are the people of God's choice, as it has been written, that God would choose the rejected and the despised. We can find no other persons fitting this description in these last days more than the so-called Negroes in America. We believe in the resurrection of the righteous.

6. WE BELIEVE in the judgment; we believe this first judgment will take place as God revealed, in America.

7. WE BELIEVE this is the time in history for the separation of the so-called Negroes and the

so-called white Americans. We believe the Black man should be freed in name as well as in fact. By this we mean that he should be freed from the names imposed upon him by his former slave masters. Names which identified him as being the slave master's slave. We believe that if we are free indeed, we should go in our own people's names—the Black peoples of the Earth.

8. WE BELIEVE in justice for all, whether in God or not; we believe as others, that we are due equal justice as human beings. We believe in equality—as a nation—of equals. We do not believe that we are equal with our slave masters in the status of "freed slaves."

We recognize and respect American citizens as independent peoples and we respect their laws which govern this nation.

9. WE BELIEVE that the offer of integration is hypocritical and is made by those who are trying to deceive the Black peoples into believing that their 400-year-old open enemies of freedom, justice and equality are, all of a sudden, their "friends." Furthermore, we believe that such deception is intended to prevent Black people from realizing that the time in history has arrived for the separation from the whites of this nation.

If the white people are truthful about their pro-

fessed friendship toward the so-called Negro, they can prove it by dividing up America with their slaves.

We do not believe that America will ever be able to furnish enough jobs for her own millions of unemployed, in addition to jobs for the 20,000,000 Black people as well.

10. WE BELIEVE that we who declare ourselves to be righteous Muslims, should not participate in wars which take the lives of humans. We do not believe this nation should force us to take part in such wars, for we have nothing to gain from it unless America agrees to give us the necessary territory wherein we may have something to fight for.

11. WE BELIEVE our women should be respected and protected as the women of other nationalities are respected and protected.

12. WE BELIEVE that Allah (God) appeared in the Person of Master W. Fard Muhammad, July, 1930; the long-awaited "Messiah" of the Christians and the "Mahdi" of the Muslims.

We believe further and lastly that Allah is God and besides HIM there is no God and He will bring about a universal government of peace wherein we all can live in peace together.

HE LIVES

discussion of all aspects of worship, some attention should be given to prayer within the Nation of Islam. Prayer is understood as a fundamental component of faith. I offer the following as an example:

"O Allah make Muhammad successful and the true followers of Muhammad successful as Thou didst make Abraham successful and the true followers of Abraham successful. For surely Thou art praised and magnified in our midst. Allah bless Muhammad and the true followers of Muhammad as Thou didst bless Abraham and the true followers of Abraham. Surely thou art praised and magnified in our midst."

In the above prayer, the Believers of the lost and found nation pray for the Messenger whom Allah (God) has raised among them; a guide to the lost and now found path of Allah. For 400 years they have been wandering in darkness, blinded by the touch of Satan, the devil.[97]

It is understood within the Nation that prayer should be performed five times each day, with two additional prayers during the night.[98] And prayer should not be conducted until the recommended components of the body are ritually washed.

Recent accounts of the Nation of Islam provide very useful insights into the Nation's life that are hard to gather from this recital of doctrine. One of these autobiographical accounts, Sonsyrea Tate's account of her childhood in the Nation, *Little X: Growing Up in the Nation of Islam*,[99] offers a good example of the influence of the Nation's doctrine in everyday life.

According to Sonsyrea, her family, beginning with her grandparents, embraced the Nation of Islam because it provided vision for life and affirmation of their basic human value. Furthermore, there was a comforting sense of family based upon shared beliefs and activities; each member of the temple was responsible for helping other members as their means allowed. Much of this doctrine was difficult to understand as a child, but attention was given to it regardless. A life of righteousness began early through the recognition of and denouncing of faults. In light of this Sonsyrea prayed:

"I have been greatly unjust to myself and I confess my faults," our prayer continued. I'd have to ask Ma what a "confess" was later on when I got home. I knew a fault was when you sneaked to do something, thinking nobody saw you. Allah was always watching and always counting up your faults. Every time I sneaked a piece of candy out of my uncles' coat pockets, that was another fault. So I had to keep saying prayers, asking Allah not to be mad at me. The grownups had bigger faults, so they had to pray five times every day. I was little, so I only had to say prayers in school.[100]

In addition to private moments such as the above, Sonsyrea remembers attending meetings throughout the week, as other children played outside. Even children had to observe order during these meetings; discipline was important. For example, no one was allowed to leave the meeting room except for use of the rest room, where children sought opportunities to talk about candy, boys, girls, and social life in general. Although Tate and her friends felt somewhat isolated from the typical dealings of childhood, they also felt "special" as a result of the Nation's protective arms and chosen-status doctrine.

This specialness and its responsibilities were reinforced through the educational process Muslim children experienced. According to Tate:

> Our reading, math, and science studies were more advanced than in public schools. We learned Arabic in level three. . . . Every day we were drilled on a few of our twenty-five Actual Facts, information about the dimensions of planet Earth and other celestial bodies. We were taught that our God, who came to North America in the form of Master Fard Muhammad, measured the Earth, all the other planets, and the distances between. This God wanted us to memorize the widths and weights of all the planets, our teachers said, because someday we black people, especially the few of us chosen for the Nation of Islam, would rule the world. We would need to understand everything about the universe in order to control it.[101]

Tate wrestled with these teachings as she grew up and became more aware of what occurred outside the Nation. For some like Tate, unsatisfying answers to questions resulted in a move away from the Nation and its teachings; others, however, remained. The appeal of the Nation's emphasis on self-worth and accountability continued to grip the imagination of some African Americans.

To summarize, the essential beliefs and praxis of the Nation entail surrender to the one God, Allah, who came in the form of Master Fard Muhammad; recognition of the prophets, with the Honorable Elijah Muhammad being the last; the mental deliverance and separation (not integration) of God's chosen people, the so-called Negroes; the judgment of God's enemies. Although fairly elusive when first encountered by the "outsider," this belief system and its connection to the Nation's praxis become clear once the underlying cosmological structure is considered in light of the Nation's complex historical development.

The cosmology embraced by the Nation of Islam became clear after Master Fard Muhammad's disappearance, and it remains relatively the same to this day.[102] That is to say, when Elijah Muhammad became the leader of the Nation of Islam, he quickly established the legitimacy of his role and the Nation's structure by asserting that Master Fard Muhammad is the self-created God (Allah) who dwells in flesh:

76 trillion years ago, before the existence of temporal and material reality, the universe was dark and motionless, void of life. Out of the womb of total darkness was issued an atom that rotated into being and thus began the concept of time. Still spinning, the atom of life matured and developed flesh and blood, brains and power. A corporeal entity, later known as Earth, incubated the dark, growing body until it achieved self-awareness and the power to create. The body, which was once an atom, became a man, a Black Man. . . . In time, the self-created man took on the name Allah or God and proceeded to create others like him in his own dark, majestic image.[103]

Allah and the other gods continued creation by forming the sun, stars, and planets close to earth (e.g., Mars), which held life forms similar to the original people of earth. However, because earth (properly called "moon" in that it combined both what we call earth and the moon) was the most important of the planets, the vast majority of Allah's creative energy was directed toward earth.

On earth, the Original people ruled from "Asia" and were divided into thirteen tribes, different but united by their blackness, their common religion—Islam—and their inherent goodness. The gods or great scientists understood that the Original people (Asiatics) would need guidance, and a written record chronicling the past and foretelling the future was created to meet this need. These records, parts of which are housed in Holy Scriptures, were written by twenty-three of the gods, and the twenty-fourth served as judge and supreme deity for the twenty-five thousand years during which history ran its course. The content of history is given to various prophets to reveal only after that historical segment is ten thousand years old. Master Fard Muhammad, Allah, is Supreme deity during our current twenty-five-thousand-year period. Fard is not, however, the "First" who began creation but is Allah, who has the same knowledge as the "First" creator:

Master Farad Muhammad is the first God to have the same power and wisdom as the First One had in the Beginning. In fact, as Master Farad Muhammad has the power to return everything to nothing and then bring forth a new and better creation from himself, he is "superior of even that First One."[104]

As humans, the gods do not live forever. That is to say, "There is no God Living Who was here in the Creation of the Universe, but They produce Gods from Them and Their Wisdom [sic] lives in us."[105] Elijah Muhammad asserts that he was the first to present the truth about God in flesh. If one pays attention to scripture, this truth is clear. According to Elijah Muhammad:

If God is a spirit and is not man, could we receive the son of man [i.e., Jesus]? Nevertheless, according to the Bible, God made man in the image of Himself and in His likeness [Genesis 1:26]. Then could God be something other than a human being? If He's a spirit, he has no life. He's no image, if He's a spirit, because a spirit neither has a form at all, nor any likeness, nor any color.[106]

This understanding of Fard as Allah was not, according to Messenger Muhammad, a creation of the Nation; rather, it is the truth given to the Nation by Master Fard himself. Elijah Muhammad recounts a conversation with Allah (Fard) in which this supreme truth was revealed:

I asked him, "Who are you, and what is your real name?" He said, "I am the one that the world has been expecting for the past 2,000 years." I said to Him again, "What is your name?" He said, "My name is Mahdi; I am God, I came to guide you into the right path that you may be successful and see the hereafter."[107]

Elijah Muhammad was appointed the Messenger of God and, in fact, the last Messenger—the one sent to bring the words of salvation to the Lost-Found Nation within the United States.[108] The Messenger's preoccupation with the Lost-Found Nation, or Asiatics living in the wilderness of North America, bespeaks the divinely ordained levels of theological anthropology.

The hierarchy of human worth was clearly defined in the Messenger's Nation. Of most importance were blacks and nonwhites who embraced Islam. These are followed by blacks and nonwhites who have not embraced Islam because they have not heard the message. Next in the hierarchy are those, black and nonwhite, who have heard the message but rejected it. The final group is composed of whites.[109] This hierarchy is more fundamentally divided into two primary units: the *creation* of Allah and that which was *made* by Yakub.[110] The former are those whom Allah seeks and for whom all other life forms exist. Furthermore, the Original people are godlike in that they operate by power, transforming situations to their liking. Hence, what separates the Original people from Allah is not characteristics so much as degree. That is to say, the Original people are wise, righteous and powerful, but Allah is all-wise and supreme in wisdom and righteousness.

The Original people are the Asiatic (Asia is the earth's original name) black race who provided the world with civilization, the tribe of Shabazz that lived in the Nile Valley and Mecca. They are the tribe that remained on this portion of the earth after a large explosion created by a discontented scientist who was displeased that the Original people spoke more than one language.

This explosion divided the moon and earth, which had been one planet called "moon," resulting in two separate bodies. This explosion also altered the time frame for the recording of history, moving it from thirty-five thousand to twenty-five thousand due to the altered circumference of the earth.[111]

The activities of another scientist named Shabazz (or Abraham according to the Bible), who wanted to strengthen the survival skills of the Original people by moving them to the jungle of Africa (East Asia), must be considered. Only those of the Shabazz tribe agreed to participate. The physical changes resulting from this experiment included the development of kinky hair, broadening of the nose, and thickening of the lips.[112] Master Fard's story indicates that this time spent in the other portions of (sub-Saharan) Africa resulted in the loss of cultural refinement and a movement toward uncivilized life entailing obedience to base instincts. Problems were not limited to this portion of the Original people, however. In other areas, religious practices not in keeping with the tenets of Islam—the original religion—were developed by the Original people. One particularly extreme religious group was forced out of Asia (known as India) and into America because of heterodoxy. This group is composed of what we commonly refer to as Native Americans or Indians.[113]

Those *made* by Yakub comprise the "white race" of devils, capable of only evil. Yakub understood as a child that he would eventually develop a race that would enslave the Original—Asiatic black—race.[114]

> Mr. Yakub was seen by the twenty-three Scientists of the black nation, over 15,000 years ago. They predicted that in the year 8,400 (that was in our calendar year before this world of the white race), this man (Yakub) would be born twenty miles from the present Holy City, Mecca, Arabia. And, that at the time of his birth, the satisfaction and dissatisfaction of the people would be: 70 percent satisfied, 30 percent dissatisfied.
>
> And, that when this man is born, he will change civilization (the world), and produce a new race of people, who would rule the original black nation for 6,000 years (from the nine thousandth year to the fifteen thousandth year).[115]

Yakub, known for his large head, gained all available information from the existing civilizations and began preaching. He preached a perverted form of Islam, promising his followers servants and luxuries. Yakub's teachings caused unrest that the city's leadership knew had to be resolved, but arresting him and his followers only increased his following. With time, a settlement was made with Yakub requiring him to relocate to another place (the Isle of Pelan or Patmos found in the Book of Revelation written by

Yakub) with his 59,999 followers. He and his followers were provided with supplies sufficient to last twenty-five years. Once relocated, Yakub instilled in his followers a dislike for those who had forced their removal, and he promised revenge if they were willing to follow his instructions and abide by his plan to graft a new race.

Yakub grafted from his followers the white race by allowing only the lighter-skinned members of his group to mate, thereby weeding out strong black genes and keeping weaker (brown) genes until white skin resulted. The process involved his doctors and ministers preventing dark-skinned followers from marrying each other, and black babies were killed. This process resulted in several important differences between Yakub's children and the Original people. Specifically:

> Their bones were fragile and their blood thin, resulting in an overall phys-
> ical strength one-third that of blacks. Weak bodies made Yakub's man sus-
> ceptible to disease, and most future ailments, "from social diseases to
> cancer," would be attributable to his presence on earth. Additionally, six-
> ounce brains made whites inherently inferior in mental capacity to the
> Original People, whose gray matter weighed an ounce and a half more. . . .
> the grafting process had made the white race both incapable of righteous-
> ness and biologically subordinate to the black people.[116]

After his death at the age of 150, the process continued through Yakub's written instructions. Eventually the process was completed and the group returned home, bringing with them their trickery and destructive ways. They polluted the Original people's thinking until they were once again removed, this time to the wilderness of Europe.[117] During this period of exile, Caucasians lost cultural refinement and the basic elements of civi-lization, reverting, in the process, to the level of monkeys—living nude or wearing animal skins, residing in caves, and walking on all fours.

Because it had been written in history that Caucasians would rule the Original people for six thousand years, Allah sent Moses and other prophets to bring Caucasians back into a state of civilization. Moses taught them that, if they followed his teachings, Allah would grant them renewed life. By means of this new station, Allah gave them dominion over the earth for the prophesied number of years. As the Book of Genesis records, God said:

> Let us make man in our image, after our likeness: Let them have domin-
> ion over the fish of the sea; and over the fowl of the air; and over the cat-
> tle, and over all the earth; and over every creeping thing that creepeth
> upon the earth": and God said unto them: "Be fruitful and multiply; and
> replenish the earth, and subdue it." (Genesis 1:26, 28)[118]

According to Messenger Muhammad, we are currently in the sixteen-thousandth year of the current twenty-five-thousand-year cycle. The time of the white race divides into three segments: (1) the first two thousand house the time of Yakub and Moses; (2) the second two thousand entail the time to the rise of Jesus; (3) the third two thousand years cover the period up to the coming of Allah in the form of Master Fard Muhammad.[119] And we now stand in the period marked by final judgment, when the Original people will be restored to their former greatness through the teachings of the Honorable Elijah Muhammad.

Muslims do not believe in life beyond the grave; thus talk of resurrection and paradise refer to the rebirth of "the Lost-Found" through the Nation of Islam's teachings and the righteous life lived by the chosen after judgment. Hence, little attention is given to the dead and to funeral activities. Rather, emphasis is placed upon life on earth and the needs of the living. This emphasis on earthly existence was initially expressed by the Honorable Elijah Muhammad in terms of a black nation on separate soil—several of the American states or some other land—and also, at times, as a black nation within a (U.S.) nation. The Messenger argued that the United States, in payment for the "free" labor of black slaves, should finance this black nation for twenty-five years as reparation payment. Integration was trivialized and denounced as unproductive and against the welfare of Asiatic black people. Only by separating will Asiatic black people fully develop and achieve the divine role established for them by Allah.

With the death of the Honorable Elijah Muhammad on February 25, 1975, there were several splits in the Nation of Islam; two are of primary importance.[120] His heir, son Wallace Deen Muhammad, dismantled the Nation's structure and theology that was not in line with orthodox Islam as practiced elsewhere in the Islamic world.[121] Wallace Muhammad actually began this theological revision during his imprisonment for draft evasion (1960–63).[122] It was not until his father's death, however, that he could express these thoughts without sanction. According to Wallace Muhammad, in bringing African Americans to self-knowledge, Fard Muhammad and Elijah Muhammad could not provide orthodox Islam because of the mental slavery under which African Americans still labored. This bondage had to be removed prior to spreading orthodox Islam. Elijah Muhammad's work helped develop the necessary changes in the black community that allowed Islam to take root; Wallace Muhammad would finish this task. Once installed as Supreme Leader of the Nation, he pub-

---

Figure 8. Cosmology of the Nation under Elijah Muhammad

Name	Identity
Master Fard Muhammad	Allah (Supreme 24th Scientist)
23 God-Scientists*	Gods who write history
Honorable Elijah Muhammad	Last Messenger
Angels in the Mother Plane	Black helpers of God
Original people (created of Allah)	Asiatics
Made people (of Yakub Adam)	Caucasians
Other life forms	Earth and Elsewhere

---

*The Wise Scientists or gods are at times referred to as "angels."

---

licly rethought the Nation's cosmology, beginning with Master Fard. This theological restructuring effort was ritually manifest in his move from Savior's Day, the celebration of Master Fard's birth, February 26, to "Ethnic Survival Day."

Wallace Muhammad's goal was to deemphasize the "divine" status of Fard Muhammad. A speech given by Wallace in the 1990s gave a concise statement on Fard's new position with the Nation:

> the father of the Nation of Islam reappeared late in his life, repented "for what he had done and made an effort . . . to bring about the end of his own work." To help him undo the vastly unorthodox version of Islam that Fard and Elijah Muhammad had foisted upon blacks, Warith Muhammad appointed Fard the imam of the mosque in Oakland, California, where he was known as Muhammad Abdullah.[123]

In the course of the transition to orthodox Islam his father, Elijah Muhammad, lost his position as the last prophet. In keeping with the larger Islamic world, this role belonged to the Prophet Muhammad, who received the final revelation in the form of the Qur'ān.

In addition to cosmological changes, Wallace Muhammad dismantled the rigid structure of the Nation by abolishing the Fruit of Islam and changing the Nation's name, in 1976, to the World Community of Islam in the West.[124] The change in the organization's name was accompanied by a shift toward traditional Islamic personal names and the renaming of the "so-called Negroes" to Bilalians after an African Muslim close to the Prophet

Muhammad.[125] Sonsyrea Tate recounts the understanding of these changes within the Washington Temple:

> Our new leader explained that what we had learned and practiced all those years before his father's death was called a First Resurrection. Black people had to be awakened from a mental state of death, from not knowing ourselves and loving ourselves, and move toward doing positive things for ourselves. Now we were moving into the Second Resurrection, and we were supposed to come alive even more and think for ourselves—individually—and read the Holy Qur'an and Bible for ourselves and discipline ourselves.[126]

These doctrinal and attitudinal changes were accompanied by physical changes to the temples that were now referred to as *Masjiids*. Tate reports:

> The brothers got rid of our flag and blackboard with all our symbols, then they tore down the stage so our minister could stand on even ground with the rest of us when we prayed. . . . all the chairs had been taken out, replaced by carpet for us to sit on. . . . The Masjiid was full with lots of people who joined us now that we didn't have so many rules and restrictions. People who had left the Nation were coming back since they wouldn't be forced to sell papers and buy special uniforms. And Orthodox Muslims of all colors came, too.[127]

In 1982, the organization underwent another name change, becoming the American Muslim Mission. This was accompanied by further decentralization and increased conversation with Christian churches.[128] Even with these radical changes, many initially followed Wallace Muhammad's program because he had been selected by the Honorable Elijah Muhammad; among them was Louis X (formerly Louis Walcott).

Louis Eugene Walcott was born in Boston on May 11, 1933, and was raised by his mother, who had come to the United States in the 1920s and married Walcott's father, a Jamaican named Percival Clarke, although Walcott is named for her lover, Louis Walcott. Although financial resources were scarce, Walcott's mother, Mae Manning, provided him and his brother with music lessons and stressed the importance of a good education. Those who remember him as a young man growing up in the Roxbury section of Boston speak of his confidence, talents, and determination. Walcott spent his early years in St. Cyprian's Episcopal Church as an acolyte, member of the choir, and musician (he played the violin). He planned to continue his musical training at Juilliard, but financial difficulties resulted in Walcott attending school in North Carolina instead. Walcott was there for two years before dropping out and getting married in 1953. He attempted to earn a living through his musical abilities. But he was not prepared for the demands of music executives and the politics of the music business, and so the music career never matched his aspirations.

The year 1955 marked his introduction to the Nation of Islam by an old friend, Rodney Smith. Exposed to the teachings of Marcus Garvey as a child he could relate to the words of the Messenger, although he was troubled by the Messenger's lack of eloquence. Walcott remembers thinking that the Messenger's grammar was unimpressive when

> suddenly, Muhammad . . . looked up. . . . "Brother, don't pay attention to how I speak. Pay attention to what I'm saying. I didn't get the chance to go to the white man's fine schools, because when I tried to go, the doors were closed. But if you take what I say and place it into the beautiful way of speaking you know, you can help me save our people."[129]

Louis Walcott joined the Nation because its leadership demonstrated vision and an agenda not present in the Christian church. Through the guidance of Malcolm X, whom he encountered during a meeting in Boston, he became a noteworthy minister who combined the fire of the Nation's theology with his musical abilities as expressed in the song "A White Man's Heaven Is a Black Man's Hell." Eventually, Louis X moved away from music and gave full attention to preaching. His speaking abilities gained him the Messenger's attention and resulted in Louis X's rise through the Nation's ranks: lieutenant, assistant minister, moving from a captain in the FOI to a minister in Boston (Temple No. 11), to minister of Mosque No. 7 in New York in 1964 and later the Messenger's National Representative (1967). During these years, Louis X continued to embrace the Nation's teachings and its leadership, ignoring contradictions and the Messenger's personal flaws.[130]

Louis X (whose name was changed by Muhammad to Louis Farrakhan) remained loyal until the Nation itself, under Elijah Muhammad's son, began a radical shift away from the original teachings. As friction between Louis Farrakhan and Wallace Muhammad grew, Wallace sought to bring Farrakhan under control by transferring him out of the prestigious New York mosque and to Chicago as Muhammad's ambassador and minister to a small and struggling mosque.[131] Wallace Muhammad gave this alteration in Farrakhan's status symbolic expression by changing Farrakhan's name to Abdul Haleem Farrakhan. As ambassador, Farrakhan traveled across the globe, and during these travels he realized that racism also held a grip on Islamic nations. This insight convinced him that the message of the Honorable Elijah Muhammad was the only way to rid the world of white supremacy.[132]

A break with Wallace Muhammad was inevitable. Arthur Magida in his biography of Louis Farrakhan, argues that before reestablishing the Nation under the theological framework offered by Elijah Muhammad, Farrakhan attempted to move back into the music business, but reading about Elijah Muhammad in *This Is the One* sparked a desire to continue the Messenger's work.[133] Whatever the case may be, Louis Farrakhan, without open hostility, resurrected the Nation of Islam in 1978,[134] because the condition of African Americans was getting worse through an increase in white supremist activities, the reneging on programs that had been earmarked for the advancement of African Americans, and the moral decline of Islamic groups.[135] After legal battles and the selling of several pieces of property by Wallace Muhammad, Louis Farrakhan was able to purchase the most important Chicago mosque, which he renamed Mosque Maryam, and the former home of the Honorable Elijah Muhammad.

According to Farrakhan, there was historical precedent for his undertaking. He contends that the Prophet Muhammad fled to Medina and established a Nation of Islam after his wife's death, and Elijah Muhammad (the Messenger of Allah) appeared dead to escape his enemies and thereby establish the next phase of the Nation of Islam. (One could also include as a median period Elijah Muhammad's "disappearance" for seven years early in the Nation's history and the disappearance of Master Fard.) Farrakhan, selected by Elijah Muhammad through visions and direct words, had the task of working for the building of this post–Elijah Muhammad phase of the Nation. In so doing, Farrakhan continued the divinely appointed line of Messengers and builders of Islam.[136]

Farrakhan's Nation regarded Master Fard Muhammad as Allah incarnate, maintaining the celebration of his birth on February 26. This is in keeping with the Messenger's pronouncement. However, the Honorable Elijah Muhammad became the Christ, whose role is noted by a Savior's Day celebration on October 7 of each year. Farrakhan claims that the Christians' Jesus is not the Chosen One, because his deeds do not point to the saving of the world. He is, rather, a marker pointing to the Messiah. And this Messiah is the Honorable Elijah Muhammad, who still lives and is preparing to return according to prophecy. Farrakhan states:

> I, Louis Farrakhan, am saying to the world that the Honorable Elijah Muhammad is not physically dead. I am further stating that he was made to appear as such as written in the Bible and in the Holy Qur'an, in order that the Holy Qur'an, in order that the Scriptures might be fulfilled.[137]

Farrakhan argues that he knows the true cosmological order of the universe not simply through scripture and second-hand sources, but because the Honorable Elijah Muhammad spoke to him directly. As part of this process, Farrakhan was anointed to continue the work of the Honorable Elijah Muhammad.

> On September 17, 1985, Minister Farrakhan was in the quiet Mexican hamlet of Tepotzlan and received a vision in which his divine power was further reinforced. In the vision, Farrakhan walked up a mountain to an Aztec temple together with some companions. When he got to the top of the mountain, a UFO appeared. . . . The circular space ship did not come directly over the mountain but stayed off the side, and a voice called Farrakhan to come closer. . . . He obeyed, and as he walked closer, a beam of light, resembling the sunlight piercing through a window, came out of the wheel. Farrakhan was told to relax and was brought up into the plane on this beam of light. . . . After docking, the door opened and Farrakhan was escorted by the pilot to a door and admitted into a room, which was totally empty except for a speaker in the ceiling. From that speaker Farrakhan heard the well-known voice of the Honorable Elijah Muhammad, which confirmed his being alive. Farrakhan was authorized to lead his God-fearing people through the latter days.[138]

In short, this vision served two purposes: (1) it affirmed Farrakhan's understanding of cosmology, and (2) it secured his place within this cosmology as the Messenger appointed to lead the people until the judgment. It is possible, however, that Farrakhan's role will extend beyond Messenger to Messiah, following the same path taken by the Honorable Elijah Muhammad. This point was made during an interview between Mattias Gardell and Minister Farrakhan in which Farrakhan said: "I am the man everybody is looking for. I am a Messiah. Elijah Muhammad was raised by Master Fard Muhammad to become the Messiah and he raised me to become the little Messiah. Read the scriptures, there are two Messiahs coming in the Latter Days."[139]

The maintenance of Elijah Muhammad's teachings under the guidance of Louis Farrakhan, involved a recognition of the message's symbolic importance along with a subtle move toward more orthodox practices. As Martha Lee observes, Farrakhan's movement toward orthodoxy took place on several fronts. It was theologically premised on the connection between the Prophet Muhammad and Elijah Muhammad insofar as the former's life was the model for the latter's actions. In addition, the importance of the Qur'ān as the basis of knowledge for both orthodox Muslims and the Nation was highlighted. In terms of ritual, this shift was premised on the

Messenger's gradual embrace of more orthodox worship activities and patterns, and by the development, under the leadership of Louis Farrakhan, of a Qur'ānic study program referred to as "Self Improvement: The Basis for Community Development."[140]

From Farrakhan's perspective, the link between the Nation and Islam as practiced in the East is natural and historically progressive, yet it is his given role to further the process begun by the Honorable Elijah Muhammad. Although he tends toward orthodoxy, Farrakhan maintains the relevance of the Nation's original teachings by claiming that the presence of Elijah Muhammad was Allah's response to current needs. Were he still alive, the Prophet's (nephew of Abu Talib) call for divine justice would necessitate involvements in keeping with the Nation's program. Therefore, the Orthodox world is moving against God by denying the last prophet— Elijah Muhammad—because of racism. Mattias Gardell provides insight into this:

> In two Hadith, the Prophet Muhammad mentions the time we are now living in. One refers to the latter days, when the sun of Islam will rise in the West. The other relates to the specific people honored to realize its fulfillment. Muhammad said, "I heard the footsteps of Bilal going into Paradise ahead of my own." The interpretation of this hadith is evident. "He didn't mean his own personal footsteps," Farrakhan explained, "he was white. He was an Arab. And he was saying that it is the Blacks who are going to lead the Arab world back to the faith that they had forsaken, and lead them into the Paradise their God promised to them by the prophet Muhammad (PBUH) and the Qur'an.[141]

Farrakhan also found it necessary to reformulate the Nation's theological anthropology. He argues from the Bible and the Qur'ān that in the beginning Allah created the human—Adam/atom—from black mud:

> According to the Qur'an, Allah says in the Qur'an, He created the man out of Black mud. Well then, if Elijah Muhammad asked the question, who is the Original Man? And the answer is, the Original Man is the Asiatic Black man, the maker, the owner, the cream of the planet earth, the God of the universe. The Qur'an doesn't say different. 'Original Man' means, that which is first, that which is the prototype from which all other types come. He's not mankind, he's not a species of man, he is the man from which all other species have their beginning.[142]

And from this Original black person came all other humans, including the Caucasian. This perspective on creation is layered with allusions to the creation of people who would bring mischief into the world. Farrakhan's reading of the Qur'ān removes some of the direct references to figures such as Yakub while maintaining symbolism that easily incorporates the Honorable Elijah Muhammad's account. That is to say, the metaphorical depictions in Muhammad's message took on historical concreteness during the early stages of the Nation. And in the new Nation, under the leadership of Farrakhan, these metaphorical pronouncements and symbolism maintain their status as signs and symbols that point, in subtle ways, to the Bible and the Qur'ān's teachings. According to Farrakhan:

> I advise everyone to get a Holy Qur'an and read it along with your Bible. Let me quote from the Qur'an. Allah was talking to the angels, and He tells the angels He's going to make a man. And they ask Him, "What will you make other than that which will create mischief and cause the shedding of blood?" [Keep in mind Yakub's conversation with his uncle. The wording is similar.] Then God said to the angels, "I know what you don't know. He may cause mischief and shed blood in a certain stage of his development, but after I get him past that stage, he's going to be greater than that. He's my glory. [This may refer to Allah's use of Caucasians to accomplish the divine plan.][143]

In 1981, six thousand were present at the new Nation's first Savior's Day. The growth, however, did not entail an end to conflict with Wallace Muhammad. Peace would not last; rhetorical battles would occur. During

---

Figure 9. Cosmology according to Louis Farrakhan

Name	Identity
Master Fard Muhammad	Allah (Supreme 24th scientist)
*23 God-scientists	Gods who write history
Honorable Elijah Muhammad	Christ—Messiah
Minister Louis Farrakhan	Messenger
Angels in the Mother Plane	God's helpers
Original people (Adam)	Asiatics
Humans made from the Original people	Caucasians
Other life forms	On earth and elsewhere

---

*Not referred to in Farrakhan's cosmology as frequently as in the Honorable Elijah Muhammad's cosmology. This chart shows the nature of divine "call" and Messenger status through the elevation of Minister Farrakhan as well as the increasingly "divine" status of the Honorable Elijah Muhammad.

the 1980s, Imams from Muhammad's movement began to condemn the work of Farrakhan as being outside the Islamic faith. And members of the new Nation of Islam had less than flattering things to say about Wallace Muhammad, who was referred to as a "thief" and "pretender." It was not until Imam Muhammad and Louis Farrakhan met and discussed their differences that an agreement to disagree was achieved.

Under the leadership of Farrakhan, the Nation of Islam has continued to grow and his lectures are heard on various radio stations and on more than ninety television stations. Beginning with small groups that grew into mosques, the message of the Nation spread, with the Nation's newspaper *Final Call* as a vital means of dissemination. Currently the Nation of Islam is present in every state and Washington, D.C., and its internal structure mirrors this growth. Under the leadership of Louis Farrakhan, the Nation of Islam's organizational structure has expanded to the following:

> National Representative of Elijah Muhammad—Louis Farrakhan
> The National Council of Laborers—Farrakhan's Council:
>> The Nation's Ministries:
>>> Minister of Finance
>>> Minister of Commerce
>>> Minister of Defense (Fruit of Islam [FOI])
>>> National MGT (Muslim Girl Training) Captain
>>> Minister of Education
>>> Minister of Youth
>>> Minister of Health
>> Six Regional Representatives

As has been noted, Farrakhan's Nation of Islam embraced the teaching of the Honorable Elijah Muhammad, but the praxis of the new Nation differed in significant ways. In addition to active political involvement, the socioeconomic agenda outlined by Farrakhan betrays the middle-class values and capitalist leanings that were present, but understated, in the Nation from its earliest years.[144] In other words, the Nation's denouncement of white supremacy and its trappings did not preclude an embrace of the "American Dream," the basic principles of democracy approved of by a growing "mainstream" audience. This is not to say that the new Nation has avoided conflict with the "mainstream" powers. Farrakhan has made his share of enemies, including much of the Jewish community as well as Christian church communities. But on a positive note, the presence of Minister Benjamin Muhammad of Temple No. 7 (formerly Benjamin

Chavis) has the potential to create praxis related links with the African American (Christian) religious community. And perhaps Benjamin Muhammad's past ties with the NAACP and other related organizations will provide grounds for conversation with liberal Jewish groups. Furthermore, the Million Man March demonstrated Farrakhan's appeal as a leader whose influence extends well beyond his own organization. As a consequence, he remains a figure to contend with.[145]

In 1993, Farrakhan published *A Torchlight for America* as a means of identifying the problems plaguing U.S. society as well as ways to avoid the total destruction with which these problems threaten us.[146] Farrakhan begins by asserting that the condition of the United States stems from the improper conduct of its political and business leaders, who give more attention to their financial greed and personal aspirations than to the welfare of their constituency.[147] Hence, although petty crime receives much attention,

> even larger than the drug industry and street crime, in terms of dollars, is white-collar crime. The Savings and Loan (S&L) bailout alone is half a trillion of the taxpayers' dollars. Michael Milken and Ivan Boesky beat the economy out of billions of dollars with their junk bond scheme that bankrupted the S&Ls. This kind of crime has eroded public confidence and placed an added burden on all taxpayers. Yet these crimes are rarely punished severely.[148]

Farrakhan warned that the West's misconduct would result in the downfall of once great nations as their ability to benefit from the raw materials of Africa, Asia, and Latin America decreased. The socioeconomic structure and fabric of the United States is disintegrating at an alarming rate and utter destruction and God's judgment will follow. The crisis now faced in the United States is due to its mistreatment of African Americans. And the outcome of its supremist attitudes and behavior is destruction: "It's dangerous to enslave a people and be the perpetual source of opposition to truth, which is the means for freeing the people from ignorance, yet say you believe in God. God has always come to the aid of the oppressed."[149]

Farrakhan argues that the American people are unaware of their actual condition because African Americans have been labeled the source of confusion and decline. In keeping with the Nation's teachings under Elijah Muhammad, Farrakhan asserts that the solution to this problem, the reversal of this destructive pattern, has been revealed by Elijah Muhammad. African American leaders from all vantage points must unite around the common theme of self-help and self-determination, and in this way crush racist attitudes.

Movement toward socioeconomic stability begins with proper education based upon knowledge of God, which entails knowledge of self. Each subsequent subject in the educational curriculum relates to the student because the student is the subject.

> When we see the curriculum as an outgrowth of self, then we can identify with the curriculum, giving us an incentive to learn. In the Muhammad University of Islam school system, our students' learning is facilitated because they identify with the subjects. They are taught that they are the subject. They are taught, "I am chemistry." Not, "I am a student of chemistry," rather, "I am biology. I am economics. . . . When we relate the forces within self to the forces that lie outside the self, this connects us to subjects we are studying in a manner that we can ultimately master those subjects.[150]

When the educational process is not underpinned in this way, notions of white superiority and black inferiority, flawed morals, and excessive attention to external trappings such as fashion ensue. Students complete their education, enter the workforce, form social relations, and perpetuate these warped notions. But education that is sensitive to the God-self relationship will denounce sexist, racist, and classist practices because they do damage to humanity's essential self and prevent the development of progressive civilizations. This does not entail the type of integration suggested by Civil Rights groups, but it does involve self-determination and true democratic practices. Healthy relations between the "races" are a byproduct of respect for and proper relations with one's own "race." Farrakhan asserts that the teachings of Elijah Muhammad spoke to this reality through his recognition of humanity's divine nature, the divinely ordained roles of men and women, and the relationship between all human communities.

A Torchlight for America clearly echoes Farrakhan's proclamation that the Nation can provide redemption because of its knowledge and determination. Farrakhan, like Elijah Muhammad before him, urges the West to allow the Nation to implement the structures and practices necessary for the development of a healthy society. Only the Nation's teachings on these issues have proven successful in changing hearts and minds, as evidenced by its work with prisoners and other so-called "undesirables." Farrakhan clearly states the Nation's potential:

> We must understand that our suffering uniquely prepares us not as slaves, or former slaves, or followers, or second-class citizens, but to be the examples and leaders for humanity. We can help both the former slave

and the former slave master with what we have been taught by the Honorable Elijah Muhammad and through our peculiar suffering within this racist society.[151]

If the United States took seriously the teachings of Elijah Muhammad, it could serve as the core of heaven—the new earth—because it would exemplify a proper relationship with Allah (God) and the various segments of humanity.

But if the United States cannot deal with its own citizens, how can it possibly hope to develop adequate foreign-relations policies? Such questions, combined with the Nation's concern for justice and equality, have resulted in an increased involvement in politics. Many have argued that the Nation of Islam is political only in rhetoric. True, the Nation of Islam in its early incarnation avoided direct political involvement, although Farrakhan alluded to the possibility when he suggested, referring to Adam Clayton Powell, Jr., that "a Muslim politician is what you need."[152] Under Farrakhan, Allah and Allah's Messenger were to provide for the sociopolitical welfare of the black nation because Islam's principles entail justice, freedom, and equality that political movements seek to secure.

Under Minister Louis Farrakhan's leadership and his direct participation in the 1988 presidential campaign, Muslims were encouraged to register to vote and actively participate in the political process. Yet the political involvement of the Nation has extended beyond the Jesse Jackson campaigns. In fact, in 1990 Farrakhan and the Nation, ran a candidate, Dr. Abdul Muhammad, for Congress from the Prince George's County District of Washington, D.C.; George X Cure ran for a delegate seat in Washington, D.C.; and Shawn X Brachern ran for a seat on the D.C. Board of Education. This political involvement is combined with increased attention to economic progress for the Nation and the United States. The hygiene products and other business ventures of the Nation, including security operations, indicates that the Nation has cautiously embraced capitalism and rethought "nationhood." The latter is now more readily used as a reference to an African–American centered state of mind.

THE NATION OF ISLAM IN MINNEAPOLIS[153]

Many of those who expressed an interest in the Nation may have arrived in the Twin Cities from locations such as Gary, Indiana, and Chicago, Illinois, where the Nation had taken root. Such a movement into the Twin Cities, spurred by the economic potential of those open to the Nation's program, certainly generated a core group of believers who could easily spread the word. And life in a new context—premised upon a Minnesotan avoidance of confrontation on hard issues and questions, fostered concerns that were forcefully addressed by the Nation's doctrine. The presence of the Nation in Minneapolis, as in other cities, continued to grow during the Black Power Movement. One of those who came to the Nation through the Black Power Movement is Minister James Muhammad (b. 1950).

As a child and a member of St. Philip's Episcopal Church, Minister James was sheltered from some of the harsher aspects of racism, although his parents, an interracial couple, were aware of the debilitating effects of racism. Yet he remembers his time in St. Philip's as less than satisfying. He knew he was "not getting the spirit"; the service did not move him. It was "hollow." At this point, believing there were no alternatives to Christianity, he embraced atheism and continued to seek the truth as a student at Macalester College, where he had won an academic scholarship. Here, he found what he needed from a faculty member who suggested to him the Nation of Islam.[154] He unquestioningly accepted the teaching of Elijah Muhammad during his first visit to the local mosque in South Minneapolis because these teachings were necessary if he were to live a righteous life. "Islam is truth."

Minister Muhammad grew dissatisfied with the questionable conduct of the Minneapolis group's leadership.[155] At the age of twenty-one, he challenged its inconsistencies and was forced out of the mosque. Although readmitted, he decided to move closer to the Honorable Elijah Muhammad. Leaving his job and college, and taking his wife and child with him, he headed to Chicago. The Honorable Elijah Muhammad "died" during Minister James's sojourn. But he, like many others, believed that Elijah Muhammad was not dead but was with Allah (Master Fard) receiving information on the second phase of his ministry and that he would return. James Muhammad calculated that Elijah Muhammad would return in 1978. Until then, Minister James planned to "hang tough," knowing that Elijah Muhammad's son's, Wallace Muhammad's, appointed role was to draw out those who were not truly committed to the teachings of the Honorable Elijah Muhammad. However, with time, the alterations made by Wallace Muhammad began to move in destructive directions. Disappointed and frustrated, Minister James moved back to St. Paul and "back into the world," embracing counterproductive behavior. He did not reenter the Nation until Minister Ava Muhammad's 1990 visit to the Twin Cities following Farrakhan's speech at the University of Minnesota in 1989.[156]

Minister James provided security for Minister Ava Muhammad and, inspired by her teachings, began moving back into Islam. That same year he submersed himself in the teachings of the Honorable Elijah Muhammad and began to make these teachings available to other interested parties through a study group in the basement of Grace Temple Church. He began teaching because his children pointed out that the Messenger's message was misused and distorted by some of their schoolmates. After a few initial meetings of this group, some attendees from Minneapolis asked him to become their official teacher.

According to Minister James Muhammad, as he and the others grew in knowledge, a need for worship as well as study emerged. The study group is currently located at 3122 Lyndale in Minneapolis. It is in a very neat storefront, brick with green and brown painted trim, with the symbol and sign of the Nation on the front. The mosque proper is a plainly furnished room consisting of chairs with an aisle separating the women's and men's seating. In front is a white rostrum, and behind the rostrum is the Nation's flag—red background with a five-pointed star and crescent moon. Each person is searched before entering the mosque and then allowed to take a seat.

When the service begins, the assistant minister greets everyone with "Peace be unto you," and the congregation responds, "Peace be unto you, sir!" Military efficiency, respect, and discipline are displayed. After this

The Minneapolis study group's building, located at 3122 Lyndale Avenue. Photo by the author.

greeting the assistant minister leads the congregation in prayer, each person stands with hands out, palms up, head bowed, and feet at a forty-five-degree angle. After prayer all are seated and the assistant minister talks on the need for atonement for the violence inflicted on blacks by blacks. After announcements by another member of the study group, Minister James Muhammad mounts the rostrum and greets everyone with the greeting of peace, giving honor to Master Fard Muhammad and the Honorable Elijah Muhammad. His remarks are similar to the following:

> In the name of Allah, the Beneficent, the Merciful, the One God to whom all praise is due, the Lord of the worlds, the Creator of all things, the Revealer of all Truth, the Sender of all Prophets. . . . I personally thank Allah for His intervention in our affairs, in the Person of Master Fard Muhammad, the Great Mahdi, to whom praise is due forever. And I thank this Great One for searching in our midst for one to lead, teach, and guide us out of the hell of a four hundred and thirty-six year sojourn in a house of strangers. The man of whom I speak is the Honorable Elijah Muhammad.[157]

After this, the minister lectures on general themes within the Nation's doctrine: the Original man; the nature of whites and U.S. society; the nature of knowledge; proper diet and its effect; treatment of blacks by blacks; and what it means for blacks to be connected to God and be gods. He also talks about the devil that dwells in each of us and the need to remove it. Minister James argues that African Americans must do for themselves by gaining the truth and acting properly, with self-control. His energetic and passionate "truth telling" is met with affirmation from the men gathered (There is little comment from the sisters.). Some of the brothers even correct the minister when wrong names are given.

After the minister's lecture, he asks for a show of hands by those who recognize the truth of Islam. This is followed by an invitation to become a part of the Nation. During each of my visits, someone has come forward and asked to be a part of the Nation. Exact membership numbers are not provided by the minister, but, because it is seeking registration as a mosque, there must be at least forty adult members, and the numbers are probably higher than this.[158]

This segment of the service is followed by comments from those new to the Nation. On one given Sunday, the minister brings to the front two young men and talks about the progress they are making. Their progress is greeted by applause and verbal encouragement from the brothers and sisters. Once again, Minister James greets the assembly with the words of peace before departing for his office. Once he leaves, the treasurer collects the charity offering. After this, one of the sisters makes announcements concerning an upcoming event and then leads the final prayer. After the prayer, the sisters exit first, and then the brothers put the chairs away before leaving. There is a great deal of activity following the service, including a communal meal and conversation with Minister James. Women and children who leave during the course of these activities are walked, by the Fruit of Islam, to their cars.

In addition to Sunday activities, the mosque houses daily self- and community-improvement activities. Wednesday nights are used for community development such as the "Men of March," cofounded by James Muhammad as a spin-off of the Million Man March mandate, and on Friday there are self-improvement activities and congregational prayer at noon. Saturday is extremely busy, with mosque activities involving those who must work during the week. Besides worship and study, this group also advances the political involvement of the Nation of Islam as outlined by Farrakhan. Minister James informed me that the Director of Protocol for the study group was running for political office in North Minneapolis. Such spiritual leadership, according to the Nation, is the basis of all proper government.

The study group seeks to bring believers into a full recognition of Islam that extends beyond mere observance of the pillars of the faith. Muslims must put the teachings of Islam into daily practice; anything less is a mockery of the Nation's teachings. The truth of Islam is life. But, Minister James admits, this is a life comprised of struggle.

THE NATION OF ISLAM AND THE PROBLEM OF EVIL

What can be said about Allah and human existence in light of moral evil?[159] In the Yakub story presented earlier, moral evil is first "named," and one glimpses God's involvement in and response to the suffering of the Original people. In the words of Elijah Muhammad:

> Our slavery at the hands of John Hawkins and his fellow slave traders and suffering here in the Western Hemisphere for four hundred years was actually all for a Divine purpose: that Almighty Allah (God) might make Himself known through us to our enemies, and let the world know the Truth that He alone is God.[160]

Through this action, the greatness of God is proven. In the words of Aminah McCloud: "In Islam, sovereignty rests with God. What is good, evil, right or wrong is determined by God. Values and 'the laws which uphold those values' are determined by God."[161] In addition to offering God's sovereignty as a response to the problem of evil, the Nation also contends that this problem is resolved by God's (Master Fard Muhammad's) and His Messenger's (Elijah Muhammad's) direct participation in suffering. Concerning the suffering of God, Elijah Muhammad says:

> He (Mr. W. F. Muhammad, God in person) chose to suffer 3 1/2 years to show his love for his people, who have suffered over 300 years at the hands of a people who by nature are evil and wicked and have no good in them. He was persecuted, sent to jail in 1932, and ordered out of Detroit, on May 26, 1933. He came to Chicago in the same year and was arrested almost immediately on his arrival and placed behind prison bars.
>
> He submitted himself with all humbleness to his persecutors. Each time he was arrested, he sent for me so that I might see and learn the price of Truth for us, the so-called American Negroes (members of the Asiatic nation).[162]

And concerning his own suffering on behalf of the chosen, Elijah Muhammad says:

> You shoot off your mouth trying to make a mockery of me. How can a man retrieve the drowning man? He doesn't have a boat to go out there, nor a [life jacket] to put around his neck; so, he has to leap in there and battle the water and suffer as he suffers. This is what I'm doing. I am battling that which you battle. This shows the love of me for you. If God makes the man go through all of your suffering, it is to approve His choosing, to let you know that, "I chose one who loves you like I love you, myself, and that he's willing to go through even death to lead you out of the hands of the enemy."[163]

If God and his Messenger suffered on behalf of the chosen, who are the Asiatics to assume that they should not suffer as well? Allah is good by nature and is the "best knower"; hence, what takes place in the world takes place with the permission of God. And ultimately it must benefit the Asiatic blacks because they are favored by a good and righteous God. On one level, the suffering of the chosen is pedagogical in that it prepares them for greatness. In fact, Allah has favored and chosen the Original people precisely because of the suffering they have endured, and in this manner the Original people are contemporary suffering servants. According to Farrakhan:

> Whether you know it or not Black man, God has chosen you. Not because of your Blackness, but He's chosen you because you have suffered in the furnace of affliction. And now, as Reverend Jackson said, the more you burn gold, you never burn it, you only purify it by removing its dross.

You are pure gold, Black man. Chosen by God, now, to do a mighty work.[164]

Suffering encountered by the chosen, however, is not always a "teaching moment." The Nation also claims that Asiatic blacks suffer because they lost true knowledge of themselves by willingly moving away from Islam. Yet Elijah Muhammad contends that the Original people are not the true source of moral evil in the world, for the production of such misery is against their nature: "The black people are by nature the righteous. They have love and mercy in their hearts even after trying to live the life of the devils—this is still recognized in them. When they are fully in the knowledge of self, they will do righteousness and live in peace among themselves."[165] The Original people are, however, responsible for this evil when they refuse the truth out of fear; hence, they are capable of both good and evil. That is to say, Allah created humanity in His image, but this entails an imperfect participation in His righteousness. The germs of both evil and good are present in the Original people.[166] Elijah Muhammad refers to the potential for evil in identifying the Original people's suffering as God's punishments for their imitation of the Caucasians' bad example:

> It is so strange now today to see that the Black Man of America desires not to be separated from his enemy, but desires that the enemy and himself live together in love of each other. . . . Therefore, Allah (God) has to strike both parties, the white man (devil) and the Black, blind, deaf, and dumb lovers of their enemy, with a severe chastisement, in order to open their blind eyes, as he did in Jesus' parable of the rich man and the poor man.[167]

From the Original people created by Allah, Yakub grafted the Caucasian race, which was completely evil. The Caucasian race's presence sheds light on the problem of evil by helping to isolate the origin and nature of sin. As Mattias Gardell points out, however, Farrakhan interprets the Messenger's teachings to mean that because the Caucasian race was made and not created, they may achieve redemption. Because Caucasians' evil deeds are in part the consequence of their creator's (the Original people's) choices, they cannot be blamed for an evil nature acquired at birth. If they surrender their supremist ideas and acknowledge the Messiah (Elijah Muhammad), they can regenerate themselves and put off the day of judgment.[168]

This is possible but unlikely. Consequently, God's judgment on the children of Yakub will restore balance to the world and remove moral evil. The Caucasian race will be destroyed (because of ideology not biology) by the "Mother of Plane" that is currently positioned one mile above the surface of the earth. This Plane, built by Fard after leaving the Nation, will at the appointed time release fifteen hundred smaller battleships and bombs. The bombs will be drilled into the surface of the earth and will cause destruction of the wicked ones, while the righteous will be removed to the wheel-like Mother Plane during this purging process.[169] The date initially set for this destruction was 1914, but Allah granted additional time for the Lost-Found Nation to hear the truth of Islam. Since this initial date, the time of judgment has been extended several times. Nonetheless, it will occur, but not without warning to Asiatics in the form, for example, of natural disasters.

Elijah Muhammad often taught that approximately 144,000 Asiatics would be saved; however, this number has changed, no doubt due to the continued efforts of the Nation to bring Islam to the Original people.[170] Yet, even with these efforts, some of the Original people will be lost.

The post-judgment earth will form after one thousand years of purging, and the Original people will dwell in righteousness. Elijah Muhammad describes this paradise as follows:

> The present brotherhood of Islam is typical of the life in the hereafter, the difference is that the brotherhood in the here-after will enjoy the spirit of gladness and happiness forever in the presence of Allah. The earth, the general atmosphere will produce such a change that the people will think it is a new earth. It will be the heaven of the righteous forever![171]

Whether one thinks of the free will of the Original people or the destined behavior of the white race, it is clear that problems in the world are attributable to humanity's improper manipulation of the truth. According to Farrakhan:

> It is not that God has failed. It is really not that truth has failed. However, like the person who takes the grape from the vine, in its purity it is energy, but when the hands of man begin to work with the grape, then we give the people an intoxicating drink. The corruption of men's hands have made religion an intoxicating drink that has people drunk with rituals, drunk with song, drunk with dance, but not right.[172]

The above quotation along with the following sums up the Nation's collective response to moral evil in terms that explicitly recognize the nature and causation of the question:

> We have grown beyond our bitterness, we have transcended beyond our pain. . . . It's easy for us to say, "The white man did this, the white man

did that, the white man did the other. . . ." Yes he did all of that, but why did God let him do that? That's the bigger question. Since we are not man enough to question God, we start beating up on the agent who is fulfilling prophecy. But if we can transcend our pain to get up into God's mind, and ask God, "God, why did you let our fathers come into bondage? God, why did you let us die in the Middle Passage? God, why did you suffer us to be in the hulls of ships? . . . We have a right to question God. . . . And if we question Him like Job did, God may bring you up into His own thinking. And if God were to answer us today He would say to Black people, "Yes, I allowed this to happen, and I know you suffered, but Martin King, my servant, said, undeserved suffering is redemptive." . . . You're the lost sheep, but the whole world is lost. . . . So my children, I cause you to suffer in the furnace of affliction so that I might purify you, and resurrect you from a grave of death and ignorance. I, God, put in your soul, not a law written on stone, but I have written a law on the tablets of your hearts. So I'm going to make a new covenant with you. . . . You are ready now, to come out of your furnace of affliction. You are ready now to accept the responsibility, not just of the ghetto; God wants to purify you, and lift you up, that you may call America and the world to repentance.[173]

Thus Farrakhan conceives of African Americans as the new suffering servant, whose ordeal has secondary benefit for the sufferers and primary benefit for all others.

4

▲▼▲▼▲▼▲▼▲▼▲▼▲▼▲▼▲

WHAT IF GOD WERE ONE OF US?
Humanism and African Americans for Humanism

HUMANISM IN EUROPE

Humanism, although not defined as such until the nineteenth century, developed in Europe as early thinkers, many of whom were Christian clerics, attempted to enhance the process of intellectual inquiry and its relationship to life issues by bringing Christian doctrine and "pagan" resources together. In this respect, early humanist-like thought as well as humanism of the medieval period were geared toward problem solving within the framework of a strong and determined church.[1]

As an example of this growing humanism, Petrarch "discover[ed] the cultural and literary modes present within the inherited resources of classical culture with which to articulate the ambiguities of life in this world and to set forth, tentatively at least, remedies. For Petrarch, the solution of earthly problems should in no way be separated from any soul's eternal destiny," because grace, intellect, and existential hardship were all present in the human quest for life."[2] He sought assistance for this task in the writings, for example, of Cicero because Cicero's rhetoric provided a necessary meditative device that facilitated a move toward divine grace. Cicero's skills served to define the interior-pedagogical concerns of Renaissance humanists.[3] Although useful motivation for the pious life, Petrarch held in tension Cicero's paganism:

> Cicero's rhetoric became Petrarch's model for his own conception of the role of the Christian scholar and teacher, which in turn became paradigmatic; but he never forgot that Cicero was not a Christian. This point he makes clear . . . rejecting Cicero's pagan teaching that virtue was in one's own power, whereas fortune was in the hands of others: "God . . . shut off the road to truth to him which a little later he deemed suitable to open to

us"; and excepting from his praise of Cicero in his *De ignorantia* all that was not Christian.[4]

From this time on, humanists in addressing religious and theological thought felt a need to respond to methodological issues that directly affected attitudes toward action. The centrality of human life in a less than ideal world is present within humanism at this stage in that humanist scholars saw little value in abstract theological discussion when people were struggling to live ethically. Religious conversation and theological language had to address the moral struggles of humanity: "humanists . . . did not write for professional theologians or for monks insulated from the daily tribulations of secular life. Their audiences consisted of men who had to strive for salvation among the competing demands of merchant, political, and professional life where temptations could not be avoided and where moral pressures were constant."[5] Humanists brought talk of God and talk of humanity into the same conversation. These two were inseparable with respect to questions of moral living. Thus sterile scholastic concerns were replaced with conversations about the "substance" of social realities. As John F. D'Amico says: "Humanism was able to find within its recovery of the ancient past, especially rhetoric, the means to present its own particular view of Christian thought, and this theology grew throughout the fifteenth century, ending only with the twin blows of the Reformation and the Counter-Reformation."[6]

At the time of the Reformation Erasmus attempted to bring humanist concerns into a rethinking of church structures. He was concerned with church thought and action that worked against concrete issues of moral conduct in the world. To combat this attitude, he emphasized the merits of learning, Scripture, the Church fathers and so forth, as an avenue to a much needed Christian morality.[7] As in the renaissance, humanists of this period still understood humanism in terms of the liberal arts—the acquaintance with ancient thought as a way of addressing current moral questions. It would not be until later, with such thinkers as Wilhelm von Humbolt, that humanism would consciously move away from traditional "religious" orientations and toward the dominance of experience as the key to truth.

Along this line, the Enlightenment and beyond would emphasize reason in a way that appealed to humanity's ability to progress and further human-centered thought. The ground for current humanist trends was laid by the work of philosophers such as Feuerbach and Marx. Feuerbach claimed that the notion of God arose from unfulfilled human longings addressed by a projection of ideal human values.[8] Marx accused religious organizations and their doctrine of running contrary to demands of social transformation. In the twentieth century, this "antireligious" sentiment continued to grow with what Lewis W. Spitz and others refer to as "new humanism"—human-centered and aggressively antireligious.[9]

Although humanism is usually discussed in terms of its leading intellectual representatives, it is also notably "a credo for average men and women seeking to lead happy and useful lives."[10] But what does humanism actually look like? How does it function? Corliss Lamont outlines basic components of humanism and, in this way, attempts to remove some of the ambiguity surrounding the term and the way of life it entails. According to Lamont, humanism, whether understood as scientific, secular, naturalistic, or democratic, is grounded in the aesthetically rich natural world, its evolving nature and observable laws. Furthermore, humanity is regarded as an inseparable component of nature. And although human life is fraught with hardships, humanity is capable of addressing its problems through appeal to reason and the scientific method. In this way, humans create and fulfill their own personal *and* collective well-being. Humanism is committed to the development, through continual self-reflection and critique, of a healthy world based upon democratic principles:

> In an era of continuing crisis and disintegration like that of the twentieth century, men face the temptation of fleeing to some compensatory realm of make-believe or supernatural solace. Humanism stands uncompromisingly against this tendency, which both expresses and encourages defeatism. The Humanist philosophy persistently strives to remind men that their only home is in this mundane world. . . . And Humanism is interested in a future life, not in the sense of some fabulous paradise in the skies, but as the on-going enjoyment of earthly existence by generation after generation through eternities of time.[11]

Lamont's attempt to define humanism raises interesting questions. Many who would embrace the principles he outlines are opposed to the label of humanism, and others are opposed to any label. Others who claim the label of humanist are opposed to any hint that humanism is a religious orientation as opposed to a philosophical stance. Many of those in this group oppose religious labels because of what they consider the failure and harm done by organized religion. Yet others want to consider humanism a religious orientation, not as a reaction to fears but because of the way humanism provides "direction." How does one bring these and others together under a common label? Lamont offers a broad understanding:

Broadly speaking, whenever a thinker in any field treats the this-worldly welfare of man as paramount, he treads on Humanist ground. For Humanism the central concern is always the happiness of man in this existence, not in some fanciful never never land beyond the grave; a happiness worthwhile as an end in itself and not subordinate to or dependent on a Supreme Deity, an invisible King, ruling over the earth and the infinite cosmos.[12]

HUMANISM IN THE UNITED STATES

Life in the U.S.A. historically held great promise, but it also fostered anxiety and uncertainty in that the struggles that formed this country, from the Revolutionary War to the Cult of True Womanhood, raised fundamental questions of life's meaning and purpose. In wrestling with these questions and the resulting anxiety, humanist principles proved useful. In the words of Corliss Lamont:

> There is a great deal in the American tradition that is fundamentally Humanist in character. In fact, our Declaration of Independence gave resounding affirmation to the social aims of Humanism when it proclaimed that "all men" have the inalienable right to "life, liberty and the pursuit of happiness." . . . The author of the Declaration himself, Thomas Jefferson [hoped that the Declaration would be] the signal of arousing men to burst the chains under which monkish ignorance and superstition had persuaded them to bind themselves, and to assume the blessings and security of self-government.[13]

In some quarters, fear over decreasing religiosity, centered on discomfort with freethinkers and the like, continued. Those who held to humanist principles had to be mindful of the Christian orientation of much of the population. Attempts to demolish Christianity, therefore, were perilous ventures seldom undertaken. There were those, nonetheless, who challenged believers to rethink Christianity and defend it in ways that recognized its weaknesses and inconsistencies. And, although the South developed a more evangelical orientation as a result of the Second Great Awakening, the North, particularly New England, maintained a strong concern for reason and morality as the guiding principles of religious thought and activity. New Englanders, notably elite Bostonians, found much wanting in Christian doctrines:

> Original sin, the atonement, and the Trinity had been abandoned one by one as irrational; in fact many of the liberals had become Arians and a few

Socinians by the end of the century. By interpreting rather than abandoning Scripture, they had come to believe in one rational and beneficent deity, who had sent Jesus, an intermediary being perhaps slightly more than man but less than God, to teach men the truth.[14]

Humanist sentiment continued to grow, particularly in the Midwest, from this early period into the age of philosophers such as John Dewey and clergy such as John H. Dietrich. Dietrich and those like him gave much attention to explicating humanism by reaching back through history while also holding to the present and thinking of the future. Prominent in Dietrich's work was the effort to "popularize" the message and equip it with a religious framework, including a liturgy. In this way he sought to understand the religious diversity of the United States, while harnessing this diversity to a common concern for life. Dietrich argued from his pulpit in Minneapolis that:

> "By religion I mean the knowledge of man and our duties toward him." That is humanism. It does not deny the right to believe in God and learn what you can about that which we designate as God, but it places faith in man, a knowledge of man, and our duties toward one another first. It is principally a shifting of emphasis in religion from God to man. It makes the prime task of religion not the contemplation of the eternal, the worship of the most high, the withdrawal from this world that one might better commune with God; rather the contemplation of the conditions of human life, the reverence for the worth of human life, and the entering into the world that by human effort human life may be improved.[15]

Some of these United States humanists, including Dietrich, Dewey, and Curtis W. Reese, further clarified their efforts through the 1933 *Humanist Manifesto,* which outlined the fifteen basic tenets of humanism.[16]

Many humanists developed their belief structures as individuals while others, over time, united in organizations such as Ethical Culture Societies and most notably the Unitarian Universalist Association. The oldest Ethical Culture Society is located in New York City, but there are numerous others across the country with an agenda geared "to assert the supreme importance of the ethical factor in all relations of life—personal, social, national and international—apart from any theological or metaphysical considerations." This agenda, at its core, is concerned with the "knowledge and practice and love of the right."[17] Humans, the argument goes, without the possibility of divine assistance, have no choice but to unite in an effort to develop healthy and beneficial ways of interacting in and with the world through proper values and ethical codes.[18] In general terms, these humanists were nontheistic, meaning not that they rejected the existence of a god. . . , but that the personal god of traditional Christianity had no place in their system. Man was considered autonomous; and God was not so much denied as ignored. Second, they rejected supernaturalism in any form, insisting that the natural world—the world described by science—was the only real world, and that humankind had no separate, spiritual identity apart from nature. Third, aware of how greatly science had transformed the world and how, again and again, the claims of faith had been relinquished before the advance of science, the humanists accepted science as providing the only proper method for describing the universe and interpreting its meaning.[19]

The Unitarian Universalists Association has a nationally recognized body, developed through a merging of Unitarian and Universalist churches in the late twentieth century. Unitarianism was a movement with European roots that insisted upon the oneness of God and the humanity of Jesus Christ. It drew from the work of Michael Servetus, who proclaimed, during the Reformation, that the Trinity is a misconception. He was put to death for heresy, but his ideas continued in locations such as Poland, England, and the United States in the eighteenth century. Initially, Unitarians were content to espouse their beliefs as members of Congregationalist churches in England and the United States (particularly New England). In 1825, however, they established themselves within their own institutional framework.[20] Unitarianism in the United States was promoted by influential figures such as Theodore Parker and Ralph Waldo Emerson. Unitarianism as such was not explicitly humanistic, but its theological liberalism contained an openness to inquiry that easily incorporated the activism that marked humanism and social reform efforts of this period. In addition, this openness allowed those who believed in God, as well as those who denied God, a place in the church as well as in social transformation.[21] With time, the Unitarian organization began giving less attention to the concept of God, relying instead on human potential and accountability.[22] Humans were required, then, to develop ways by which life could be lived and lived well.

Unitarians were not alone, however, in their radical appeal to the value of humanity. Universalist churches emerged in the eighteenth century and provided another forum for humanist endeavors. Universalists rejected the concept of eternal punishment brought about by failure to accept the "correct" faith, and instead believed that God grants salvation to all of humanity. A common need for a stronger organizational base, combined with theological connections between these two organizations, resulted in a 1961 merger—the Unitarian Universalist Association.[23]

The effectiveness of these organizations came with a price. Humanists, particularly those calling themselves "secular," have served as scapegoats. Neo-orthodox thought, fundamentalism of various types, the collapse of communism and socialism in parts of the world—all contributed to a radical questioning of humanism's role in the fostering of collective life. Many began to argue that humanism's lack of a recognizable spiritual center or "object" of focused attention would result in its demise, and that traditions with a stronger spiritual base would replace it. Donald H. Meyer writes: "In the late 1970s the religious right in America finally identified the source of all the moral corruption and religious skepticism that had plagued the country since the middle of the twentieth century: secular humanism."[24] Regardless of questions concerning its legitimacy, humanism continued and continues to provide what some consider the best moral and ethical vision for life.

When the make-up of humanist organizations is even briefly probed, a question begs attention: Has humanism only functioned within white communities, or have others embraced it as a viable and vital response to the human condition? African Americans, for one, have embraced humanism—although they have not always used this term—as a dynamic response to social ills faced. Benjamin E. Mays observes:

> The Negro's incredulity, frustrations, agnosticism, and atheism do not develop as the results of the findings of modern science nor from the observation that nature is cruel and indifferent; but primarily because in the social situation, he finds himself hampered and restricted.[25]

AFRICAN AMERICANS AND HUMANISM

As demonstrated earlier in this book, African slaves in the United States used versions of theism to make sense of life's absurdities; but this was not the case for all slaves, for the hypocrisy of some slave owners, and the contradictions between the political and economic-driven interpretations of the gospel and Africans' essential sense of self, caused some to question the validity of theism. In 1839 Daniel Payne expressed his concern that slaves would completely give up faith if they were not introduced to the true gospel message:

> The slaves are sensible of the oppression exercised by their masters and they see these masters on the Lord's day worshipping in his holy Sanctuary. They hear their masters professing christianity; they see these

masters preaching the gospel; they hear these masters praying in their families, and they know that oppression and slavery are inconsistent with the christian religion; therefore they scoff at religion itself—mock their masters, and distrust both the goodness and justice of God. Yes, I have known them even to question his existence. I speak not of what others have told me, but of what I have both seen and heard from the slaves themselves. . . . A few nights ago between 10 and 11 o'clock a runaway slave came to the house where I live for safety and succor. I asked him if he was a christian; "no sir," said he, "white men treat us so bad in Mississippi that we can't be christians." . . . In a word, slavery tramples the laws of the living God under its unhallowed feet—weakens and destroys the influence which those laws are calculated to exert over the mind of man; and constrains the oppressed to blaspheme the name of the Almighty.[26]

Thus it seems fairly clear that the early presence and rationale for humanism within African American communities is based on the hypocrisy of nominally Christian slave owners. They turned to a nontheistic solution to the challenge of reorienting human destiny and fostering equality.

It is possible that hush arbor meetings, secret slave gatherings, and field work arrangements allowed for conversation that was humanistic in orientation; however, little evidence of this has been recorded, because it would have been considered unimportant. (For more information on hush arbor meetings, see chapter 5, pages 196–98.) Payne's statement, along with allusions in, for example, some blues tones and African American folk wisdom, point to the presence of humanism in early African American communities, but it is not until the African American renaissance (i.e., the "Harlem Renaissance" of the twentieth century that nontheistic orientations are widely presented.

The Great Migration and the First World War, for example, questioned the sense of progress and optimism that marked the pre-war period. Some who questioned the war were still willing to participate in the U.S. war effort because they hoped that it would result in democratic rule throughout the world. Yet, as history proved, the war did not change the oppressive nature of U.S. social relations or reduce the inequality of U.S. eco-political interactions. Disillusionment with U.S. religious and political rhetoric naturally resulted from this failure, and it was amplified by what has been noted elsewhere as the "de-radicalization" of African American churches. Based upon this inward gaze of African American churches, an inversely proportional relationship between outreach and social problems developed. Consequently, answers to the questions posed by life in the

United States took on a harder and rougher texture through the development of the Harlem Renaissance (or, more accurately, the African American Renaissance) and its characteristic rejection of sanitized depictions of life. This Renaissance also opened discussions concerning the impotence of traditional religious practices. According to Arthur Fauset, "The church, once a *sine qua non* of institutional life among American Negroes, does not escape the critical inquiry of the newer generations, who implicitly and sometimes very explicitly are requiring definite pragmatic sanctions if they are to be included among church goers, or if indeed they are to give any consideration at all to religious practices and beliefs."[27]

James Weldon Johnson developed a perspective revolving around the human condition and the human, alone in the world, as responsible for correcting societal problems. He spoke, nonetheless, of the church and its life because it was familiar and had touched him early. Yet, the culture of African Americans and others as chronicled in his *God's Trombones: Seven Negro Sermons in Verse* did not assert an embrace of God; rather it was a mark of his respect for the work of human hands. Logically speaking, an appreciation for cultural production as such is not an endorsement of the doctrinal assumptions and theological stance of the African American church. Johnson was concerned with maintaining the cultural identity and value of African Americans as shapers of American cultural reality, and this required a response to minstrel-like caricatures of African American culture. Hence, Johnson's *God's Trombones* is better understood as a defense of African American folk art than as a testimony of personal belief. Johnson is quite clear on this point.

> My glance forward reaches no farther than this world. I admit that I throughout my life have lacked religiosity. I do not know if there is a personal God; I do not see how I can know; and I do not see how my knowing can matter. As far as I am able to peer into the inscrutable, I do not see that there is any evidence to refute those scientists and philosophers who hold that the universe is purposeless: that man, instead of being the special care of a Divine Providence, is dependent upon fortuity and his own wits for survival in the midst of blind and insensate forces. . . . All that is clearly revealed is the fate that man must continue to hope and struggle on. To do this, he needs to be able at times to touch God; let the idea of God mean to him what ever it may.[28]

Johnson developed this perspective fairly early. Although his grandmother, and later his father, attempted to secure his involvement in church, Johnson rebelled. The church held little appeal for Johnson:

As he grew older, James became increasingly discontented with the whole business of religion. He was irked by the constant round of church-going forced upon him by his well-meaning grandmother. . . . When he was nine, James allowed himself to be "saved" at a revival meeting, but, he admitted later, he acted largely out of a desire to please his grandmother. . . . His doubts concerning religion and the church increased with each year. He could not, however, resolve the tension solely out of his narrow experience with his family or church. It would take a few years, and a sense of life styles beyond the provincialism of Jacksonville, for Johnson to find his answer in agnosticism.[29]

Johnson's agnosticism was most likely enhanced, prior to his years at Atlanta University, through his work with Dr. Thomas Osmond Summers, who embraced science and rejected religion. Through Summers's library, Johnson "found the works of Thomas Paine and Robert G. Ingersoll, America's best known agnostics. He read Paine and Ingesoll avidly as nourishment for his earlier vague dislike of conventional religion. By his freshman year, Johnson was one of the two acknowledged agnostics at Atlanta University."[30]

James Baldwin also contributed to the advancement of humanism as a system with ramifications for daily conduct, while advancing African American culture. Again, he acknowledged African American religious (Christian) expression as an undeniable fixture within African American culture, but he also regarded it as problematic in ways that prevent personal involvement. For Baldwin, the Church offered a means of dealing with his fears: "all the fears with which I had grown up, and which were now a part of me and controlled my vision of the world, rose up like a wall between the world and me, and drove me into the church."[31] He hoped that church involvement would also provide comfort from the sense of depravity that pervaded his mind with respect to his sexuality and general life as a second-class citizen. He sought affirmation of his value and his "beauty." He felt himself needing "to belong" somewhere, to someone; and he felt that he could not hold out much longer. Like everyone around him, he would surrender to something; and if surrender was inevitable, why not to the church? Reflecting on his turn to the church, Baldwin says:

My friend was about to introduce me when [the pastor] looked at me and smiled and said, "Whose little boy are you?" Now this, unbelievably, was precisely the phrase used by pimps and racketeers on the Avenue when they suggested, both humorously and intensely, that I "hang out" with them. Perhaps part of the terror they had caused me to feel came from the fact that I unquestionably wanted to be *somebody's* little boy. I was so frightened, and at the mercy of so many conundrums, that inevitably, that summer, someone would have taken me over; one doesn't, in Harlem, long remain standing on any auction block. It was my good luck—perhaps—that I found myself in the church racket instead of some other.[32]

From Baldwin's perspective, this turn to the church was logical and relatively safe in light of the other options available in Harlem.

After some years, Baldwin came to realize that the church did not provide the solace he had sought as he lay on the church floor on the day of his conversion. He was "able to see that the principles governing the rites and customs of the churches in which I grew up did not differ from the principles governing the rites and customs of other churches, white. The principles were Blindness, Loneliness, and Terror, the first principle necessarily and actively cultivated in order to deny the two others."[33] He could fool himself and others only for so long; even preaching and the excitement (and acceptance) he found in the pulpit could not ultimately satisfy his needs and push aside his sociotheological questions. He was still lonely and afraid. Hence, Baldwin writes, "when I faced a congregation, it began to take all the strength I had not to stammer, not to curse, not to tell them to throw away their Bibles and get off their knees and go home and organize, for example, a rent strike."[34] Baldwin preached for three years, but he ultimately left the church and found what the church could not provide: orientation and meaning through his writing. For him, "religion" in general and Christianity in particular failed to meet the basic needs of believers. It was equipped to offer them what only pushed them further into absurdity, alienation, and race-based demise. As Baldwin expressed his orientation, he belonged to nothing other than his writing. Thus humanity is his concern and the humanizing of life his orientation. This comes through in a conversation he had with Elijah Muhammad:

> I said, at last, in answer to some other ricocheted questions, "left the church twenty years ago and I haven't joined anything since." . . . "And what are you now?" Elijah asked. I was in something of a bind, for I really could not say—could not allow myself to be stampeded into saying that I was a Christian. "I? Now? Nothing." This was not enough. "I'm a writer. I like doing things alone." . . . "I don't, anyway," I said, finally, "think about it a great deal."[35]

In addition to Johnson and Baldwin, the work of J. Saunders Redding is important.[36] Redding asserts that God and the Christian faith have played a dubious role in the development of the United States. Both social transformation and the oppressive status quo have been proclaimed "God's will."

In this capacity, God has served to both humanize and dehumanize. And what is so striking about all of this is that God resides in the collective consciousness as an "implicit assumption." That is, according to Redding, God "is a belief that operates just by being, like a boulder met in the path which must be dealt with before one can proceed on his journey. . . . God is a catalyst, and He is also a formulated doctrine inertly symbolized in the ritual and dogma of churches called Christian."[37] Yet even in light of the manner in which God is woven into the fabric of American life, Redding has his doubts:

> I do not know how long I have held both God and the Christian religion in some doubt, though it must have been since my teens. . . . I can only think that it came as a result of some very personal communion with God, established perhaps by a random thought, a word, or a certain slant of light through the yellow and rose and purple windows.[38]

Also, reflecting on the energetic worship and hysterics of black worship, "realized with deep shame that what the Negroes did on this holy day made a clowns' circus for the whites. The Negroes' God made fools of them. Worship and religiosity were things to be mocked and scorned, for they stamped the Negro as inferior."[39]

Although he was not fully aware of the exact progression of thought that led to his final rejection of religion, it seemed the inevitable response to the existential realities of life as an African American. There is an air of comfort accompanying his admission that he "simply rejected religion. I rejected God. Not my instincts, but my deepest feelings revolted compulsively—not because I was I, a sort of neutral human stuff reaching directly to experience, but because I was a Negro."[40] Even with this admission the continued appeal to God within his own family and a significant segment of the African American community required an understated rejection, or a truce with the notion of God, a truce that emerged not from a reversal of opinion but as a means of maintaining community connections:

> It was also years before I made a sort of armed truce with religion and with God. I stepped around God determinedly, gingerly, gloating that I was free of Him and that He could not touch me. Indeed, I had to step around Him, for He was always there. He was there, foursquare and solid, at the very center of my father's life. . . . He was in various people I met and felt affection for. He was in the affable, tremulous sweetness of the first love I felt; in the drowning ecstasy of the first sexual experience; in the joy of imaginative creation. But I moved around Him warily, laughing, mocking His pretensions, determined that He would not betray me into

Negroeness. If there lingered still in the deep recesses of my real self some consciousness of a religious spirit, then the ideal self—the Negro-hating me—did all it could do to exorcise it.[41]

For Redding, religion shortcircuited the drive toward social transformation. Whereas religion was virtually absent from social issues, God is, unfortunately, present and supportive of the status quo. Redding appears to regard God as a human construct that holds promises of liberation that it can never fulfill.[42]

The development of humanism among African American writers is not limited to males; figures such as Alice Walker have also worked along these lines. According to Trudier Harris, Alice Walker, and others make use of this orientation in constructing their characters; they

pattern their [characters'] lives according to values Peter Faulkner recognizes as humanism in "its modern sense of an ethic which places human happiness as its central concern and is skeptical about the supernatural and transcendental. . . . The emphasis is on mutual human responsibility. . . . The spirit of humanism is flexible and undogmatic, refusing to sacrifice human happiness to any rigid orthodoxy. . . . Humanism is a philosophical position, not a matter of casual goodwill, and its basis is the belief in human responsibility and human potentiality."[43]

This position comes across in Alice Walker's work—for example, in novels such as *The Color Purple* and *The Third Life of Grange Copeland*—and in her own life. Walker recalls

I seem to have spent all of my life rebelling against the church or other people's interpretations of what religion is—the truth is probably that I don't believe there is a God, although I would like to believe it. Certainly I don't believe there is a God beyond nature. The world is God. Man is God. So is a leaf or a snake.[44]

Alice Walker's humanism is deeply contemplative. It is, in essence, a worshipful appreciation for humanity and for the earth in general. This type of reverence for life gives it god-like status in that it must remain at the forefront of our thoughts and actions, centering our every move within a profound sense of awe. What is called for, according to Walker, is a recognition of life as beautiful and beautifully connected to all things. Such a system, I believe, is not a broadened theism; but it is in keeping with the basic principles of humanism as outlined here: healthy existence for all as the goal and proper ethical conduct with respect to nature (i.e., radical environmentalism) directs humanity toward that goal. Walker speaks to this appreciation for nature with respect to the silencing of women in the Christian church:

> The truth was, we already lived in paradise but were worked too hard by the land-grabbers to enjoy it. this is what my mother, and perhaps the other women knew, and this was one reason why they [women] were not permitted to speak. They might have demanded that the men of the church notice Earth. Which always leads to revolution. In fact, everyone has known this for a very long time.[45]

Walker's appreciation of the well-being of all creation as the center of religious life and devotion is present in her reflections on her baptism at age seven. She recounts:

> The "God" of heaven that my parents and the church were asking me to accept, obscured by the mud, leaves, rot, and bullfrog spoors of this world [sic]. How amazing this all is, I thought, entering the muddy creek. And how deeply did I love these who stood around solemnly waiting to see my "saved" head reappear above the murky water. *This experience of communal love and humble hope for my well-being was my reality of life on this planet.* I was unable to send my mind off into space in search of a God who never noticed mud, leaves, or bullfrogs. Or the innocent hearts of my tender, loving people.[46]

Some humanists find it useful, if not necessary, to find a body of "believers." That is, their conversion experience is often furthered by communal interaction that affirms the conversion as the correct decision. Many African Americans logically looked for a like-minded community in the academy, others moved toward political involvement in, for example, the Communist Party:

> Doubt, frustration, and denial of God's existence arise also from social crises. God must not be interested in helping the group to achieve the needs necessary for existence. God does not exist; if He does, He is indifferent to the needs of the group. They arise at the point where physical security is denied; economic privilege cut off; the free exercise of the ballot prohibited; segregation in every area sustained by custom and law; and, the free development of spiritual powers almost completely stifled. . . . The negation of the idea of God may . . . drive Negroes into the communistic camp, whereby more militant or violent means would be used to achieve political and economic status.[47]

Within this camp one can include the early Langston Hughes. Although I believe he changed his opinion as a consequence of the "Red Scare," it is clear that his communist leanings facilitated an independence from the

Christian faith as outlined in pieces such as "Goodbye Christ."[48] Although many debate whether Hughes was personally committed to communism, this poem provides a critique of Christianity and a rejection of its theological underpinnings and instead reflects a humanism held by many African Americans.[49] Granted, there is a tension between this early poem and his later work, but Faith Berry explains it this way:

> his attraction to communism has been as misinterpreted as his posture toward Christianity. His reaction to both was to what each proclaimed: He watched communism hail the classless society, the distribution of wealth, the equality of all, regardless of race or color; he saw Christianity preach the brotherhood of man, alms for the poor, freedom to the oppressed, the kingdom of God. He found Christianity full of broken promises and communism unable to fulfill its promises. Christianity was old. Communism was young. He reached out to both in his youth only to find two Gods that failed. Those who see a dichotomy, a bifurcation, a contradiction, between an early poem such as "Goodbye Christ" in 1932 as opposed to his more reverent religious works of later years should remember he was always searching for justice for all.[50]

I wish to suggest that the atheistic stance of the Communist Party and its rhetorical appeal to African Americans (thin as it was) provided a forum and "home" for African American humanists who found churches hopelessly out of touch with the times. Documents preserved at the Schomburg Center for Research in Black Culture, in New York City (e.g., Universal Negro Improvement Association Papers) and other locations document Party organizing activities in African American communities such as Harlem during the 1920s and 1930s.[51] The Communist Party was reluctant to "attack" African American churches because of their strength within African American communities which could hamper Communist efforts; nonetheless, some African Americans who joined the Party were more than willing to critique Christian churches even when they were church members. According to Robin D. G. Kelley,

> Afro-American Communists shared with the rest of the black working-class community a grass-roots understanding of exploitation and oppression which was based more on scripture than anything else. The prophetic Christian tradition, so characteristic of the Afro-American experience, has historically contained a vehement critique of oppression. Ironically, this radical, prophetic tradition of Christianity was a major factor in drawing blacks into the Communist Party and its mass organizations.
>
> References to God and the bible were not uncommon among Alabama's black radicals. In 1933 the Daily Worker (13 April) received an

interesting letter from a black Communist from Tallapoosa County, thanking "God and all the friends of the Negro race that are working for the defense and rights of the Negroes. I pray that we may succeed in our struggle for Bread, Land and Freedom." . . . Furthermore, not only were most black Communists in Alabama churchgoing Christians; for quite some time, Communists in Montgomery opened all their meetings with a prayer.[52]

Furthermore, some churches actively worked with the Communist Party: "Although the Communists never had a sympathetic ear from the larger, well-established black churches, several ministers and working-class congregations of smaller Baptist churches in and around Birmingham provided critical support for the Communists and the International Labor Defense in opposition to a state-wide anti-sedition bill."[53] Kelley points out, however, that this support was mixed with a critique of clergy, who spent their time gaining wealth and preaching against transformation.[54]

Some took this critique further and rejected the Christian church and its doctrine as non-liberating.[55] Communist Party member Hosea Hudson's reflections on his Communist involvement support this point: some African American communists were atheists or humanists. Although black communists such as Hudson were active in the church, some ministers attempted to prevent the use of churches for what they considered "trouble-making" speeches and activities. At one point Hudson stopped attending church because of such sentiments, but he recalls starting to attend again between 1937 and 1938. His comments to church members, most likely meant to spark discontent with the Church's otherworldly stance, remained troubling:

> I challenge one or two deacons one Sunday afternoon. We all sitting around talking. I told them, I said, "It ain't no such thing as no God. You all go around here singing and praying," I said, "and they regular lynching Negroes, and you ain't doing nothing about it."[56]

Hudson recalls that this stance was even shared by some Party members who never attended church:

> I had heard other Party people talking. Some of them had never been members of no church, talking about there wont no such thing as God: "Where is he at? You say it's a God, where is he at? You can't prove where he's at." Negro Party people said that to me, Murphy and Horton and Raymond Knox. We'd have big discussions. One Sunday I said I was going to church. "What you going for? What you going for?" I said, "I'm going to serve God." They said, "Where is God at? You can't prove it's no

God nowhere." They said, "Where is God?" I said, "In heaven." "Well, where is heaven?"[57]

In rejecting God, the humanists Hudson knew in the Party assigned humanity responsibility for social transformation. Hudson found it difficult to respond to these charges. In his words:

> I just didn't have a [sic] answer. And them was the kind of questions they put. "If God is such a just God, and here you walking around here, ain't got no food. The only way you can get food is you have to organize. So if you have to organize to demand food, why you going to pray to God about it? Why don't you go on and put your time in organizing and talk to people?"[58]

Hudson found these arguments challenging, but he never lost his belief in God. His remarks, however, suggest agnosticism:

> I never did finally stop believing in God. I haven't stopped believing yet today. I don't argue about it. I don't discuss it, because it's something I can't explain. I don't know whether it's a God, I don't know whether it's not a God. But I know science, if you take science for it, and all these developments, I can't see what God had much to do with it. . . . So it's something beyond my knowledge to deal with. And I don't deal with it. I don't try to deal with it.[59]

As the disillusionment with the Communist Party expressed in Ralph Ellison's *The Invisible Man* and the work (and life) of Richard Wright indicate, the Party—by the time African Americans participated in noticeable numbers—had withdrawn from a strong interest in the "negro question" and were concerned primarily with the "Moscow line."[60] Although some African Americans undoubtedly remained within the Party hoping for a change, others moved in the direction of black nationalism as a means by which to embrace a materialist critique of U.S. society and the question of race.[61]

In the late twentieth century the Black Power Movement, particularly the second wave of the Student Non-violent Coordinating Committee (SNCC) and the Black Panther Party, serves as an example of this turn toward black cultural nationalism. I believe that the shift away from the Christian-based Civil Rights movement marked by the second wave of SNCC and its thundering call for black power point to deep theological differences between SNCC and the larger Civil Rights movement. It is more than likely that the theistic motivations espoused by Dr. Martin Luther King, Jr., and others, did not adequately address the concerns of some of the more radical elements of the movement. The break, therefore, marks a transition from the theism of the Civil Rights movement toward materialist analysis and human-centered solutions. Although I am unwilling to stress this point too forcefully, I suggest that SNCC's underlying framework was humanist in nature regardless of whether this term was actually employed.

The late 1960s witnessed a methodological and epistemological shift within SNCC. Gone were the integrationist goals that made it compatible with the Civil Rights movement; gone was its reliance upon Christian doctrine and paradigms for action. The rhetoric found in early issues of SNCC's newspaper, *Student Voice,* was replaced with calls for self-determination through black power. But in 1960, SNCC described its philosophy in the following terms:

> We affirm the philosophical or religious ideal of nonviolence as the foundation of our purpose, the pre-supposition of our faith, and the manner of our action. . . . Love is the central motif of nonviolence. Love is the force by which God binds man to himself and man to man. Such love goes to the extreme; it remains loving and forgiving even in the midst of hostility. . . . By appealing to conscience and standing on the moral nature of human existence, nonviolence nurtures the atmosphere in which reconciliation and justice become actual possibilities.[62]

Veering away from this agape paradigm, SNCC embraced its own version of black nationalism predicated upon a strong appeal to the acquisition of power. According to Stokeley Carmichael and Charles Hamilton:

> [Black power] is a call for Black people in this country to unite, to recognize their heritage, to build a sense of community. It is a call for black people to begin to define their goals, to lead their own organizations and to support those organizations. It is a call to reject the racist institutions and values of this society. The concept . . . rests on a fundamental premise. *Before a group can enter the open society, it must first close ranks.* By this, we mean that group solidarity is necessary before a group can operate effectively from a bargaining position of strength in a pluralistic society.[63]

Although inadequately defined in terms of social transformative thrusts and foci, black power, for some of its advocates, did adopt rather clearly defined theological assumptions based upon humanist leanings and articulated in the language of self-determination. One example is the thought of James Forman, an important member of SNCC.

In his autobiography, *The Making of Black Revolutionaries,* James Forman describes his "conversion" to humanism as a move that did not hamper but rather informed his praxis. He notes that during his time at

Wilson Junior College in Chicago his doubts concerning the existence of God grew and were intensified by contact with questionable black preachers whose self-centered ways sparked his distaste for ministry and the church. Says Forman, "God was not quite dead in me, but he was dying fast."[64]

After returning from military service some years later, Forman came to a final conclusion concerning the existence of God:

> The next six years of my life were a time of ideas. A time when things were germinating and changing in me. A time of deciding what I would do with my life. It was also a time in which I rid myself, once and for all, of the greatest disorder that cluttered my mind—the belief in God or any type of supreme being.[65]

Outlining the rationale for his "disbelief," Forman notes that during a philosophy course he set firm upon the following:

> I reject the existence of God. He is not all-powerful, all-knowing, and everywhere. He is not just or unjust because he does not exist. God is a myth; churches are institutions designed to perpetuate this myth and thereby keep people in subjugation.[66]

Foreman did not reach this conclusion because God had not responded to his petitions; rather, his conclusion was based upon the historical condition and needs of a large community. His rejection of God was not a surrender to absurdity but a call to arms. For him humanism required a strong commitment on the part of people to change their present condition:

> When a people who are poor, suffering with disease and sickness, accept the fact that God has ordained for them to be this way—then they will never do anything about their human condition. *In other words, the belief in a supreme being or God weakens the will of a people to change conditions themselves.* As a Negro who has grown up in the United States, I believe that the belief in God has hurt my people. *We have put off doing something about our condition on this earth because we have believed that God was going to take care of business in heaven.* . . . My philosophy course had finally satisfied my need for intellectual as well as emotional certainty that God did not exist. I reached the point of rejecting God out of personal experience and observations.[67]

Critiques of the African American churches based upon materialist approaches to social transformation were also present in the ideological platform of the Black Panther Party. In fact, the attraction of some SNCC workers to the Black Panther Party led by Huey Newton, Bobby Seales, Eldridge Cleaver, and others, was based upon a common concern with transformative activity that held as its measuring stick the welfare of African Americans and other oppressed groups. The Party, however, had a more clearly materialist platform and was much more certain of its armed and revolutionary stance. This commitment to human struggle as the key to social transformation reveals theological underpinnings that are humanistic in nature. Reflecting on the ultimate demise of many Black Panthers, Bobby Seales sums up the goals of the Party, goals that speak to humanist desires:

> We need activists who cross all ethnic and religious backgrounds and color lines who will establish civil and human rights for all, including the right to an ecologically balanced, pollution-free environment. We must create a world of decent human relationships where revolutionary humanism is grounded in democratic human rights for every person on earth. Those were the political revolutionary objectives of my old Black Panther Party. They must now belong to the youth of today.[68]

Drawing heavily from Marx, Fanon, Engels, Lenin, Mao, and others, the Party initially denounced the church, labeling it counterproductive. In the words of Huey P. Newton:

> As far as the church was concerned, the Black Panther Party and other community groups emphasized the political and criticized the spiritual. We said the church is only a ritual, it is irrelevant, and therefore we will have nothing to do with it. We said this in the context of the whole community being involved with the church on one level or another. That is one way of defecting from the community, and that is exactly what we did. Once we stepped outside of the whole thing that the community was involved in and we said, "You follow our example; your reality is not true and you don't need it."[69]

The Party softened its position, however, when it recognized the central role the church played in the African American community's life. Like the Communist Party, the Panthers recognized that recruitment would be difficult if open hostility existed between the Party and the black churches. Therefore, the Panthers fostered a relationship of convenience and sociopolitical necessity, but without a firm commitment to the church's theology. Newton rationalized this involvement by arguing a different conception of God, God as the "unknown" whom science will ultimately eliminate. In this sense, God does not exist in the affirmative; God is the absence of knowledge:

> So we do go to church, are involved in the church, and not in any hypocritical way. Religion, perhaps is a thing that man needs at this time because scientists cannot answer all of the questions. . . . the unexplained

and the unknown is God. We know nothing about God, really, and that is why as soon as the scientist develops or points out a new way of controlling a part of the universe, that aspect of the universe is no longer God.[70]

Another voice from the Black Panther Party that denounced claims of God's existence and involvement in human affairs was Eldridge Cleaver. Although Cleaver would later give attention to the Mormon Church and Reverend Moon, his earlier thoughts on God and humanity are still worth noting. Reflecting on his incarceration in 1954, he writes:

> In Soledad state prison, I fell in with a group of young blacks who, like myself, were in vociferous rebellion against what we perceived as a continuation of slavery on a higher plane. . . . While all this was going on, our group was espousing atheism. Unsophisticated and not based on any philosophical rationale, our atheism was pragmatic. I had come to believe that there is no God; if there is, men do not know anything about him. Therefore, all religions were phony. . . . Our atheism was a source of enormous pride to me. Later on, I bolstered our arguments by reading Thomas Paine and his devastating critique of Christianity in particular and organized religion in general.[71]

Although Cleaver at one point became a Muslim "chained in the bottom of a pit by the Devil," his sense of religion was utilitarian. He writes: "To me, the language and symbols of religion were nothing but weapons of war. I had no other purpose for them. All the gods are dead except the god of war."[72] His connection to the black Muslims would give way as soon as it failed to provide a useful political tool.

Whether successful or misguided, the Black Panther Party's humanism is notable. The notion of divine assistance is rejected and humans given sole responsibility for altering the world. In the words of Bobby Seale:

> It is necessary for young people to know that we must use organized and practical techniques. We cannot let ourselves continue to be oppressed on a massive scale. We are not trying to be supermen, because we are not supermen. We are fighting for the preservation of life. We refuse to be brainwashed by comic-book notions that distort the real situation. The only way that the world is ever going to be free is when the youth of this country *moves* with every principle of human respect and with every soft spot we have in our hearts for human life. . . . We know that as a people, we must seize our time. . . . Power to the People! Seize the Time![73]

Some may question what distinction, if any, this study suggests between humanism and atheism. I acknowledge that in this text the line between the two is blurred, but I do not hold that a humanist must necessarily be an atheist. As I demonstrated in *Why, Lord? Suffering and Evil in Black Theology*, humanism does comes in a theistic form called "soft humanism."[74] Much of the religious stance embraced in the various forms of liberation theology involves the type of partnership between humans and God promoted by "soft humanism." Hence, humanists can be theists; humanism is not necessarily reducible to atheism. Within this study, a blurring of the boundary exists between the two because my concern is with what they share in common: the basis for both humanism and atheism is belief in the need for humans to act in responsible ways that do not assume the presence of a superhuman force.

BLACK HUMANISM AND THE UNITARIANS

Although African Americans have held humanist perspectives and operated accordingly for centuries, the use of the term *black humanism* is fairly recent. Because the Unitarian Universalist Association already accepted itself as humanist, it makes sense that one of the first references to black humanism would surface within its struggles with race during the late twentieth century. *Empowerment: One Denomination's Quest for Racial Justice, 1967–1982* links the use of the term *black humanism* with the Black Unitarian Universalist Caucus, which was created to respond to racial issues within the UUA:

> By 1970, the BUUC leadership was beginning to refer to its philosophy of empowerment as "Black Humanism." Hayward Henry [former SNCC organizer and member of the board of Second Boston Church] first discussed Black Humanism in the February 1970 newsletter, *BUUCVine*. . . . Mr. [Benjamin] Scott went on to describe the black interpretation of the [humanist] principles. Black humanists understood humanism as a process, an existential process by which one finds and lives his humanity. To be human is to direct one's own life; therefore, Black Humanism calls for a seizure of decision making and implementation for oneself. Gaining power is an essential element of humanism.[75]

Such a statement allowed for the fundamental elements of religiosity—direction or orientation toward human development and empowerment. In addition, this religiosity takes into account the "unique" demands and existential context of African Americans; the value of their "blackness" was brought into human-centered thought and action. So conceived, black humanism constitutes an African American religion, a form of religious practice that used the UUA to provide institutional structure.

African Americans bring to Unitarian Universalism a sense of urgency in response to the black experience of oppression, a hope born of having survived that experience, and a basic life-affirming joy that can transcend many moments of despair. What Unitarian Universalism offers the African Americans is, as David Eaton, minister of All Souls' Unitarian Church in Washington, DC, has said, "a more vital reservoir of spiritual awareness [and] a deeper spiritual life."[76]

It is difficult to measure the casual participation of African Americans in the UUA, but formal involvement is easier to monitor. And clearly African Americans are conspicuously absent. Still, various African Americans have found in the Unitarian Universalist Association a comfortable home. Attention has already been given to the development of the UUA in the United States, and so we will move directly into African American humanists within this religious body. As a cautionary note, the participation of African Americans in this Association must be kept in perspective. Mark D. Morrison-Reed offers sobering thoughts on this relationship:

Unitarian Universalism's only significant penetration into the black community has been limited to a dozen inner city churches. Frequently churches of the liberal faith located in urban communities are unable to attract blacks, and in other areas there are few blacks. [There are no all-Black churches in the UUA.] The typical congregation has several black families at most, and often none at all. In 1968 when black involvement in the denomination was at a high point, blacks numbered 1,500 of the denomination's 180,000 members, less than 1 percent.[77]

Rather than focusing on the reasons for such small numbers of African Americans in UUA churches, attention will be given here to the nature of African American involvement based upon the UUA's assumed commitment to intellectual inquiry, reason, and tolerance.[78] We begin with Egbert Ethelred Brown's work in Harlem.

After frustration with Unitarians in Jamaica, Brown traveled to Harlem in hopes of bringing liberal religion to African Americans in New York City. Before his arrival in Harlem in 1920, there existed the Unity Congregational Society, but this Unitarian church could not adjust to the black Harlem created by the Great Migration. Yet Brown found a Harlem engulfed in progressive possibilities arising from the efforts of the NAACP, Marcus Garvey's UNIA, and the Communist Party. He held numerous jobs to support his family while he attempted to establish a Unitarian church, with little support from the American Unitarian Association. Brown devoted a significant amount of time to his ministry and fostered a sense of religiosity that was connected to a longing for justice and political-social equality; at the same time he drew on the input of the few socialists, communists, and Garveyites who crossed his path. The forum format for services provided a comfortable environment for social activists and others who were interested in opportunities to talk about the conditions faced by African Americans. Mark Morrison-Reed recalls, "We know there were initially the left-wing radicals, many Jamaicans, but only a few black Americans. On a number of occasions Brown mentioned people who had forsaken organized religion until they found the Harlem church. The overwhelming impression is that people came for political and intellectual reasons."[79]

Gatherings usually consisted of thoughtful talks, rebuttals, and discussion; missing were the emotional outbursts and otherworldly orientation that marked many churches in this same section of New York City. In the words of Morrison-Reed: "while Brown railed at the black churches in Harlem for pursuing otherworldly concerns, he endeavored to make the connection between religion and politics intimate."[80] The church's format and focus created problems, however. Brown's answer was variation:

> He reported that services were modified from year to year, always with the hope of attracting new people. Over the years they varied between a traditional religious service, with hymns, prayers, scripture readings, doxology, sermons, and benediction, and a forum situation, with a strongly secular orientation that included a brief service before the sermons and a discussion afterward. The church's letterhead called the church a temple and a forum. But it was largely upon the forum element that the reputation of the Harlem Unitarian Church was built. It drew people through the quality of its speakers and the open dialogue, yet its character as a forum also left it vulnerable to the kind of disruption described earlier. Moreover, it left some members desiring a service that was more religious in content and format.[81]

Some who desired a more religious service complained to Unitarian officials about the atheistic tone of the church. I believe that the atheist ethos was a natural outgrowth not only of Brown's leadership but of the perspective of many participants, the communists and socialists among them. In keeping with this perspective, Brown believed that African Americans needed to be freed from "the emotionalism and superstition and otherworldliness of the old time religion." Furthermore, he regarded the Harlem Unitarian church as "a church-forum where the honey-in-heaven and harassment-in-Hades type of religion is not tolerated. There are no 'amen corners' in this church, and no 'sob sister bench.'" Rather, this church called for human action and accountability for the condition of the world.[82] Its self-understanding is present in its charter statement:

> This Church is an institution of religion dedicated to the service of humanity.
>
> Seeking the truth in freedom, it strives to apply it in love for the cultivation of character, the fostering of fellowship in work and worship, and the establishment of a righteous social order which shall bring abundance of life to man.
>
> Knowing not sect, class, nation or race, it welcomes each to the service of all.[83]

In the 1940s Brown began losing the few members he had to larger, more prominent churches such as Community Church. According to Morrison-Reed, "He touched lives, promoted radical causes, exposed others to a broad spectrum of issues, affected the tenor of his time in some small ways, but left no temple of liberal religion in Harlem."[84] Until his death in 1956, Brown continued to struggle with this church.

Lewis A. McGee began the Free Religious Fellowship (initially named the Free Religious Association) in Chicago in 1947, after having been a part of the Chicago Ethical Society. McGee developed this Fellowship in response to a lack of liberal religion on Chicago's South Side. It began as a discussion group composed of African Americans living on the South Side, and from that it grew. Most of the members of this fellowship, unlike Brown's church in Harlem, were African American with some white and Japanese members.[85] Morrison-Reed describes the make-up of McGee's Fellowship as follows:

> Most of these individuals had been reared within Christian orthodoxy; the largest group originally came from the African Methodist Episcopal church or other Methodist churches. These people left the orthodox faith when they found that science raised issues their churches did not answer and that the church could not give an adequate explanation for the oppression of black people. These blacks were ready to hear the humanist perspective McGee offered, and sought a community that would assist the inquiring mind. Moreover, these were people whose lives were no longer confined to the black community. Their broadening outlook required a religion that supported their quest but did not confine them as orthodoxy had.[86]

As with Brown's church in Harlem, some members of McGee's Fellowship were involved with the Communist and Socialist Parties, reinforcing a humanist if not atheist perspective within the Fellowship. During the years of U.S. communist hunting, however, this caused problems, which resulted in surveillance of Fellowship activities. In spite of increased stress created by external forces, McGee's Fellowship was more successful than Brown's church for several reasons, the most obvious being a changed attitude within the Unitarian Association concerning integrated churches and black Unitarians in general.

At first the services were held in the home of Harry Jones, whom McGee met at the Chicago Ethical Society:

> The topics presented, in order, were "Why Make a New Approach to Religion," "The Liberal Way in Religion," "Liberalism Faces a Hostile World," "What Is Unitarianism" and "Free, for What?" In each case [McGee] led off with a twenty minute talk and then asked for questions or discussions. These gatherings were marked by a growing interest which became more and more sharply defined toward the possibility of a Unitarian Fellowship.[87]

Many assume, incorrectly, that humanist fellowship is limited to cerebral activity with little commitment to more than thought. McGee's Fellowship, for example, was committed to social action. Under McGee's leadership members of this organization acknowledged that religious involvements necessitate social activism. And so McGee and other members of the Fellowship involved themselves in the NAACP, the Civil Rights movement, and other transformative efforts. In the words of McGee:

> We believe in the human capacity to solve individual and social problems and thus to make progress. We believe in a continuing search for truth and hence that life is an adventurous quest. We believe in the scientific method as valid in ascertaining factual knowledge. We believe in democratic process in our human relations. We believe in ethical conduct. We believe in a dynamic universe, the evolution of life, the oneness of the human family and the unity of life with the material universe. . . . We believe in the creative imagination as a power in promoting the good life.[88]

The Fellowship maintained as its goal the application of humanist principles within African American communities. Even after McGee's retirement the Fellowship continued to function on Chicago's South Side.

The UUA's appeal to social justice is similar to that within African American Christian churches, except that justice is demanded and premised upon an anthropocentric appeal to accountability and progress, and not on the dictates of Scripture lived through God.

AFRICAN AMERICANS FOR HUMANISM

In addition to the UUA, another strong, albeit often understated, humanist organization is "African Americans for Humanism" (AAH). Norm Allen, Jr., the director of AAH and its sponsoring organization, the Council for Secular Humanism, assert that the humanism they practice is secular. Nonetheless, even within this context humanism as defined above can be considered a religious system because of the manner in which it provides orientation or direction for life.

Norm Allen was born into a Baptist household in Pittsburgh, but one that allowed for freethinking because it was only loosely affiliated with the church. He remembers being allowed to ask questions freely. At the age of ten, he asked questions about the plurality of religious traditions and about which one was correct. His mother replied that all we can do is to ask questions and follow our convictions. Allen then asked, "What if I reject God?" In response, his mother said that this would be fine, if it were based upon his questions and done in accordance with his convictions. Allen recalls that, growing up during the Black Power Movement, he was influenced by the teachings of the Nation of Islam and the Black Panther Party that questioned the reality and value of Christianity. From this information, Allen says, the "seeds of doubt were planted."[89]

As Allen grew older, he maintained his doubts but did not lose faith. At the age of eighteen, during his first year of study at the University of Pittsburgh, he became a "born-again" Christian, deeply moved by the Jewish and Christian Scriptures.[90] In reading the Scriptures he found contradictions, but by placing emphasis on faith, he maintained his Christian convictions. In addition to Scripture, Allen began reading *Plain Truth* magazine, which challenged the assumptions of many religions and sparked new questions for him, and the writings of J. A. Rogers and others who questioned Christianity. Thus Allen began to question the value of Christian faith and tradition. This was all buttressed by classroom readings on Bertrand Russell. As a result of this, Allen became a deist, yet one who maintained some sense of a personal deity.

Allen explains his growth into humanism was based upon his reading of *Free Inquiry* magazine beginning in 1980. This, combined with his readings on atheism and nationalism, moved him away from deism and introduced him to the basic principles of humanism. The final break with deism came through a personal "testing" of his God-concept. He began relying on his own capabilities and recognized that the situation's outcome did not differ when he prayed for assistance and when he relied on his own energies. He recalls that this break was not a traumatic experience but a relief, and that it was not a result of bitterness or personal loss but rational rejection of ideas that were not pragmatically and scientifically sound.[91] Allen's acquaintance with *Free Inquiry* also sparked his involvement with humanist organizations. The magazine made it clear that humanism should be concerned with all of humanity, but there was no African American representation in this magazine or in its sponsoring organization.

In 1989, Allen wrote a letter to Paul Kurtz, the editor of *Free Inquiry,* voicing his concerns. In response, the assistant editor invited Allen to write an article, in Summer 1989, addressing the issues outlined in his letter. In July 1989, Kurtz invited Allen to come to Buffalo, New York, and organize a subdivision of the larger organization (Council for Secular Humanism) that would address the questions and concerns of African American humanists. Allen arrived in September 1989 and began to create an International Advisory Board and the African American Humanist Declaration. The result was the organization called African Americans for Humanism (AAH). After initial organizing issues were addressed, outreach was established as a

The cover for an issue of the AAH newsletter, edited by Norm Allen, Jr. Reprinted by permission.

means of spreading information to potentially interested partners through travel, lectures, articles, a book (*African American Humanism: An Anthology*), and the *AAH newsletter.* Composed primarily of urban middle-class males, AAH has developed branches in Kansas City, Seattle, and other American cities, as well as in Ghana, Zaire, Uganda, and Kenya.

In an article on "Humanism in the Black Community," Allen advanced his reasons for what he perceived as the inadequacy of Christianity to respond to the suffering of African Americans:

> The black syndicated columnist and television commentator Tony Brown once remarked, "If not for the black church, black America wouldn't have had a prayer." But he also could have added that if not for European Christianity and the evils of slavery and racism that it fostered, there would have been no need for the black church. Christianity has caused more problems for blacks than it has solved. . . .
>
> Despite the many negative aspects of Christianity, it helped blacks to survive slavery; many people are impressed by the overwhelming strength of black spirituality despite the horrors of slavery. But there is no reason to be impressed. Blacks had tremendous faith in God, not despite slavery but because of it! Throughout history poor people have tended to be deeply religious; their beliefs have often made them apathetic to their plight and easy for the rich to dominate. This was the case with blacks during slavery. . . . Blacks are very proud of their deep religious convictions, but convictions are usually obstacles to new and productive ideas. The ultimate value of a religion is not how long it has helped a people to survive, but how far it has helped them to advance.[92]

Allen asserts that humanism is a viable alternative helping humanity toward its own fulfillment.

The African-American Humanist Declaration of 1990 provides useful insight into the nature, content and function of humanism as a praxis oriented religious system. The writers of this Declaration proclaim, "Today the world needs a critical, rational, and humane approach to living. This is what humanism is all about."[93] Norm Allen and the other African American humanists involved in the drafting of the Declaration contend that humanism provides a systematic response to major problems plaguing U.S. society, such as alcohol and substance abuse and economic development issues, by increasing the recognition of human accountability and potential for fostering useful change. AAH is committed to a mature and complex community in which individuals are respected and exposed to vital and viable life options. In seeking improvement of life options for African Americans, it aims to:

- Fight against racism in every form.

- Incorporate an Afrocentric outlook into a broader world perspective.

- Add depth and breadth to the study of history by acknowledging the great contributions made by people of African descent to the world, with the purpose of building self-esteem among African-Americans and helping to demonstrate the importance of all peoples to the development of world civilization.

- Develop eupraxophy, or "wisdom and good conduct through living" in African-American community by using the scientific and rational methods of inquiry.

- Solve many of the problems that confront African Americans through education and self-reliance, thereby affirming that autonomy and freedom of choice are basic human rights.

This cover advertises the Declaration written by African Americans for Humanism. Reprinted by permission.

- Develop self-help groups and engage in any humane and rational activity designed to develop the African-American community.

- Emphasize the central importance of education at all levels, including humanistic moral education, developing a humanistic outlook, and providing the tools for the development of critical reason, self-improvement, and career training.[94]

AFRICAN AMERICAN HUMANISM AND THE PROBLEM OF EVIL

I am not convinced that religion is dying wholesale, because religion provides a language or grammar for making sense of the world in life affirming ways.[95] Rather than dying, religion emerges in new forms of expression. Some who acknowledge this still avoid humanism because they believe that it robs adherents of valuable hopes and comforts. John Dietrich states, however: "Humanism robs man of nothing that actually exists. It takes from him only his comforting illusions and substitutes from them consolations that are real and hopes that are realizable."[96] Humanism challenges activities and thought that do not appear liberating in nature. Organized traditional religions, therefore, have come under increasing attack because of their perceived failure to combat continued socioeconomic and political turmoil. Although the churchs' role in promoting such transformative events as the Civil Rights movement must be acknowledged, humanists will point to more examples of the churches' failure to engage relevant questions and issues.

Theistic forms of religious expression resolve the problem of moral evil in the world through some interaction between god(s) and humanity. This resolution, however, stimulates additional questions for the humanist. In the words of Raymond Knox:

> . . . here they lynching Negroes——-if God's all that good, how come he don't stop the police from killing Negroes, lynching Negroes, if God is all that just?[97]

Or, as James Baldwin articulates the question:

> And if one despairs—as who has not?—of human love, God's love alone is left. But God—and I felt this even then, so long ago, on that tremendous floor, unwillingly—is white. And if His love was so great, and if He loved all His children, why were we, the blacks, cast down so far? Why? In spite of all I said thereafter, I found no answer on the floor—not *that* answer, anyway—and I was on the floor all night.[98]

Humanism resolves the problem of evil through an appeal to human accountability. Humans have created the conditions presently encountered and humans are responsible for changing these conditions.

For African American humanists history demonstrates that this goal is noble but its achievement is far from guaranteed. African American humanists' sense of optimism based upon human potential for transformation is more guarded than that present in white humanist thought because of black people's history of disproportionate suffering.[99] Nonetheless, African American humanists hold that humanity has no choice but to continue seeking progress. The alternative is stagnation. Praxis, then, is a requirement of life: the goal is to make the world healthy and supportive of all life.

Norm Allen rejects the notion of redemptive suffering. Suffering understood as good or redemptive is a dangerous idea, he asserts, because it promotes complacency and increased suffering.[100] Suffering, understood strictly as a matter of humans improperly interacting with other humans, is corrected by humans behaving morally and ethically.[101]

5

▲▼▲▼▲▼▲▼▲▼▲▼▲▼▲▼▲

HOW DO WE TALK ABOUT RELIGION?

Religious Experience, Cultural Memory, and Theological Method

> African American culture was vibrantly alive, and had been alive for more than 300 years. Through that span, African Americans combined African legacy with American culture, and along the way they left stories in the ground.[1]

The foregoing chapters of this book promote a sense of religious diversity that calls into question traditional understandings of theology and theological method as necessarily grounded in a Christian community of faith. Up to this point, a response to this challenge has only been intimated. But in this final chapter, a revised sense of theological reflection is explicitly presented by giving attention to four points: (1) a discussion of current uses of cultural production in African American theology; (2) a rethinking of collective memory and cultural resources, arguing that collective cultural memory is fragile; (3) assessment of the theological ramifications of fragile cultural memory; (4) an outline of archaeological resources and the nature of a theology of fragile cultural memory and religious diversity.[2]

AFRICAN AMERICAN THEOLOGY AND CULTURAL PRODUCTION[3]

Liberation theologies are committed to cultural production as vital material for theological reflection. African American theological reflection is no exception to this stratagem. From its first conception as an academic enterprise, it has spoken of the significance of African American history, culture, and experience for the theological enterprise. The first systematic treatment of black liberation theology by James H. Cone establishes this commitment to cultural resources.[4] According to Cone:

It is clear, therefore, that the most important decisions in theology are made at this juncture. The sources and norm are presuppositions that determine the questions that are to be asked, as well as the answers that are to be given. . . . Because a perspective refers to the whole of a person's being in the context of a community, the sources and norm of black theology must be consistent with the perspective of the black community.[5]

Cone's commitment to cultural production as theological resource is not a simple embrace of black nationalistic tendencies popular during the 1960s and 1970s, but a recognition of culture realities as the framework through which divine revelations are manifest. Consequently, to miss the importance and content of culture is to overlook the presence of God in the world.[6]

Notwithstanding the logic and rhetorical strength of Cone's argument, the scope and depth of his attention to African American cultural production was questioned by Cecil Cone.[7] According to Cecil Cone, black theological reflection is vulnerable because of a reliance on "nonreligious" orientations that are reflective of and reactive against European notions of freedom and community.[8] As a corrective, he suggests a conscious turn to African American religious experience and cultural production and the avoidance of white European approaches and cultural concerns. In this way black theology becomes *black* by taking seriously claims about the revelatory value of black cultural experience and production. Blackness here is understood as referring both to physical blackness and to a unique set of cultural and historical realities that mark and distinguish this segment of the U.S. population. Joseph Washington also indirectly raised questions concerning the blackness of black theology by questioning the blackness of black folk religion.[9] He concluded that black folk religion is viable but requires a radical commitment to biblical theology as foundational in the quest for liberation. Furthermore, there must be a return to the roots of black religious and cultural experience as expressed in the black Christian church, in the essential religious presence of the black community.[10]

In response to these critiques, many African American theologians placed more emphasis on the cultural roots of African American churches and African American communities.[11] This attention to cultural production as theological resource, however, usually did not move beyond those elements that are readily apparent and well documented. Even agendas that question assumptions of theological normality do so using only the more visible resources, cultural production close to the surface of the cultural terrain. What develops is a rather static and reified notion of cultural "blackness" based upon a limited collective cultural memory.[12] The work of Maurice Halbwachs explicates this assertion. He writes: "The memory of the religious group, in order to defend itself, succeeded for some time in preventing other memories from forming and developing in its midst."[13] What ultimately occurs, then, is a sense of personal and cultural identity that takes into consideration only a limited number of cultural markers, and theology easily becomes apologia or advocacy for the religious implications of this reified cultural image.[14]

This practice has been questioned in recent work by Dwight Hopkins and others who rethink black culture's content and forms of expression. For example, in his article "Theological Method and Cultural Studies: Slave Religious Culture as a Heuristic,"[15] Hopkins argues for an understanding of culture as a "total way of life" that embraces an ever broadening cultural terrain:

> [C]ulture . . . is religious and constituted by a dynamic, non-hierarchical interplay of macro-, micro-, linguistic, and identity concerns. Theological method details the path by which people develop a conscious and intentional understanding of a community's belief in and practice with the ultimate as it is envisioned by their religious culture.[16]

Furthermore,

> the task of theological methodology is made more difficult by the lack of recognizable road signs which are missing in this strange and unfamiliar land of religious thinking and practices of the challeted blacks.[17]

Hopkins understands culture as complex conversation and exchange taking place on a variety of levels. His explicit connection of culture with individual and communal identity is also useful because it fosters an understanding of the development of culture in connection with the development of personality and in light of various socially constructed factors. This implicit appeal to social evolution and political economy is helpful because it highlights the difficulty of marking out the inroads that black culture has made on the rough U.S. terrain.

FRAGILE CULTURAL MEMORY AND CULTURAL PRODUCTION

How is the complex range of cultural productions and activities uncovered and used in theological reflection? A move toward answering this question begins with a rethinking of culture, cultural production, and cultural memory. Culture is tangled collections of signs in motion that reveal the meanings we give to life.[18] The term *culture* comes from the Latin (*colo, colere, coli, cultum*) meaning "to till the ground, to tend and care for."

> [I]n antiquity it had already gathered the wide range of extended senses it still has today. Culture is the familiarized, tamed, gardened, version of the world. . . . It includes not only the *cultivation* of the soil, *agriculture,* but also the *culture* of new varieties of domesticated plant, the careful *cultivation* of acquaintanceships and skills, of one's own "person" and one's own soul, and therefore also *high culture,* the arts and sciences, and above all the *cult,* the care and tending of the gods.[19]

This concept of culture also points to the ways in which cultural production and cultural life are housed and transformed. The key is memory or the meaning-making portraits that explain and "connect" the various remnants and artifacts we come across as individuals and as groups.[20] With each articulation of these cultural memories, they are moved that much further from the moment of their conception and their cultural context. The past is reconstructed by groups and individuals, and what emerges helps shape identity and perceptions of the present. Direct contact with the context of cultural artifacts is lost because time continues to move forward and representations replace realities.

The development of collective cultural memory in the United States serves as an example of this loss of collective cultural memory. The early North American terrain held untapped wonder and possibility, particularly in the West. This created a sense of progress and possibility that overshadowed the importance of a historicized past, a contextual story. Memory became static and disassociated with the (arti)facts.[21] Although this seemed beneficial at the time, selective memory and disregard for the past actually resulted in a shallow self-identity and consciousness that facilitated the denial of worth to African Americans, Native Americans, and women. For example, prior to 1870,

> [a] few whites, . . . at least considered the Indians' tragic part in the American past and present, even though they responded inconsistently to such issues as friend or foe? Victim or villain? By contrast, the African-American appears silently and unobtrusively in some historical art concerning the War for Independence. But any claims that might appear on behalf of black participation in national history would have to be made by blacks themselves and could expect to be largely ignored.[22]

With time, the turmoil of the present and the uncertain future (as demonstrated, for example, by the Civil War and reconstruction) were addressed through an appeal to a more comfortable and certain story.[23] Yet, again, "minority" communities were forgotten. And during the early twentieth century, this problematic use of memory made the philosophies of racial inferiority and separation that much easier to espouse. The ramifications of the work of such revisionists as Thomas Dixon and Harvard's Louis Agazizz for oppressed communities are clear. According to Charles Long:

> one of the basic ingredients within the philosophical and cultural meaning of the conquerors is the evaluation of history. . . . Those who are forced to undergo this history are not subjected simply to economic and political exploitation; they are simultaneously forced to undergo an evacuation of their cultural meaning and to possibility for cultural creativity and stability. This evacuation is matched by the presentation of the conquered people and culture as "problems of knowledge."[24]

Although this process does not completely obliterate cultural memory and meaning within African American communities, it does problematize the nature of both. In short, African American cultural memory is fragile and cultural artifacts decontextualized.[25] African American communities continued to nurture their own cultural production by making sense of their cultural memories that were distorted during years of bondage and continued discrimination. Continued existence required this process. In the words of Frederick Douglass: "Memory was given to man for some wise purpose. The past is . . . the mirror in which we may discern the dim outlines of the future."[26] With time, others would seek to maintain collective black cultural memory in organizations. One example is the "Negro Society for Historical Research" (renamed the Schomburg Center for Research in African American life), developed in New York in 1911 as a depository.[27]

As important as this exercising of collective cultural memory is, it does not bring about a complete transmission of cultural information. Pieces are lost or neglected along the way according to what groups and individuals consider important or unimportant. In short, cultural memory is distorted by the necessity of interpretation. Whether one argues that the present shapes our perceptions of the past (social construction) or the past shapes the present (construction through commemoration), the fact remains that a clear and uncontaminated link between the past and present does not exist.[28] Robert O'Meally and Geneviéve Fabre are correct: "Whether deliberately or not, individual or group memory selects certain landmarks of the past—places, art work, dates, persons, public or private, well known or obscure, real or imagined—and invests them with symbolic and political significance."[29] Perceiving the world, which collective cultural memory helps us to do, always entails a loss of some pieces, the removal of what does not, at the moment, appear useful or helpful.[30] Memory is not disinterested; it is conscious construction. According to Toni Morrison:

> Over and over, the writers pull the narrative up short with a phrase such as, "But let us drop a veil over these proceedings too terrible to relate." In shaping the experience to make it palatable to those who were in a position to alleviate it, they were silent about many things, and they "forgot" many other things. There was a careful selection of the instances that they would record and a careful reading of those that they chose to describe.[31]

Cultural memory is again problematic not only because it is composed of decontextualized cultural artifacts, but because we use cultural memory to decode and interpret those artifacts.

Furthermore, history in some sense is cultural artifacts catalogued and filed. It involves freeze-framing cultural production and artifacts that actually move throughout a rather undefined and unstable contextual framework. History is, at best, an inadequate way of presenting cultural artifacts. It pretends to remember and chronicle all, forgetting nothing of merit. And in "organizing" cultural memories, history ultimately destroys them through a faulty process of "clarification."[32] History is not a victimless crime; yet I would not want to focus rigidly on oppressive social factors as the sole cause, although they certainly play a role in the fragile nature of collective cultural memory. African American collective cultural memory is fragile for an additional reason that is connected to oppressive circumstances but not completely explained by or reducible to these circumstances. Due to generational shifts "certain sites of memory were sometimes constructed by one generation in one way and then reinterpreted by another. These sites may fall unexpectedly out of grace or be revisited suddenly and brought back to life."[33]

The fine points have been overlooked by many African Americans. Not every black person, for example, can " 'play the dozens' and appreciate the undertones of Dolomite's comic routine."[34] In addition, much of what has been collected concerning African American culture and cultural memory has gone through several translations before reaching print or another final form. For example, many WPA workers who collected very good information received materials from generations who had forgotten (for many reasons) nuances accompanying the cultural artifacts they shared. In this way standing both within and outside a cultural system has negative consequences. As Karen Fields reminds us:

> Nothing is more fully agreed than the certainty that memory fails. Memory fails, leaving blanks, and memory fails by filling blanks mistakenly. In filling blanks mistakenly, memory collaborates with forces separate from actual past events, forces such as an individual's wishes, a group's suggestions, a moment's connotations, an environment's clues, an emotion's demands, a self's evolution, a mind's manufacture of order, and yes, even a researcher's objectives.[35]

This in no way suggests that fragile memory is worthless; rather it is simply fragile. But this fragility does necessitate attention to the manner in which we use memory. Says Fields: "It is important to refine continually our methods of observing and thinking about memory as a matter of scholarly or scientific enterprise."[36] Much progress can be made in theological reflection by first recognizing the incomplete and fragile nature of collective cultural memory. And I believe that Frantz Fanon and African American existentialism can help with this process.

My intention is not to take Fanon's analysis as a direct representation of conflict over African American cultural memory, but to suggest that Fanon's psychological and existential approach to cultural memory and identity in the face of cultural hostility is a useful tool.[37] And African American existentialism points to the necessity of understanding the condition of African Americans as an introduction to their collective cultural memory.

Early in *Black Skin, White Masks,* Fanon makes a statement that, in a symbolic manner, captures the existential dilemma cast in terms of cultural production: "The white man is sealed in his whiteness. The Black man in his blackness. . . . There is another fact: Black men want to prove to white men, at all costs, the richness of their thought, the equal value of their intellect." According to Fanon, this dilemma results in a fracture of the human "soul" by which memory is split between an urge toward blackness—conceived in cultural terms—and the continual presence of European cultural ideas.[38] Within this cultural quagmire, oppressed groups seek to resurrect cultural artifacts and place them in a context by which identity is established. Even in light of this seemingly promethean task, Fanon does not give up on the ability of groups to reconnect or recover cultural realities that buttress a useful individual and collective identity. Although he refers to the African context, Fanon's words are not lost on the U.S. situation:

> Somewhere beyond the objective world of farms and banana trees and rubber trees, I had subtly brought the real world into being. The essence of the world was my fortune. Between the world and me a relation of

coexistence was established. I had discovered the primeval One. My 'speaking hands' tore at the hysterical thought of the world. The white man had the anguished feeling that *I was escaping from him and that I was taking something with me.*[39]

"Cultural estrangement"[40] is not complete. There are cultural artifacts that the whitenizing of history does not wipe out. These resilient artifacts allow for a certain sense of rightful cultural place, and I cannot help but believe that African American collective cultural memory is a matter of "escaping . . . and . . . taking something." Something, but not everything, is taken.

Intellectuals who think that they gather artifacts and construct firm collective cultural memory are mistaken, because "[they] only [catch] hold of . . . outer garments. And these outer garments are merely the reflection of a hidden life, teeming and perpetually in motion."[41] Fanon makes an interesting observation that sheds additional light on the ontology of fragile cultural memory.[42] He recognizes that the physical body itself is a cultural artifact, complete with scars, piercings, the memories housed in its essential form. One could easily relate this understanding of body to Hortense Spiller's understanding of flesh as "that which holds, channels and conducts cultural meanings and inscriptions." According to Spiller, enslavement seeks to strip the body of its flesh, but this is never completely accomplished. Rather, the flesh is transformed; it is hidden from view, covered by protective layers.[43] Hence, cultural memory is visible yet hidden. An additional problem emerges: the invisibility of African Americans has put their cultural artifacts up for grabs. The artifacts are conceived as belonging to no one and thus they are even more difficult to collect and interpret. Recognition of this should spark new theological questions concerning collective cultural memory's locations and nature. In the words of Fanon, "O my body, make of me always a man who questions!"[44]

Theological soundness is dependent upon the perpetual quest for cultural roots and the epistemological soundness noted in existentialist thought. The benefit of the cultural quest is uncertain, but it should drive theological reflection onward. Fanon's observations on the quest for an Aztec past by Mexican scholars are apt: "Because they realize they are in danger of losing their lives and thus becoming lost to their people, these [intellectuals], hotheaded and with anger in their hearts, relentlessly determined to renew contact once more with the oldest and most pre-colonial springs of life of their people."[45] Such a task would be difficult enough if African Americans conducted this work in solitude, but it is complicated by the presence of a larger cultural norm (the dominant society) that often blocks this work by co-optation and the denial of the artifacts' importance. From Hegel to the present, African American culture and its manifestations have been questioned. As Richard Wright comments on this troubled terrain:

> Not only had the southern whites not known me, but, more important still, as I had lived in the South I had not had the chance to learn who I was. The pressure of southern living kept me from being the kind of person that I might have been. I had been what my surroundings had demanded, what my family—conforming to the dictates of the whites above them—had exacted of me, and what the whites had said that I must be. Never being fully able to be myself, I had slowly learned that the South could recognize but a part of a man, could accept but a fragment of his personality, and all the rest—the best and deepest things of heart and mind—were tossed away in blind ignorance and hate. . . . Yet, deep down, I knew that I could never really leave the South, for my feelings had already been formed by the South, for there had been slowly instilled into my personality and consciousness, black though I was, the culture of the South.[46]

Wright rejected the dominant culture's rejection of him and went in search of cultural artifacts, cultural meaning—identity. But how do theologians engage in this same enterprise? How do they leave the metaphorical "South" in search of cultural artifacts and collective cultural memory by which to inform their thought? The search should take them into new terrain and, with more critical insight, over old terrain.

THEOLOGICAL RAMIFICATIONS

African American writers have often taken the lead in promoting theological and religious questions and concerns. In their writings they have closely investigated cultural memory and artifacts. As Toni Morrison came to realize: "Memories and recollections won't give . . . total access to the unwritten interior life of these people [African American forebears]."[47] At this point Morrison imaginatively suggests something of fundamental importance: "[using] literary *archaeology,* on the basis of some information and a little bit of guesswork you *journey to a site to see what remains were left behind and to reconstruct the world that these remains imply.*"[48]

Mindful of Morrison's words, I suggest an alternative way of interpreting African American religion (and its often understated diversity) and culture by theologically embracing the creative and life-affirming, yet fragile, manifestations of African American culture.[49] I call this approach *theology of fragile memory and religious diversity;* in some presentations I have also referred to it as *archaeological theology*. In either case, it is a theological enterprise because theological concerns remain high-level, and archaeological sensibilities and tools are used simply to enhance this theological agenda.[50] With respect to this theological approach, the first order of business is to outline its preliminary tasks. For the purposes of this chapter, I will concentrate on three: (1) attention to methodological shifts; (2) rethinking the religious terrain; attention here is given to the "hush arbor meetings" as exemplary; (3) implementing a process based upon (1) and (2).

ON THEOLOGY AND ARCHAEOLOGY

Initially the term *archaeology* referred to the systematic and descriptive analysis of ancient societies. During the nineteenth century, however, the term was expanded and archaeologists became those who examined the material remains of perished civilizations. In short, "the purpose of archaeology is to extract history from the monuments and artifacts of the past, to write history from the often inadequate relics that time has spared."[51] This took various forms and centered on various parts of the world. A eurocentric bias was usually obvious, particularly in the work of those interested in non-Western cultural traditions. Others during the nineteenth century were concerned chiefly with adventure and treasure, spending time only with pyramids and romanticized past civilizations.[52] In the 1960s "New Archaeology" developed and was more concerned with the manner in which people interacted with the environment and other groups, and the role of cultural production in facilitating this exchange.[53] Additional attention is now given, through "New Archaeology," to the politics of archaeology and the manner in which archaeological methodology can be fitted to the agendas of women and African Americans, among others.

I suggest an archaeological method marked by "cultural resource management" based upon political economy because it is mindful of the sociopolitical and economic factors influencing culture and archaeological analysis. Cultural management that accompanies the type of archaeological endeavor favored here—rescue archaeology—will help theologians move beyond present patterns by seeking not simply to "absorb" or add new materials, but by attempting to synthesize materials. Theologians can then work with materials that are usually excluded from the accepted record as well as familiar materials that must now be reevaluated.[54]

Because of the commodification of Africans through slavery, my sense of archaeological method also responds to a cultural-commodity point of departure connected to political economy ideas. It argues that every object can be commodified and the object's value is dependent upon a given location of exchange.[55] Borrowing from Charles E. Orser, I would like to extend the meaning of value to include use, exchange, and aesthetics. Orser gives the example of iron pots found on sites once housing slave quarters. The use and exchange value of these pots is connected to kitchen or cooking services. But slave accounts indicate that these pots were also used to capture sound during worship services. This is aesthetic value that sheds additional light on cultural production during slavery.[56] In short, archaeological focus is placed on the manner in which religious rhetoric was placed in the service of economic agendas within the context of slavery. It demonstrates, I believe, the ways in which cultural artifacts and memory point to untapped theological connotations. Hence, attention to archaeological method can mean a richer understanding of African American life extending beyond a select and distorted representation, a movement away from current biases, for example, in the depiction of African American religiosity. This in turn can mean a broader and more complex theological analysis of cultural production and African American life in general.

I suggest beginning this enterprise with a rethinking of hush arbor meetings. I have selected hush arbor meetings because of their central role in the discussion of cultural artifacts and memory associated with African American liberation theology and African American religion in general. William E. Montgomery offers a depiction of a typical hush arbor meeting:

> If their masters refused to permit them to hold their own worship services, slaves would steal away into the woods and congregate in what they called hush arbors or brush arbors, which were sanctuaries constructed of tree branches or in secluded cabins. . . . Black preachers related to them in their vernacular, and the singing and dancing provided them with excitement and pleasure.[57]

As Montgomery notes, not all hush arbor meetings took place without the knowledge of whites. In fact, whites at times gave slaves permission to hold their own meetings in order to avoid having to share space, and after emancipation many blacks built similar structures to use until more permanent locations were available. It is likely that these not-so-secret meetings are the hush arbors thought of with respect to the early stages of black Christianity in the South. Referring again to Montgomery, one sees this implicit movement from hush arbor to black Christian churches in the South. Concerning the religious ramifications of emancipation, he writes:

Control of their churches was as much a part of being self-reliant as own-ing their own land and exercising legal and political rights. . . . And it was dramatically stated in the action of the Reverend Morris Henderson, a for-mer slave who was freed in February, 1865, and who led his Baptist con-gregation out of the church building in Memphis that whites had allowed them to worship in and moved into a rude shelter of tree limbs and branches known as a brush arbor. . . . They could listen to and react to their own preachers in their own way, singing, dancing, and shouting as the spirit moved them. And, of course, a church structure was already in place. It needed only to be formalized, in the case of the slaves' "invisible" church.[58]

Montgomery and others draw from Albert Raboteau, who provided one of the earlier and best treatments of Christian slave religion, making explicit use of the "invisible institution" (i.e., hush arbor meetings) as a paradig-matic religious move on the part of enslaved Africans.[59] Raboteau argues that the invisible institution arose as slaves felt the need to develop their own religious thought outside oppressive structures of economically driven "false Christianity," to use Frederick Douglass's terminology. He does acknowledge some diversity of opinion within slave communities; yet it leads back to the Christian church. During the closing decades of the ante-bellum period the so-called invisible institution of slave Christianity came to maturity."[60] Raboteau, like most, acknowledge the various religious "resources" brought to the "New World" by slaves, but this material, it is argued, is nonsubstantial. The work of Raboteau and others has served as the paradigm of black religious history. What has resulted from this is a preoccupation with Christian forms of expression to the neglect of other viable alternatives. Granted, religious (Christian) activity during the ante-bellum period is documented by slaves. Nevertheless, when one keeps in mind prior statements concerning collective cultural memory, one cannot assume that this documentation contains all occurrences of religious prac-tice. And what was not reported may have been housed in decontextual-ized and misunderstood cultural artifacts. My argument is not that secret slave meetings were non-Christian; I cannot be certain of this any more than others can be certain that Christianity dominated these meetings—cultural memory is not that reliable. Rather, I am arguing for a hermeneu-tic of suspicion, understanding that assumptions commonly accepted con-cerning religious expression in slave communities is problematized by archaeological excavation. For example, archaeologist Kenneth Brown, in his work with a mid-nineteenth-century village in Texas, unearthed a room that "contained many artifacts similar to those used to fill *minkisi* [or sacred medicines]."[61] This points to the presence of Bakongo influence and the strong presence of African religious items and practices.

Furthermore, as of the 1960s there was increased interest in cultural artifacts of colonial African Americans, and this material is ripe for archaeological theology's probing. For example, Leland Ferguson, in *Uncommon Ground: Archaeology and Early African America, 1650–1800,* speaks of the excavation of slave quarters that should spark the interest of theologians who make use of African American cultural artifacts in their work. He writes that among the things found have been slave quarters

> with secret cellars and others with foundations for African-styled clay walls. Lying buried where they were used, these artifacts directly reflect the activities of daily life. With the exception of a few early slave narratives, this newly found archaeological record is as close to the slave's personal story as we have ever been.[62]

Furthermore:

> while objects like engraved spoons and African-style shrines seldom were mentioned in written documents, artifacts excavated on plantation sites, coupled with . . . discoveries of Bakongo-style marks on bowls from low-country sites suggest that the preserved remains of many shrines and rituals must be buried underground across the South. Archaeological evidence of African-style religious practices in America reinforces and makes tangible [a] sense that slaves brought to the Americas not only a variety of practical skills, but also elements of their African spiritual beliefs.[63]

Archaeological method applied to theology is useful because it facilitates hard questioning of assumed cultural history and theological reflection dependent upon it.

Gaining access to this material and including it in theological analysis requires searching all angles: written historical records and autobiographical accounts, architectural information, folktales, folklore, field trips to various sites, anthropological findings, archaeological findings, imagination, and so forth. Theology as I envision it suggests a use of all available resources and the recognition that our findings are missing "something." The framework for this theological method is as follows: (1) decide upon issues and select work sites, possible locations of cultural artifacts; (2) conduct surveys of the sites, suggesting initial theories and ideas; (3) record findings; (4) analyze the findings using an appropriate hermeneutic and theological sensibilities.

Many argue that archaeology by nature entails interpretative work. I, however, prefer to include an explicit hermeneutic that works in keeping with the basic principles of my proposed theological method. I suggest nitty gritty hermeneutics.[64] Simply put, nitty gritty hermeneutics is an interpretative tool comfortable with disruption because it recognizes the fragile nature of memory and cultural artifacts. The artifacts, then, are less likely to be forced into contextual categories simply because the categories are widely known and embraced. "Its guiding criterion is the presentation of black life with its full complexity, untainted by static tradition. . . . the term nitty-gritty denotes a hard and concrete orientation in which the 'raw natural facts' [in this case cultural artifacts] are of tremendous importance, irrespective of their ramifications."[65] It recognizes that the act of interpretation, like love-making, is unpredictable, passionate, and messy—without apology.

NOTES

INTRODUCTION: THEOLOGY AND THE CANON OF BLACK RELIGION RETHOUGHT

1. Anthony B. Pinn, *Why, Lord? Suffering and Evil in Black Theology* (New York: Continuum Publishing Company, 1995), 20. For a more detailed discussion of these ideas see Anthony B. Pinn, "Rethinking the Nature and Tasks of African American Theology: A Pragmatic Perspective," an article for "Pragmatism and Recent African American Religious Thought," a special edition of *American Journal of Theology and Philosophy*, forthcoming. I will do more work on this area in *Earth Bound: Toward a Theology of Fragile Cultural Memory and Religious Diversity* (working title), to be published by Fortress Press.

2. James H. Evans, *We Have Been Believers: An African-American Systematic Theology* (Minneapolis: Fortress Press, 1992), 26–27.

3. Shiva Naipaul, *Love and Death in a Hot Country* (New York: Penguin, Inc., 1985), 8.

4. Gordon Kaufman, *In Face of Mystery: A Constructive Theology* (Cambridge, Mass.: Harvard University Press, 1993), 225.

5. Ibid., 227.

6. Ibid.

7. Gordon D. Kaufman, *An Essay on Theological Method*, rev. ed. (Missoula, Mont.: Scholars Press, 1995), 1–2. Although this text is still useful, Kaufman has further developed his methodological approach in two recent texts: *In Face of Mystery* and *God—Mystery—Diversity: Christian Theology in a Pluralistic World* (Minneapolis: Fortress Press, 1996). These texts, particularly *God—Mystery—Diversity,* are influential particularly in the final chapter of this book and in *Earth Bound* mentioned in n. 1.

8. Kaufman, *An Essay,* 8.

9. Kaufman, *God—Mystery—Diversity,* 10.

10. Theophus H. Smith, *Conjuring Culture: Biblical Formations of Black America* (New York: Oxford University Press, 1994).

11. Albert J. Raboteau, *Slave Religion: The "Invisible Institution" in the Antebellum South* (New York: Oxford University Press, 1978), 80–81.

12. Yvonne P. Chireau, "Hidden Traditions: Black Religion, Magic, and Alternative Spiritual Beliefs in Womanist Perspective," in Jacquelyn Grant, ed., *Perspectives on Womanist Theology,* Black Church Scholars Series 7 (Atlanta: Interdenominational Theological Center Press, 1995), 72.

13. Lawrence W. Levine, *Black Culture and Black Consciousness: Afro-American Folk Thought from Slavery to Freedom* (New York: Oxford University Press, 1977), 56–57.

14. Charles Long, *Significations* (Philadelphia: Fortress Press, 1986), 7.

15. Gayraud Wilmore, *Black Religion and Black Radicalism: An Interpretation of the Religious History of Afro-American People,* 2d ed. (Maryknoll, N.Y.: Orbis, 1983), 161.

16. Naipaul, *Love and Death,* 104–5.

17. I note that the case studies presented here have a potential problem in that interviews are limited, for the most part, to leaders of the particular communities. This was necessary because of my interest in information concerning the origin and doctrine of each community. It is my belief that leaders (and in most cases here, the founder) of each movement are in the best position to provide this information. I do acknowledge, however, that subsequent study by myself and others should also take into consideration the manner in which participants in these communities process and live this history and doctrine.

CHAPTER 1: SERVING THE *LOA*

1. W. J. Argyle, *The Fon of Dahomey: A History and Ethnography of the Old Kingdom* (Oxford: Clarendon Press, 1966), 3–6.

2. Ibid., 7–12. For additional information on Dahomey see Melville J. Herskovits, *Dahomey: An Ancient West African Kingdom*, 2 vols. (Evanston: Northwestern University Press, 1967).

3. Argyle, *The Fon of Dahomey*, 12.

4. Robert Farris Thompson, *Flash of the Spirit: African and Afro-American Art and Philosophy* (New York: Random House, 1983), 166.

5. Vodu can also refer to "spirit" or sacred objects in general. See, for example, Alfred Metraux, *Voodoo in Haiti*, trans. by Hugo Charteris (New York: Oxford University Press, 1959), 27. See also Harold Courlander and Remy Bastien, *Religion and Politics in Haiti* (Washington, D.C.: Institute for Cross-Cultural Research, 1966), 12–13, 25 (n. 1).

6. Herskovits, *Dahomey* 2:101.

7. There is some difficulty in reaching an exact understanding of Mawu-Lisa's nature. See Argyle, *The Fon of Dahomey*, 176.

8. Ibid. 175.

9. Ibid., 188–93.

10. Detailed information on the vodun is available in Herskovits, *Dahomey*.

11. Thompson, *Flash of the Spirit*, 176.

12. Herskovits, *Dahomey*, 233–35.

13. In 1508, the indigenous population numbered roughly 60,000, and by 1548, there were roughly 500 remaining.

14. C. L. R. James, *The Black Jacobins: Toussaint L'Ouverture and the San Domingo Revolution*, 2d ed. (New York: Vintage Books, ca. 1963; reprint 1989), 6.

15. Thomas O. Ott, *The Haitian Revolution, 1789–1804* (Nashville: University of Tennessee Press, 1973), 3–5.

16. See Leslie G. Desmangles, *The Faces of the Gods: Vodou and Roman Catholicism in Haiti* (Chapel Hill: University of North Carolina Press, 1992), 21–22, 23, 27.

17. Cited in ibid., 26–27.

18. The reader interested in more information on Haitian vodou should consult Harold Courlander, *The Drum and the Hoe: Life and Lore of the Haitian People* (Berkeley: University of California Press, 1960).

19. Joseph Murphy notes that Harold Courlander divides vodou into three connected categories: (1) rites associated with Dahomey; (2) rites associated with Dahomey and others such as the Ibo; (3) all rites including the sources of both Rada and Petro. These latter terms are discussed in some detail later in this chapter. See Joseph Murphy, "Haitian Vodou," in *Working the Spirit: Ceremonies of the African Diaspora* (Boston: Beacon Press, 1994), 15; Courlander and Bastien, *Religion and Politics in Haiti*, 11–13. Also see Milo Rigaud, *Secrets of Voodoo*, trans. Robert B. Cross (San Francisco: City Lights Books, 1953), 9–13; George Eaton Simpson, section on Vodun belief system, *Religious Cults of the Caribbean: Trinidad, Jamaica and Haiti* (Rio Piedras, Puerto Rico: Institute of Caribbean Studies, University of Puerto Rico, 1980); Maya Deren, *Divine Horsemen: The Living Gods of Haiti* (New York: McPherson & Company, 1953), 57–71. Deren, unlike many authors, suggests that Vodoun was also influenced by the religious beliefs and practices of the indigenous population. For her discussion of this see Appendix B (271–86) of *Divine Horsemen*. For regional approaches to the topic of Vodou see, for example, Michel S. Laguerre, *Voodoo Heritage*, Sage Library of Social Research 98 (Beverly Hills: Sage Publications, 1980).

20. This political, historical and ecclesiastical development is nicely outlined by Desmangles, *Faces of the Gods*, 38–47. Also see Bastien, "Vodoun and Politics in Haiti," 41–67, in Courlander and Bastien, *Religion and Politics in Haiti*.

21. "A Small Guinea Transplanted in America: A Disgrace," cited in the document section of Laennec Hurbon, *Voodoo: Search for the Spirit*, trans. Lory Frankel (New York: Harry N. Abrams, 1995), 134–35. Also see Desmangles, *Faces of the Gods*, 33–57.

22. Cited in Metraux, *Voodoo in Haiti*, 336–37.

23. Ibid., 340–41.

24. Laguerre, *Voodoo Heritage*, 24.

25. Cited in Thompson, *Flash of the Spirit*, 179.

26. As Desmangles (*Faces of the Gods*, 94–98) points out, the Rada *lwas* or the Rada *nanchon* (nation) of *loas* is so large partly because it has drawn in *lwas* from other little remembered *nanchons* such as the Wangol and Naga. Others have been absorbed by the Petro *nanchon*.

27. See Thompson, *Flash of the Spirit*, 165–66. For a discussion of Dahomey vs. Congo (etc.) influence see David Geggus, "Haitian Voodoo in the Eighteenth Century: Language, Culture, Resistance," *Jahrbuch für Geschichte von Staat, Wirtschaft und Gesellschaft Lateinamerikas* 28 (1991): 21–51. Others, such as Rigaud (*Secrets of Voodoo*, 9), mention the contribution of other African peoples but without the detailed discussion offered by Geggus.

28. It is important to note that not all of the *loas* are African. The understanding of the *loas* (*lwas*) is derived from contact with a variety of sources. As a result, *loas* (*lwas*) such as Mademoiselle Charolette emerged. She is a white woman who, when present during ritual activities (as rare as this is), tends to speak French and behave in the manner of European high society.

29. Simpson, *Religious Cults of the Caribbean*, 238.

30. Deren, *Divine Horsemen*, 16, 56.

31. The debate concerning the relationship between Catholic saints and *lwas* is longer and much more detailed than can be presented here. Some argue that the connection is superficial (dissimulation at best), used by the slaves to maintain their African gods within an environment hostile to them. Others argue that the relationship is much more essential or syncretistic than that. Connected with this is the argument concerning whom devotees are possessed by. Many assert that devotees are possessed by the *lwas*—the African deities. Simpson (*Religious Cults of the Caribbean*, 287), however, argues that he knows of practitioners in the northern section of Haiti who are possessed by saints such as St. John, St. Peter, and St. Anthony. According to Simpson, some believe that the saints and *loas* are enigmatic beings and that the *loas* are displaced angels who select certain humans to worship them, and this worship is based upon fear. Nevertheless, even those who hold this belief at times discuss the saints and *loas* as if they were synonymous terms (ibid., 244–46). Within the Voodoo-Spiritual Temple discussed later in this chapter, possession often involves saints and Jesus, as well as ancestors, spirits, and *loas*. It should also be noted, in keeping with Deren's assertions (*Divine Horsemen*, 59), that there is also evidence of a syncretistic relationship between the *loas* and the Christian Trinity—Father, Son, and Holy Spirit—which corresponds to the vodun levels of cosmic authority: *loas*, ancestors, and the divine twins. Others argue that Legba, Erzulie, and Damballah are representative of the Trinity. For an example of this type of argument, see Riguad, *Secrets of Voodoo*.

Another interesting connection between vodou and the Judeo-Christian tradition involves Moses. Many argue that Moses learns vodun and is initiated by Jethro. Through this connection with vodun, Moses is able to perform the "magic" in front of Pharaoh. The place of worship constructed by Moses also resembles current vodou temples, with his staff serving as the central pole. For variations on and details concerning this story see Rigaud, *Secrets of Voodoo*, 14, 40–41; Theophus H. Smith, *Conjuring Culture: Biblical Formations of Black America* (New York: Oxford University Press, 1994), 32–54; Zora Neale Hurston, *Moses: Man of the Mountain* (New York: HarperPerennial, ca. 1939, 1991).

It should be kept in mind that the descriptions that follow are by no means complete; the genealogy and ontological status of the *loas* vary from locale to locale. Thus it is impossible to give definitive statements concerning the *lwas*. This is further problematized by their numerous manifestations. Owing to this, what I present are introductory statements meant to orientate the reader toward the complexity of vodou cosmology; these descriptions provide working definitions upon which the reader can further build with resources cited throughout the chapter.

32. See Laguerre, *Voodoo Heritage*, 44–46; Desmangles, *Faces of the Gods*, 15.

33. The rooster often found in lithographs of St. Peter is said to be a symbol of Legba and is also his companion. See Desmangles, *Faces of the Gods*, 113. It is commonly held in Haiti that

the *lwas* do not speak the same language; thus Legba functions as the medium between *lwas* and humans.

34. Depending upon the ritual, the *veves* are drawn on the ground around the central post in the *oum'phor.* They can be made with wheat flour, corn meal, wood ashes, powdered leaves, rice powder, and so forth. Although the material used to trace them may vary, only the priest or priestess may draw them. To draw them poorly will result in ineffective rituals because the *loa* are only obliged to appear when they are properly represented. The content of *veves* will vary from temple to temple. What is important is the maintenance or drawing of the *veve* in accordance with the tradition of that particular temple. The *lwas* are also represented or associated with the *govis* or jars containing items associated with the *loa* and held by a priest (*houn'gan*) or priestess (mambo). The *lwa* come into the jars in order to provide information during consultations between a *houn'gan* or mambo and a client/practitioner. Metraux (*Voodoo in Haiti,* 165–67) argues that *veves* are stylistically connected to France and the ironwork common in Europe during the nineteenth century. He suggests that the presence of *veves* as they appear in vodun are further evidence of syncretism between African (Dahomey) cultural realities and European cultural practices. According to other scholars, one will also find a picture of the Haitian president in the *oum'phor* (temple). This indicates the connection between voodoo and Haiti's political life.

35. Some accounts indicate that she is Creole; others suggest that she is Ethiopian, dark because of her association with Legba, the sun.

36. Other spellings include *Damballah* and *Danbala.*

37. Rigaud, *Secrets of Voodoo,* 90–91.

38. Desmangles, *Faces of the Gods,* 157.

39. Desmangles (ibid., 121) argues that the reference to St. John the Baptist is mistaken; the portrait is actually St. Isidore, the saint for agricultural workers.

40. Deren, *Divine Horsemen,* 110.

41. Laguerre, *Voodoo Heritage,* 95–97; Deren, *Divine Horsemen,* 38.

42. Deren, *Divine Horsemen,* 108.

43. Ibid., 38–39.

44. Ibid., 61. It is far too simplistic to suggest that Rada rituals are geared toward good and Petro toward evil. *Serviteurs*—practitioners—do not make this type of moral distinction. In fact, most practitioners work "with both hands"; life in Haiti requires the benefits of both approaches to the gods. The distinction is one of aggression, not one of moral or ethical conduct. Hence, there are some requests that are better handled by the Petro *loas* and others best handled by Rada *loas*. One provides service to the major *loa* and others who meet particular needs. It is far better to distinguish good and evil in terms of the work requested from the *loa* as opposed to locating this ontologically within the *loa*. Some argue, however, that the "pure" African *loas* respond to human requests only when approached through their particular rites (see Rigaud, *Secrets of Voodoo,* 132).

45. Other Petro manifestations include Mademoiselle Charolette. These two are interesting in part because they are European *loas*. According to Milo Rigaud (*Secrets of Voodoo,* 78), these two came to Haiti with the early colonists and eventually began manifesting in voodoo rites.

46. Deren, *Divine Horsemen,* 62. For a good study of the Haitian Revolution see James, *The Black Jacobins*. There is some debate over the genealogy of these rites and *loas*. Many argue that they are of Haitian development—a creolization. Others, such as David Geggus, argue for a strong connection between Petro and Congo rituals. He argues that it is not likely that the cult takes its name from a Don Pedro, but rather that Pedro was the name of seven Congo kings and was consequently a popular name readily found among Congo slaves. See David Geggus, "Haitian Voodoo in the Eighteenth Century: Language, Culture, Resistance."

47. Deren, *Divine Horsemen,* 273–74.

48. Simpson, *Religious Cults of the Caribbean,* 236. Also see James, *The Black Jacobins,* 86–87; Desmangles, *Faces of the Gods,* 33–36.

49. Guy S. Endore *Babouk* (New York: Monthly Review Press, ca. 1991), offers an interesting literary account.

50. Rigaud (*Secrets of Voodoo,* 66) lists twenty-three Congo *loas* and six distinguishable Ibo *loa.*

51. See Laguerre, *Voodoo Heritage,* 107–10.

52. Desmangles, *Faces of the Gods,* 63.

53. Deren, *Divine Horsemen,* 41, 44.

54. See Murphy, "Haitian Vodou," 23.

55. Deren, *Divine Horsemen,* 15–16, 27–30, 33, 36, 43–46.

56. For a detailed discussion of the hounfor and its contents see ibid., 181–84.

57. See Rigaud, *Secrets of Voodoo,* 8–10.

58. Deren, *Divine Horsemen,* 68.

59. For details and initiation accounts see Metraux, *Voodoo in Haiti,* 200–224; Katherine Dunham, *Island Possessed*; and Milo Rigaud, *Secrets of Voodoo.*

60. Deren, *Divine Horsemen,* 68.

61. Other instruments with ritual significance include the ogan and the triangle. For information on these instruments see Rigaud, *Secrets of Voodoo,* chap. 5. For more information on the ceremonies used to "renew" or "feed" the drums, see ibid., 115–20.

62. See Deren *Divine Horsemen,* chap. 4, for detailed information on vodun's priesthood. One enters the priesthood because of family line or the calling of a *loa.* In the latter case, the *loa*—through dreams, visions, misfortune, and the testimony of others—makes manifest this calling. The only way to balance life or to achieve happiness once the calling is known, is to surrender to the *loa* and provide service.

63. Ibid., 176.

64. See Rigaud, *Secrets of Voodoo,* 35–42, and Metraux, *Voodoo in Haiti,* 192–212.

65. According to Deren (*Divine Horsemen*) and Desmangles (*Faces of the Gods*), houn'gans are often members of the Masonic order and incorporate masonic knowledge and rituals (such as secret handshakes) into vodou practice.

66. Rigaud, *Secrets of Voodoo,* 31.

67. As is the case with North American spirituals, these vodou songs are layered and passed on by oral transmission, and are subject to spontaneous alterations. Thus they contain both a superficial and deeper meaning.

68. Deren, *Divine Horsemen,* 54.

69. For a detailed presentation of ritual activity see ibid., 202–28. Also of interest is the video "The Divine Horsemen," filmed by Deren.

70. At times, this power has been misused through what have been called "red sects." These groups, which go by names such as the "Hairless Pigs," make use of Petro rituals and human sacrifice not to correct wrongs but to create fear, ensure self-aggrandizement, and ultimately harm community. Their flaw, in essence, is their mutating of vodou's complexity and purpose into the strict exercise of sorcery. Consequently the members of "red sects" have been referred to as those who have rejected the tradition—*cabrit thomazos.* It is in light of such activities that the distinction between magic and religion is relevant. Religion revolves around communal renewal as opposed to individual gain; also, magic does not have religion's emphasis on metaphysical growth and development but instead involves the manipulation of forces in a purposely destructive way (Rigaud, *Secrets of Voodoo,* 164–66).

71. For a discussion of this "magic" see, e.g., Norman E. Whitten, Jr., "Contemporary Patterns of Malign Occultism among Negroes in North Carolina," *The Journal of American Folklore* 75, no. 298 (October/December, 1962): 311–25.

72. Jessie Gaston Mulira, "The Case of Voodoo in New Orleans," in Joseph E. Holloway, ed., *Africanisms in American Culture* (Bloomington: Indiana University Press, 1990), 35.

73. Albert Raboteau, *Slave Religion: The "Invisible Institution" in the Antebellum South* (New York: Oxford University Press, 1978), 76.

74. Albert J. Raboteau, "The Afro-American Traditions," in Ronald and Darrel W. Amundsen, eds., *Caring and Curing: Health and Medicine in the Western Religious Traditions* (New York: Macmillan, 1986). There is a great deal of debate concerning the African groups represented in New World slave populations. Some have given primacy to large numbers of Dahomean and Yorùbá groups; others, such as Robert Farris Thompson (*Flash of the Spirit*) argue for the existence of large numbers of Congolese and Angolan slaves in South America and the United States. Because we are more concerned with description of ritual practices and the theodicy suggested than with providing etymology for ritual terminology and detailed historiography, it is sufficient to mention the existence of this debate. For more information on the development of this debate see Thompson, ibid.; Bennetta Jules-Rosette, "Creative Spirituality from Africa to America: Cross-Cultural Influences in Contemporary Religious Forms," *The Western Journal of Black Studies* 4, no. 4 (Winter 1980): 273–85.

75. The term *voodoo* is most likely derivative of the Haitian term *vodou. Hoodoo*, then, would be an alteration of voodoo, related to changes in religious practice. Some suggest that the term *voodoo* is etymologically connected to Peter Valdo (founder of the French Vaudois or Waldenses) and thus would have been carried to the French West Indies and Louisiana. See Robert Tallant, *Voodoo in New Orleans* (New York: Collier Books, 1946; Macmillan, 1971), 19. This text should be read with caution. Others have suggested that it is connected to the European term *veaudeau*, which refers to African magical practices. For a discussion of this position see Zora Neale Hurston, "Hoodoo in America," *The Journal of American Folklore* 44, no. 174 (October–December, 1931): 317.

76. Charles Joyner, "'Believer I Know': The Emergence of African-American Christianity," in David G. Hackett, ed., *Religion and American Culture: A Reader* (New York: Routledge, 1995), 198.

77. Savannah Unit, Georgia Writers' Project, Work Projects Administration, *Drums and Shadows: Survival Studies Among the Georgia Coastal Negroes* (Garden City, N.Y.: Anchor Books, 1972), 25; Smith, *Conjuring Culture*, 34–43.

78. Raboteau, *Slave Religion,* 45–46.

79. Joyner, "'Believer I Know,'" 188.

80. For additional information on the religion of the Gullahs, see Margaret Washington Creel, *"A Peculiar People": Slave Religion and Community-Culture Among the Gullahs* (New York: New York University Press, 1988).

81. G. W. Nichols, "Six Weeks in Florida," *Harper's New Monthly Magazine* 41 (1870): 663.

82. Harry Middleton Hyatt, *Hoodoo—Conjuration—Witchcraft—Rootwork: Beliefs Accepted by Many Negroes and White Persons These Being Orally Recorded among Blacks and Whites*, 2 vols. (Washington: Distributed by American University Bookstore, 1970 [Hannibal, Mo.: Western Pub.]).

83. Hyatt, *Hoodoo* I:862.

84. Some of Hyatt's material also suggests Petro-like tendencies for St. Anthony. See ibid., 874–75.

85. Ibid., 869, 881–82.

86. Ibid., 876.

87. John Q. Anderson, "The New Orleans Voodoo Ritual Dance and Its Twentieth-Century Survivals," *The Southern Folklore Quarterly* 24 (1960): 135. Anderson makes use of Robert Tallant's *Voodoo in New Orleans*. It should be kept in mind, however, that much of what Tallant presents is the racist and religious paranoia of white Americans concerning the tradition. Thus it provides insight to the New Orleans reaction to voodoo.

88. Articles in papers such as the *Daily Picayune* during the late 1800s present accounts of these ceremonies that, when the racial bias and other stereotypical ideas are bracketed, show the "tourist-trap" nature of these ceremonies. Actual vodou had moved elsewhere, away from unworthy and prying eyes. Hurston provides insight into how information on voodoo rituals was transmitted between devotees without nonpractitioners being aware ("Hoodoo in America," 74).

89. Tallant, *Voodoo in New Orleans*, 23.

90. Raboteau, *Slave Religion*, 77; Tallant, *Voodoo in New Orleans*, 67.

91. Herskovits, *Dahomey*, 250.

92. Raboteau, *Slave Religion*, 77, 79.

93. For early statements concerning such practices as understood by popular media see, e.g., Chalmers S. Murray, "Edisto Negroes Close to Spirits," "Voodoo Gods Yet Alive on Islands," and "Voodoo Survivals Traced on Edisto," from the Chalmers S. Murray Papers located at the South Carolina Historical Society, Charleston.

94. Mulira, "The Case of Voodoo," 54. Also see Rod Davis, "Children of Yorùbá: The Religion the Bible Belt Wouldn't Allow Is Again Boiling to the Surface," *Southern Magazine* (February 1987): 35–41, 84–86. Davis blends Yorùbá and Dahomey terminology; however, several of his examples point to the development of new saints geared toward meeting the needs of African Americans in New Orleans.

95. Much interest in Marie Laveau has been generated in recent years. For a fictitious account of her life and activities, see the novel by Jewell Parker Rhodes, *Voodoo Dreams: A Novel of Marie Laveau* (New York: Picador USA, 1993). In order to enjoy this novel, the reader must be willing to relinquish a degree of historical accuracy.

96. Mulira, "The Case of Voodoo," 55.

97. Zora Neale Hurston, *Mules and Men* (1935; New York: Harper & Row, 1990), 229. Also see *Drums and Shadows*, e.g., xxiv and 54.

98. *Drums and Shadows*, 140.

99. Hurston, "Hoodoo in America," 327, 357, 362.

100. See, e.g., Hurston, *Of Mules and Men*, 195.

101. Renaldo J. Maduro, "Hoodoo Possession in San Francisco: Notes on Therapeutic Aspects of Regression," *Ethos* 3, no. 3 (Fall 1975): 429.

102. Ibid.

103. Ron Bodin, *Voodoo: Past and Present*, Louisiana Life Series 5 (The Center for Louisiana Studies, University of Southwestern Louisiana, 1990), 71. Chapter 2 suggests some overlap between vodou practices and Yorùbá religion as practiced in the United States. The U.S. context, I argue, did not allow for the same high level of differentiation present in Haiti and Cuba. In part this results from the attention given to African "nations" (of gods and people) on these two islands.

104. Another well-known practitioner is Luisah Teish, author of *Jambalaya* (San Francisco: Harper & Row, 1985) and *Carnival of the Spirit: Seasonal Celebrations and Rites of Passage* (San Francisco: HarperSanFrancisco, 1994).

105. Bodin, *Voodoo: Past and Present*, 80.

106. Articles on the museum's activities such as that on p. 6 of the New Orleans Tourist News (October 1992) reinforce suspicion. This article contains elements that suggest a romanticization and exoticization of the tradition for the benefit of tourists: "For the visitor to the Crescent City, Halloween Night will be an unmatched opportunity to see an authentic Voodoo Ritual, replete with exotic dances to the accompaniment of live drums. A spectacular snake dance—without which New Orleans Voodoo would not be what it is—will certainly be the highlight of the festivities."

107. Letter from the New Orleans Historic Voodoo Museum, 724 Dumaine, P.O. Box 70725, New Orleans, LA 70172. I thank one of my former students, Adam Posnak, for sharing a good deal of information on the Voodoo Museum with me.

108. Priest Oswan's and Priestess Miriam's thoughts on Obeah are found, e.g., in "Obeah, a Book in the Making," *Voodoo Realist Newsletter* 1, no. 5 (n.d.): 4–5.

109. Interview with Priestess Chamani, May 1996.

110. Ibid.

111. For information on Spiritual churches see Hans Baer, *The Black Spiritualist Movement: A Religious Response to Racism* (Knoxville: University of Tennessee Press, 1984); Claude F. Jacobs

and Andrew J. Kaslow, *The Spiritual Churches of New Orleans: Origins, Beliefs, and Rituals of an African American Religion* (Knoxville: University of Tennessee Press, 1991); Jason Berry, *The Spirit of Black Hawk: A Mystery of Africans and Indians* (Jackson: University Press of Mississippi, 1995).

112. Interview with Priestess Chamani, May 1996.

113. Ibid.

114. "About the Editors," *Voodoo Realist Newsletter* 1, no. 1 (n.d.): 2.

115. See Baer, *The Black Spiritualist Movement*; Hans Baer and Merrill Singer, *African-American Religion in the Twentieth Century: Varieties of Protest and Accommodation* (Knoxville: University of Tennessee Press, 1992).

116. Priest Oswan Chamani, "What does the word 'Voodoo' really mean?" *Voodoo Realist Newsletter* 1, no. 1 (n.d.): 3–4. Each issue of the *Newsletter* contains information on the meaning and content of voodoo. See, e.g., "Historical Background," *Voodoo Realist Newsletter* 2, no. 2 (1996): 1–2.

117. Priest Oswan Chamani and Priestess Miriam Williams, eds., *Voodoo Realist Newsletter* 1, no. 4 (n.d.): 4; *Voodoo Realist Newsletter* 4, no. 1 (n.d.): 1.

118. Interview with Priestess Chamani, May 1996.

119. *Voodoo Realist Newsletter* 4, no. 1 (n.d.): 4, 5.

120. Coverage of the Voodoo Spiritual Temple in the popular press includes Faith Quintavell, "True Voodoo," *The Inquirer* (December 8, 1996). *The Voodoo Realist Newsletter* is published by the Voodoo Spiritual Temple. Although I have been unable to secure a complete run of this newsletter, I have on file the following issues, which can be secured by writing to Priestess Miriam at the temple: vol. 1, nos. 1, 2, 3, and 5; vol. 2, no. 2.

121. The Voodoo Spiritual Temple has also extended its contact with the larger religious world through the Internet. Through its website, interested persons are able to secure information on the history and practices of the temple.

122. Priestess Miriam (interview, May, 1996), described Palo as a related means by which to expose oneself to the power of the spirit world. It allows one to harness the spiritual power of the universe for good or ill. Initiation does not guarantee this power, however; one must have Spirit in order to work. One can make use of negative or positive forces, both of which are considered legitimate depending upon one's objectives. Inner discipline is required in order to use Palo effectively because it centers on one's own traits, so that if one is "bad" it will make one worse. The aggression must be controlled; otherwise it is potentially dangerous, partly because of Palo's long-lasting effects. Those I spoke to connected Shango and other *orisha/loa* to Palo manifestations and activities.

123. Interview with Priestess Chamani, May 1996.

124. Ibid.

125. Karen McCarthy Brown, *Mama Lola: A Vodou Priestess in Brooklyn* (Berkeley: University of California Press, 1991), 10.

126. Desmangles, *Faces of the Gods,* 61, 96, 97.

127. Deren, *Divine Horsemen,* 89.

128. Ibid., 198.

129. Interview with Priestess Chamani, May 1996.

130. Ibid.

CHAPTER 2: ASHE!

1. Jacob K. Olupona, "The Study of Yorùbá Religious Tradition in Historical Perspective," *NUMEN* 40 (1993): 240–71. Ulysses Jenkins argues that the name Yorùbá is derived from "yo," from "yeye," and "ruba," from "rupa." "Yo" + "ruba" means "God's child causes me to live in this world." See Ulysses Jenkins, *Ancient African Religion and the African American Church* (Jacksonville, N.C.: Flame International, 1978).

2. George Brandon, *Santeria from Africa to the New World* (Bloomington: Indiana University Press, 1993), 20. Andrew Apter, *Black Critics and Kings: The Hermeneutics of Power in Yorùbá Society* (Chicago: The University of Chicago Press, 1992), presents an interesting discussion of the problematic nature of Yorùbá historiography resulting from a need to rely on mythic accounts couched in oral tradition. Apter provides economic and political rationales for changes in myth that are beyond the scope of my introductory and therefore summary presentation. Readers might find the following text of interest with respect to oral tradition as a source for history: S. O. Biobaku, *Sources of Yorùbá History* (Oxford: Clarendon Press, 1973).

Early in its history, Yorùbáland was divided into two groups, one associated with the savannah (Oyo) and one associated with the forest (Ifè).

3. J. F. Ade Ajayi and Robert Smith, *Yorùbá Warfare in the Nineteenth Century* (London: Cambridge University Press/Institute of African Studies of the University of Ibadan, 1964), 2.

4. Quoted in Robert Farris Thompson, *Flash of the Spirit: African and Afro-American Art and Philosophy* (New York: Vintage Books, 1983), 3.

5. Other accounts state that Odùdúwà was the son of Olódùmarè, the high God. In these accounts, Odùdúwà is responsible for the creation of earth using a bit of dirt and a cock. He begins this process of developing earth in Ile Ifè. In either case, what is most important here is that Odùdúwà is considered to be the ancestor of the Yorùbá.

6. Thomas Hodgkin, *Nigerian Perspectives: An Historical Anthology* (London: Oxford University Press, 1960), 59–61.

7. R. C. C. Law, "Traditional History," in S. O. Biobaku, ed., *Sources of Yorùbá History,* 27–28.

8. Sir Alan Burns, *History of Nigeria* (London: George Allen and Unwin Ltd., 1972), 27–28.

9. For a concise discussion of traditional Yorùbá religion in contemporary Nigeria, see Wande Abimbola, "The Place of African Traditional Religion in Contemporary Africa: The Yorùbá Example," 51–58, in Jacob K. Olupona, ed., *African Traditional Religions: In Contemporary Society* (New York: Paragon House, 1991). For a concise discussion of *àse* see Roland Hallgren, *The Vital Force: A Study of Ase in the Traditional and Neo-traditional Culture of the Yorùbá People* (Lund, Sweden: University of Lund Press, 1995).

10. For this section I have relied heavily on E. Bólájí Ìdòwú, *Olódùmarè: God in Yorùbá Belief* (1962; New York: Wazobia, 1994).

11. Thompson, *Flash of the Spirit,* 18.

12. For a good study of divination, see William Bascom, *Ifa Divination: Communication between Gods and Men in West Africa* (Bloomington: Indiana University Press, 1969).

13. Joseph M. Murphy, *Santería: African Spirits in America* (Boston: Beacon Press, 1988, 1993), 17.

14. Ibid., 18.

15. Thompson, *Flash of the Spirit,* 42.

16. For a very good collection of essays related to this deity, see Sandra T. Barnes, *Africa's Ògún: Old World and New* (Bloomington: Indiana University Press, 1989).

17. Ìdòwú, *Olódùmarè,* 91.

18. Ìdòwú points out that this deity was not the first associated with thunder and lightening; Jàkúta was actually the first. See ibid., 93–95. In some accounts, Sàngó is spoken of as the fourth king of Oyo.

19. Thompson, *Flash of the Spirit,* 85.

20. Ìdòwú, *Olódùmarè,* 90.

21. Ibid., 71–72.

22. Ibid., 19. It is possible that there is a connection between this deity and Odùdúwà, the first ancestor. See ibid., 18–29.

23. Ìdòwú argues that he was actually a divinity and the name was later used as a reference to the first ancestor. See Ìdòwú, *Olódùmarè,* 22–29.

24. Ibid., 192.

25. Ibid, 69.

26. Ibid., 169.

27. Ibid., 169–73.

28. Ibid., 155. For an outline of the elements of character see pp. 156–58.

29. Hallgren, *The Vital Force*; Jacob K. Olupona, "Major Issues in the Study of African Traditional Religion," in Olupona, editor, *African Traditional Religions*; 25–33; C. Osamaro IBIE, *Ifism: The Complete Work of Orunmila* (Lagos, Nigeria: Efehi Ltd., 1986); William Bascom, *Sixteen Cowries: Yorùbá Divination from Africa to the New World* (Bloomington: Indiana University Press, 1980).

30. Treatments of Yorùbá history and power relations include: Burns, *History of Nigeria*; Apter, *Black Critics and Kings*.

31. Jaime Suchlicki, *Cuba: From Columbus to Castro and Beyond*, 4th ed. (Washington: Brassey's, 1997), 13.

32. Ibid., 4–5, 17–19.

33. Herbert S. Klein, *Slavery in the Americas: A Comparative Study of Virginia and Cuba* (Chicago: University of Chicago Press, 1967), 11–12.

34. Ibid., 66. As Klein indicates, Spain had slavery policies in place before the 1492 encounter with the Americas. These policies were not developed with the demands and contextual needs of the Americas in mind, however. Hence, changes were necessary that addressed the crown's desire for control over the colonies, Spain's economic concerns, and the demands for labor and a working social structure in Cuba (57–85).

35. Ibid., 28.

36. Brandon, *Santería from Africa to the New World*, 55.

37. Kenneth F. Kiple, *Blacks in Colonial Cuba, 1774–1899* (Gainesville: University of Florida, 1976), 4–8.

38. See e.g., Brandon, *Santería from Africa to the New World*, 52–55.

39. Hugh Thomas, "Cuba, c. 1750–c.1860," in Leslie Bethell, ed., *Cuba: A Short History* (Cambridge, England: Cambridge University Press, 1993), 8–9.

40. Klein, *Slavery in the Americas*, 73.

41. The slave trade "officially" ended in 1817 for Cuba, but slaves were illegally brought to the island as late as 1835. By 1868, the Cuban population would be roughly half of Spanish origin and half Black, with some others also represented but in very small numbers. See Thomas, "Cuba," 20.

42. Brandon, *Santería from Africa to the New World*, 46.

43. Antonio Dominguez Ortiz, *The Golden Age of Spain, 1516–1659* (New York: Basic Books, 1971), 211; quoted in Brandon, *Santería from Africa to the New World*, 46.

44. Klein, *Slavery in the Americas*, 86–87.

45. *Recopilación de leyes de los reynos de las Indias*, 3 vols. (Madrid: D. Joaquin Ibara, 1791), quoted in Klein, *Slavery in the Americas*, 91.

46. Quoted in Klein, *Slavery in the Americas*, 100.

47. Ibid.

48. Ibid., 47.

49. This is not the only African-based tradition found in the Cuban context. Others include *Palo Monte* and *Palo Mayumbe* associated with slaves from the Congo. Other more recent traditions also include *Espiritismo*, which includes Kardecian spiritism with other religious elements.

50. Steven Gregory, "Santeria in New York City: A Study in Cultural Resistance," Ph.D. dissertation, New School of Social Research, 1991, 39.

51. For an interesting comparison of African-derived religions in Cuba, Puerto Rico, and the Dominican Republic, see George Brandon, "African Religious Influences in Cuba, Puerto Rico and Hispaniola," *Journal of Caribbean Studies* 7, nos. 2/3 (Winter 1989/Spring 1990): 201–31. In this discussion of Santería I do not divide the tradition's development into stages. For a study that does this see Brandon, *Santería from Africa to the New World*.

52. Brandon, *Santería from Africa to the New World*, 75.

53. Contemporary accounts of the initiation process and the "secrets" of the tradition (in Cuba, Puerto Rico, and the United States) are becoming more widely available, as initiates write books (in English) and encourage appreciation of the religion through the sharing of information. Among these are Migene González-Wippler *The Santeria Experience: A Journey into the Miraculous* (St. Paul, Minn.: Llewellyn Publications, 1992); Migene González-Wippler, *Legends of Santeria* (St. Paul, Minn.: Llewellyn Publications, 1994); Philip John Neimark, *The Way of the Orisa: Empowering Your Life through the Ancient African Religion of Ifa* (San Francisco: HarperSanFrancisco, 1993); Luis Manuel Núñez, *Santeria: A Practical Guide to Afro-Caribbean Magic* (Dallas: Spring Publications, Inc., 1992); Gary Edwards and John Mason, *Black Gods: Orisa Studies in the New World* (Brooklyn, N.Y.: Yorùbá Theological Archministry, 1985); John Mason, *Orin Òrìsà: Songs for Selected Heads* (Brooklyn, NY: Yorùbá Theological Archministry, 1992); Raul Canizares, *Walking with the Night: The Afro-Cuban World of Santeria* (Rochester, Vt.: Destiny Books, 1993).

54. Joseph M. Murphy, *Working the Spirit: Ceremonies of the African Diaspora* (Boston: Beacon Press, 1994), 84.

55. Ibid., 85. Raul Canizares' outline of religious hierarchy is also worth noting. See Canizares, *Walking with the Night* chap. 4.

56. Murphy, *Working the Spirit,* 86.

57. Murphy, *Santería,* 87. An interesting video that provides some information on initiation within the Puerto Rican context is Judith Gleason and Elise Mereghetti, "The King Does Not Lie: The Initiation of a Shango Priest," distributed by Filmakers Library, New York, 1992. Also see Murphy, *Working the Spirit,* 92–109.

58. Canizares, *Walking with the Night,* 30–31.

59. Brandon, "African Religious Influences," 76–78.

60. For a personal account of Santería in Puerto Rico, see González-Wippler, *The Santería Experience.*

61. Canizares, *Walking with the Night,* 32.

62. Ibid., 33–34. Also see Murphy, *Working the Spirit,* chap. 4.

63. Canizares, *Walking with the Night,* 35–37.

64. Ibid.

65. Murphy, *Working the Spirit,* 104–9.

66. Brandon, "African Religious Influences," 85. For information on the Afro-Cuban movement see, e.g., the work of Fernando Ortiz. English translations include Fernando Ortiz, *Cuban Counterpoint* (New York: Vintage Books, 1970).

67. Brandon, "African Religious Influences," 99–100.

68. George Eaton Simpson, *Black Religions in the New World* (New York: Columbia University Press, 1978), 19.

69. Albert J. Raboteau, "The Afro-American Traditions," Ronald and Darrel W. Amundsen, eds., *Caring and Curing: Health and Medicine in the Western Religious Traditions* (New York: Macmillan, 1986), 546.

70. Harry Middleton Hyatt, *Hoodoo—Conjuration—Witchcraft—Rootwork,* vol. 1 (Washington, D.C.: Distributed by American University Bookstore, 1970 [Hannibal, Mo.: Western Pub.]), 870.

71. Ibid. 2:1220–21.

72. Erika E. Bourguigeon, "Afro-American Religions: Traditions and Transformations," 191–202, in John F. Szwed, ed., *Black America* (New York: Basic Books, 1970), 196.

73. Murphy, *Santería,* chap. 3.

74. Ibid., 50.

75. Gregory, *Santeria in New York City,* 67.

76. Ibid., 55. Some of this information is available in Steven Gregory, "Afro-Caribbean Religion in New York City: The Case of Santería," in Constance R. Sutton and Elsa M. Chaney, eds., *Caribbean Life in New York City: Sociocultural Dimensions* (New York: Center for Migration

Studies of New York, Inc., 1994): 287–302. Also see Migene Gonzalez-Wippler, *The Santería Experience: A Journey into the Miraculous,* rev. and expanded ed. (St. Paul, Minn.: Llewellyn Publications, 1992). Canizares claims that he has evidence suggesting that Afro-Cuban groups practiced in Florida as early as 1939 (*Walking with the Night,* 122–23).

77. Canizares, *Walking with the Night,* 125.

78. Marta Moreno Vega, "The Yorùbá Orisha Tradition Comes to New York City," in *African American Review* 29 (November 2, 1995): 201–2. An interesting popular account of Santería is Karl Vick, "Gods Help Us All," *The Washington Post* (July 2, 1995): F1, F5. Another story in this issue of the *Post* is also worth noting: William Booth, "At a Miami Courthouse: A Chicken in Every Spot," F1, F2.

79. Interview with Chief Medahochi K. O. Zannu, February 1996, Milwaukee, Wisconsin.

80. See Vega, "The Yorùbá Orisha Tradition Comes to New York City." Readers should also be aware of the Caribbean Cultural Center, 408 W. 59th Street, New York, NY 10019, which published *African Religion in the Caribbean: Santeria and Voudon* (New York: Caribbean Cultural Center, n.d.).

81. Brandon, *Santería from Africa to the New World,* 104–5, 107. For interesting work on an African American house, see Mary Elaine Curry, "Making the Gods in New York: The Yorùbá Religion in the Black Community," Ph.D. dissertation, City University of New York, 1991. Curry asserts that most African American initiates are descendants of either Omi Duro or Osa Unko; both have their roots in Ofun Che in Regla, near Havanna (151).

82. Murphy, *Santería,* 54.

83. Gregory, "Afro-Caribbean Religion in New York City," 295. For more information on this particular house see Gregory, "Santería in New York City," 70–102.

84. Gregory, "Santería in New York City," 72, 77–78, 79.

85. Ibid., 69.

86. Curry, "Making the Gods in New York," 154, 159; Steven Gregory, "Santería in New York City," 5.

87. For extensive information on particular African American houses see, e.g., Gregory, "Santeria in New York City"; Curry, "Making the Gods in New York"; Brandon, *Santeria from Africa to the New World,* chap. 5; Canizares, *Walking with the Night,* 121–26; Vega, "The Yorùbá Orisha Tradition Comes to New York City."

88. Curry, "Making the Gods in New York," 48.

89. Ibid., 139, 142–53.

90. Biographical sketch of H.R.H. Oseijeman Adefunmi I provided by Oyotunji African Village.

91. Stephen C. Clapp, "A Reporter at Large: African Theological Arch-Ministry, Inc." (New York Public Library: Schomburg Collection), 10.

92. Carl M. Hunt, *Oyotunji Village: The Yorùbá Movement in America* (Washington, D.C.: University Press of America, 1979), 24.

93. Clapp, "A Reporter at Large," 11.

94. Hunt, *Oyotunji Village,* 25.

95. Interview with H.R.H. Oba Adefunmi I, April 1996, the Palace of Oyotunji African Village.

96. Biographical sketch made available by Oyotunji African Village and also based upon an interview with Oba Adefunmi I, April 1996, for which I am grateful.

97. Interview with Oba Adefunmi I, April 1996.

98. Biographical sketch provided by Oyotunji African Village.

99. Clapp, "A Reporter at Large," 5.

100. Ibid., 4.

101. As Raul Canizares indicates, however, this secrecy is questioned by many non-Cuban priests who want to adapt the tradition to its new U.S. context. See *Walking with the Night,* "Secrecy and Survival," beginning on p. 26.

102. Clapp, "A Reporter at Large," 3.

103. Gregory, "Santería in New York City," 62; S. Cohn, "Ethnic Identity in New York City: The Yorùbá Temple of Harlem," M.A. thesis, New York University, 1973.

104. Hunt, *Oyotunji Village,* 30.

105. Ibid., 30–31.

106. Adefunmi would separate from his wife in 1965 due to the demands of his nationalist perspective. In 1962, Adefunmi helped two practitioners establish a Yorùbá Temple in Gary, Indiana. One of these two men would be among the first persons initiated by Adefunmi in Oyotunji Village, in 1970.

107. Clapp, "A Reporter at Large," 25–26.

108. Edwards and Mason, *Black Gods.* The Yorùbá Theological Archministry sponsors classes on Yorùbá cooking, language, theology, and songs. Mason, along with others, is responsible for putting much of this information into English. Adefunmi's group considers itself orthodox and Mason as moderate because of his work outside African American communities. Those such as Philip Neimark (Fagbamila), a white American and head of the Ifa Foundation of North America, are held in contempt. Neimark's friend Afolabi Epega argues, however, for full inclusion of Neimark and others based upon the centrality of Ile Ifé for all human life:

> Ifa is not a black religion; it is an African religion originating from Ile Ifé in what is now the nation of Nigeria. Oosanla or Obàtálá as he is better known in the West, one of our most important *orìsàs,* was white. Ifa teaches that people of all colors where born into the earth from Ile Ifé. (Neimark, *The Way of the Orisa,* xv)

109. H.R.H. Oseijeman Adefunmi I, "Keynote Address," Columbia University, New York: January 16, 1993.

110. Clapp, "A Reporter at Large," 16.

111. Ibid., 16.

112. Ibid., 18.

113. Ibid., 5–6.

114. Ibid., 6–8.

115. Ibid., 20.

116. Interview with Chief Ajamu, April 1996, Oyotunji African Village.

117. Hunt, *Oyotunji Village,* 55. Also see Carlos Canet, *Oyotunji* (Miami: Editorial AIP, n.d.). A copy of this document is available through the University of Illinois, Urbana-Champaign.

118. Hunt (*Oyotunji Village*) outlines the levels of authority within the Village in this way: it is a monarchical socialism. The state controls all vital resources (e.g., water, land, minerals). The king represents the state and is the chief priest of the Village and the society of chiefs (the Ogboni Society). The latter provides for religious, social, political, and personal continuation of the Village. The criteria for the position of chief are priesthood and functional use of Yorùbá. There are two types of chief—district and town. District chiefs are responsible for the various segments into which the village is divided and town chiefs perform functions related to the entire village (69). Details on the governance of the Village are beyond the scope of this treatment; for more information see ibid., 70–74.

119. Ibid., 56.

120. Children start their schooling at the age of six, learning informally prior to that. Adults also take part in the Yorùbá Royal Academy. In both cases the educational format separates males and female. With respect to adults the Akinkonju Society (men) and the Egbebinrin Society (women) handle the process respectively.

121. Hunt, *Oyotunji Village,* 60.

122. Ibid., 40.

123. Ibid., 86.

124. HRH Oba Oseijeman Adefunmi I, *OLORISHA,* 7.

125. Biographical sketch provided by Oyotunji African Village.

126. HRH Oba Oseijeman Adefunmi I, *OLORISHA: A Guidebook into Yorùbá Religion* (Oyotunji Village: Great Benin Books, 1982), 1. This text provides important initiation information that readers will find of interest.

127. Medahochi K. O. Zannu, interview, March 20, 1995.

128. The first Orisa Temple was built in this new community in 1971.

129. Oba Adefunmi I, *OLORISHA*, 23. This information was also provided during an interview with Oba Adefunmi I. This astral association is not unique to this particular tradition. According to writers such as Milo Rigaud, *Secrets of Voodoo* (San Francisco: City Lights Books, 1953), this practice is also found within voodoo through the association, for example, of Baron Samedi (chief *loa* of the cemetery) with Saturn.

130. Oba Oseijeman Adefunmi I, *OLORISHA*, 7.

131. Interview with Chief Ajamu, April 1996.

132. It is likely that the *Egúngún* society did not survive in Cuba (and in Santería in the United States) because of the high cost of funeral ceremonies and other restrictions placed upon slaves.

133. Hunt, *Oyotunji Village*, 82.

134. For details see Oba Adefunmi I, *OLORISHA*, 29–36.

135. Adefunmi I, "Keynote Address," 14. Much of this training takes place in the Royal Academy, the school in the Village. As a result of fire in 1996, this structure, along with the archive/library and temple for Obàtálá, was destroyed. Efforts to rebuild are under way.

136. Oba Adefunmi I, *OLORISHA*, 27–28.

137. Thompson, *Flash of the Spirit*, 5–6.

138. Clapp, "A Reporter at Large," 27.

139. Interview with Oba Adefunmi I, April 1996.

140. Ibid.

141. Ibid.

142. Ibid.

143. H.R.H. Oseijeman Adefunmi I, "Keynote Address," 7.

144. Interview with Oba Adefunmi I, April 1996.

145. H.R.H. Oseijeman Adefunmi I, "Keynote Address," 4.

146. Interview with Oba Adefunmi I, April 1996.

147. Ibid.

CHAPTER 3: THE GREAT MAHDI HAS COME!

1. Alfred Guillaume, *Islam* (New York: Penguin Books, 1986), 4–5.

2. Ibid., 8–9.

3. Ibid., 24–25.

4. Ibid., 28–29.

5. Kenneth Cragg, *The Call of the Minaret*, 2d ed. (Maryknoll, N.Y.: Orbis Books, 1985), 70–71.

6. Guillaume, *Islam*, 31.

7. The word *Allah* means god and, in terms of etymology, is associated with the Arabian term *Ilah*, a reference to the moon god. "In Arabia Allah was known from Christian and Jewish sources as the one god, and there can be no doubt whatever that he was known to the pagan Arabs of Mecca as the supreme being. Were this not so, the Qur'ān would have been unintelligible to the Meccans" (ibid., 7).

8. Ibid., 38.

9. Cragg, *Call of the Minaret*, 72–73.

10. The recording of the prophet's words in the beginning was haphazard. Verses were written on palm leaves, stones, the shoulder-blades of animals—in short, on any material which was available. Tradition associates the collection of all this material, together with

what men had committed to memory, to Abu Bakr, the first Caliph, and alternatively to his successor "Umar who died before the work was completed" (Guillaume, *Islam*, 57)

11. Sura 4:135; quoted in ibid., 63.

12. Cragg, *Call of the Minaret*, 81–82.

13. Guillaume, *Islam*, 57.

14. The Hebrew Scriptures and Christian New Testament have value, but they have been tampered with by humans. An example of this tampering is found in the Jews' "demoting" of Jesus Christ, and the Christians' "promotion" of Jesus Christ to the status of God.

15. There is also the *sadaqāt* or voluntary contributions to the poor.

16. See Cragg, *Call of the Minaret*, 97–98, for details on the posture for prayer.

17. Ibid., 67.

18. Quoted in Guillaume, *Islam*, 67.

19. Ibid., 67.

20. Cragg, *Call of the Minaret*, 137, 138.

21. Ibid., 103–4.

22. Guillaume, *Islam*, 70.

23. Cragg, *Call of the Minaret*, 109.

24. Ibid., 29–34, 60.

25. Ibid., 96, 101.

26. Ibid., 103.

27. Guillaume, *Islam*, 79–80. Once areas were sufficiently occupied, non-Muslim residents were taxed. This resulted in a significant conversion rate, although Christians and Jews were allowed to continue their practices as people of the book.

28. For information on the development of Islam in Africa along these lines see, e.g., Douglass Grant *The Fortunate Slave: An Illustration of African Slavery in the Early 18th Century* (New York: Oxford University Press, 1968).

29. Michael A. Gomez, "Muslims in Early America," *The Journal of Southern History* 60, no. 4 (November 1994): 674.

30. Richard Brent Turner, *Islam in the African-American Experience* (Indianapolis: Indiana University Press, 1997), 16–17.

31. Gomez, "Muslims in Early America," 674–75.

32. See e.g., Noel Q. King, "Encounters between Islam and the African Traditional Religions," 296–311, in Alford T. Welch and Pierre Cachia, eds., *Islam: Past Influence and Present Challenge* (Albany: State University of New York Press, 1979).

33. Also of interest in terms of the link between African and African American Islamic experience is Turner, *Islam in the African-American Experience*.

34. Allan D. Austin, *African Muslims in Antebellum America: Transatlantic Stories and Spiritual Struggles* (New York: Routledge, 1997), 22.

35. Ivan Van Sertima, *They Came before Columbus* (New York: Random House, ca. 1976); Ivan Van Sertima, ed., *African Presence in Early America* (New Brunswick, N.J.: Transaction Books, ca. 1987).

36. C. Eric Lincoln, *The Black Muslims in America*, 3d ed. (Grand Rapids: Wm. B. Eerdmans, 1994), 257.

37. Gomez, "Muslims in Early America," 685. Also see Sir Charles Lyell, F.R.S., *A Second Visit to the United States of North America*, vol. 1 (New York: Harper & Brothers, 1849), 263.

38. Austin, *African Muslims in Antebellum America*, 14.

39. Ibid.

40. Grant, *The Fortunate Slave*, 83.

41. Mattias Gardell, *In the Name of Elijah Muhammad: Louis Farrakhan and the Nation of Islam* (Durham: Duke University Press, 1996), 34. See also Austin, *African Muslims in Antebellum America*, and Georgia Writers Project, *Drum and Shadows*.

42. Austin, *African Muslims in Antebellum America*, 96–99, 111.

43. Ibid., 6, 17; 129.

44. Ibid., 37, 40. See also Charles Ball, *Slavery in the United States: A Narrative of the Life and Adventures of Charles Ball, a Black Man* (New York: Negro Universities Press, 1969; John S. Taylor, 1837), 164–65.

45. Gomez, "Muslims in Early America," 698.

46. The debate over the strength of the retention of Islam in former slave communities is ongoing. Some scholars such as Gardell (*In the Name of Elijah Muhammad*) argue against an Islamic "memory" that connects Islamic practices during the antebellum period with contemporary manifestations such as the Nation of Islam. I disagree with Gardell and think that he focuses on the "quality" of Islamic practice within these various time periods, whereas I focus less on quality and more on quantity and possibility. It strikes me that in the Americas, the various forces that shaped religious developments do not allow for a resolution to this issue in terms of "quality" of religious experience.

47. Wilson Jeremiah Moses, "Assimilationist Black Nationalism, 1890–1925," in *The Wings of Ethiopia: Studies in African American Life and Letters* (Ames: Iowa State University Press, 1990), 102. The twentieth-century march of Islam into African American communities does not begin, however, with the Nation of Islam, although none would be as successful as the Nation of Islam. Hence, although groups such as the Ahmadiyya from Pakistan made contact during the early twentieth century, they did not attract significant numbers of African Americans. This had to be due, in part, to this movement's origins outside of the United States and, thus, its failure adequately to understand the issues to which African Americans responded through religious practices.

48. See Gayraud Wilmore, *Black Religion and Black Radicalism: An Interpretation of the Religious History of Afro-American People*, 2d ed. (Maryknoll, N.Y.: Orbis Books, 1983).

49. For information on the various African American Islamic communities within the United States see Aminah Beverly McCloud, *African American Islam* (New York: Routledge, 1995). For a concise discussion of the Moorish Science Temple of America see Yvonne Yazbeck Haddad and Jane Idleman Smith, "The Moorish Science Temple of America," 79–104, in *Mission to America: Five Islamic Sectarian Communities in North America* (Gainesville: University Press of Florida, 1993).

50. McCloud, *African American Islam*, 11; Haddad and Smith, "Moorish Science Temple of America," 87.

51. For a concise introduction to the Moorish Science Temple see Haddad and Smith, "The Moorish Science Temple of America."

52. See E. U. Essien-Udom, *Black Nationalism: A Search for Identity in America* (Chicago: University of Chicago Press, 1962), 33–36.

53. Quoted in McCloud, *African American Islam*, 13–14.

54. Ibid., 12–13.

55. Ibid., 14–15.

56. Ibid., 34.

57. Quoted in Essien-Udom, *Black Nationalism*, 35.

58. There is some debate concerning the date of Drew Ali's death. McCloud (*African American Islam*, 18) marks it as 1920, while Essiem-Udom (*Black Nationalism*, 35) notes it as 1929.

59. McCloud (*African American Islam*) asserts that the Moorish-American community considers itself a part of the larger Islamic world. For information on the current Moorish-American community see ibid. as well as publications by the community: *Moorish Guide National Edition*; *Moorish Science Monitor*; *Moorish Scribe*; *Moorish Review*; *Moorish Voice*; and *Moorish American Voice*.

60. Arna Bontemps and Jack Conroy (*Any Place But Here* [New York: Hill and Wang, 1966], 217) argue for this type of connection between Noble Drew Ali and Master Fard Muhammad. Gardell, convincingly demonstrates why Bontemps, Conroy, Marsh, and Essiem-Udom are

incorrect (*In the name of Elijah Muhammad*, 51). See Gardell chap. 3, n. 19, for reference information on the authors mentioned. Abbie Wyhte, in "Christian Elements in Negro American Muslim Religious Beliefs" (*Phylon*, 4th Quarter [Winter 1964]: 382–88), argues for this type of link. I find her argument less than convincing, however.

61. Clifton E. Marsh is not as convinced as some scholars that Fard's work is distinctive. He maintains that Fard was inspired by the work of Noble Drew Ali and knowingly made use of similar information. His book provides an interesting comparison of the Nation of Islam and the Moorish Science Temple. See Clifton E. Marsh, *From Black Muslims to Muslims: The Resurrection, Transformation, and Change of the Lost-Found Nation of Islam in America, 1930–1995*, 2d ed. (Lanham, Md.: Scarecrow Press, 1996).

62. Elijah Muhammad, "Foreword," in *The True History of Master Fard Muhammad*, ed. Nasir Makr Hakim (Atlanta: Messenger Elijah Muhammad Propagation Society, 1996), xliv–xlv.

63. One of the first treatments of the Nation of Islam is Erdmann Doane Beynon, *Master Fard Muhammad: Detroit History* (n.p., n.d.), first published as: "The Voodoo Cult among Negro Migrants in Detroit," *American Journal of Sociology* 43 (1938): 894–907. Another important and early treatment of the Nation of Islam is Hatim Sahib, "The Nation of Islam," Master's thesis, University of Chicago, 1951.

64. Gardell, *In the Name of Elijah Muhammad*, 155.

65. Other names associated with Master Fard Muhammad are Mr. F. Mohammad Ali, Professor Ford, Mr. Wali Fard, and W. D. Fard. For another theory on Master Fard Muhammad's identity see Howard Brotz, *The Black Jews of Harlem: Negro Nationalism and the Dilemmas of Negro Leadership* (New York: Schocken Books, 1970), 11–13.

66. Essien-Udom, *Black Nationalism*, 43.

67. Turner, *Islam in the African-American Experience*, 150.

68. Beynon, "The Voodoo Cult among Negro Migrants in Detroit," 895.

69. Arthur Magida, *Prophet of Rage: A Life of Louis Farrakhan and His Nation* (New York: Basic Books, 1996), 47–48.

70. This lost-found reference recalls Jesus' parable of the lost sheep and the shepherd's search for the one missing.

71. According to Essien-Udom (*Black Nationalism*, 77, n. 37), until 1935, members of the Nation of Islam dressed in a manner similar to those of the Moorish-Science Temple, but this was stopped in order to avoid confusion between the two groups.

72. With respect to the possibility of the influence of early Islamic thought on twentieth-century developments, the following is useful: "Given the fact that Sandersville [the birthplace of Elijah Muhammad] was fairly close to the Georgia coast, where a crude form of Islam was practiced by descendants of slaves who had been Muslims in Africa, and the fact that Elijah's father's first name, Wali, was an Arabic term for a holy man or saint who performed 'miraculous feats,' Islam may have appealed to Elijah Muhammad [early leader of the Nation of Islam] because he was exposed to its vocabulary and concepts as a child" (Magida, *Prophet of Rage*, 35–36).

73. Claude Clegg, *An Original Man* (Boston: St. Martin's Press, 1996), 17. The two spellings of Muhammad are found in this text.

74. Essien-Udom, *Black Nationalism*, 79.

75. Clegg, *An Original Man*, 22.

76. Ibid., 23.

77. This tension might have reached a critical level even prior to Fard's departure if it had not been for other problems, such as the association of the Nation of Islam with human sacrifice. For information on this, see Benyon, "The Voodoo Cult among Negro Migrants in Detroit," 903–4; and Clegg, *An Original Man*, 29–33.

78. In part this trouble involved a literal interpretation of what the Nation considers the symbolic killing of four "white devils." Master Fard taught that the Muslim who "killed" four devils would receive free passage to Mecca. The Nation claims that this symbolism involves the

elimination of a demonic mentality of supremacy, not the physical harming of Caucasians. Nonetheless, sacrificial murder by a few who claimed membership in the Nation resulted in the arrest of Fard and a string of legal problems for the Nation. In addition, some took literally Master Fard's teaching that Muslims should willingly sacrifice themselves for the good of the religion. For information on this, see Beynon, "The Voodoo Cult among Negro Migrants in Detroit," 903–4; C. Eric Lincoln, *The Black Muslims in America*, 3d ed. (Grand Rapids: Wm. B. Eerdmans, 1994), 204–5; Magida, *Prophet of Rage*, 49–52; Gardell, *In the Name of Elijah Muhammad*, 55–57; Martha Lee, *The Nation of Islam: An American Millennarian Movement* (Lewiston, N.Y.: Edwin Mellen Press, 1988; Syracuse University Press, 1991), 24–25.

79. Because of this chapter's concentration on the development of the Nation of Islam, attention is not given to Malcolm X other than to mention his role in its growth. For information on Malcolm X, see Malcolm X, *The Autobiography, as Told to Alex Haley* (New York: Ballantine Books, 1965); George Breitman, ed., *By Any Means Necessary* (New York: Pathfinder, 1970); Bruce Perry, ed., *Malcolm X: The Last Speeches* (New York: Pathfinder, 1989); Bruce Perry, *Malcolm: The Life of a Man Who Changed Black America* (Barrytown, N.Y.: Station Hill Press, 1991); James H. Cone, *Martin and Malcolm and America: A Dream or a Nightmare?* (Maryknoll, N.Y.: Orbis Books, 1991); Michael E. Dyson, *Making Malcolm: The Myth and Meaning of Malcolm X* (New York: Oxford University Press, 1995).

80. Elijah Muhammad's romanticized notions of the Middle East were shattered by his first-hand contact with that area, which exposed him to the manner in which humanity was exploited by those he had once considered fair, just, and righteous people. Nonetheless, the appeal of his message increased.

81. Elijah Muhammad, *Message to the Black Man in America* (Philadelphia: Hakim's Publications, 1965), 189.

82. See ibid.

83. Lincoln, *Black Muslims in America*, 27.

84. Ibid., 74.

85. See Elijah Muhammad, *Our Saviour Has Arrived* (Newport News, Va.: United Brothers Communications Systems, 1996).

86. Essein-Udom, *Black Nationalism*, 201.

87. Early in its history, several from the Middle East who sought access to various temples were denied admittance. Yet others were not only admitted but played key roles in training Muslims in Arabic and other essentials. When they were denied admittance, it was often explained to them that: (1) those seeking entrance already had knowledge of Islam and that the temple gave primary attention to those with little or no knowledge of the religion; (2) many Eastern Muslims in the United States have lost sight of the true teachings of Islam.

Elijah Muhammad made these and other views known through newspapers such as the *New Crusader*, the *Herald-Dispatch*, the *Amsterdam News*, and the Nation's various publications. At one point, as expressed in *Message to the Black Man*, Caucasians were denied admission to public functions because of harassment by white law enforcement groups.

88. Reprinted in Essein-Udom, *Black Nationalism*, 200.

89. Ibid., 191–92.

90. Muhammad, *The True History of Master Fard Muhammad*, 34.

91. For an early account of the University of Islam, see "Detroit's University of Islam," *Salaam* 1, no. 1 (July 1960): 7–13.

92. For additional information on the University of Islam and education within the Nation of Islam see Essein-Udom, *Black Nationalism*, chap. 9.

93. Muhammad, *Message to the Black Man*, 39, 41.

94. Muhammad, *How to Eat to Live* (Chicago: Muhammad's Temple of Islam No. 2, 1967).

95. Clegg, *An Original Man*, 103.

96. Muhammad, "Mr. Muhammad Speaks," *Salaam* 1, no. 1 (July 1960): 14.

97. Muhammad, *Message to the Black Man*, 157.

98. Ibid., 135–60.

99. Sonsyrea Tate, *Little X: Growing Up in the Nation of Islam* (San Francisco: HarperCollins, 1997). Also of interest is Conrad Muhammad's conversion account found in Richard Wormser, *American Islam: Growing Up Muslim in America* (New York: Walker and Company, 1994), 77–81.

100. Tate, *Little X*, 8–9.

101. Ibid., 37.

102. Zafar Ishaq Ansari offers an interesting perspective on the Nation's theology (1934–74) in "Aspects of Black Muslim Theology," *Stuida Islamica* 53 (1981): 137–76.

103. Clegg, *An Original Man*, 41–42.

104. Gardell, *In the Name of Elijah Muhammad*, 146.

105. Muhammad, *Our Saviour Has Arrived*, 97.

106. Ibid., 3.

107. Muhammad, *Message to the Black Man*, 17.

108. In many of his talks and visions, Elijah Muhammad also made mention of angels or those who help God. He argued that these should not be understood as "spooky" beings but rather as assistants sent by God from the Mother Plane positioned above the earth.

109. John T. McCartney, *Black Power Ideologies: An Essay in African-American Political Thought* (Philadelphia: Temple University Press, 1992), 173.

110. At times the Nation claims that Allah created the Original people and they participate in Allah's essence. In this context the making of Adam is regarded as a reference to Caucasians, the children of Yacub (or Yakub). At other times, however, the Nation teaches that Adam is the "father" of the Original people created by God. See Gardell, *In the Name of Elijah Muhammad*, 165–68.

111. Ibid., 145.

112. Muhammad, *Message to the Black Man*, 31–32. Interestingly enough, the Nation often spoke of Africa in negative terms as the location of "animal"-like people who lack civilization and training.

113. Within the Original people, a distinction exists between men and women. The Nation argues that women are viewed not as inferior but as special and deserving protection from men. Nonetheless, there are clear roles for men and women: men are the head of the home and provide for the needs of the family, while women are responsible for the maintenance of the home as well as the children. The Nation's theological anthropology is unapologetically tied to a notion of set roles for women and men, and disorder and strife stem from the rejection of this natural order. These roles are continued in the Nation's current theological stance, as attested to by the recent Million Man's March and the Million Women's March.

114. For more information on the Yakub account see Clegg, *An Original Man*, 49–56. Also of interest is *Malcolm X, Yakub History: The Nation of Islam Speech* (Stone Mountain, Ga.: T.U.T. Publications, 1997).

115. Muhammad, *Message to the Black Man*, 110–11.

116. Clegg, *An Original Man*, 51.

117. According to Elijah Muhammad, the name *Europe* can be deciphered in this way: "EU stands for hills and cavesides of that continent and ROPE means a place where that people were bound in" (*Message to the Black Man*, 267).

118. Ibid., 121.

119. Muhammad, *Our Savior Has Arrived* 14.

120. Also of note is the Five Percent Nation of Gods and Earths that split from the Nation of Islam in the 1960s. For information see Yusuf Nuruddin, "The Five Percenters: A Teenage Nation of Gods and Earth," 109–32, in Yvonne Yazbeck Haddad and Jane Idleman Smith, *Muslim Communities in North America* (Albany: State University of New York Press, 1994).

121. For information on Warith Muhammad's agenda see W. Deen Muhammad, *Challenges That Face Man Today* (Chicago: W. D. Muhammad Publications, 1985).

122. Ibid., 74.

123. Magida, *Prophet of Rage,* 56.

124. See Marsh, *From Black Muslims to Muslims,* Appendix A.

125. See, e.g., Wallace D. Muhammad, "Self-Government in the New World," Bilalian News 1, no. 19 (March 19, 1976): 23–26, reprinted in Milton Sernett, ed., *Afro-American Religious History* (Durham: Duke University Press, 1985), chap. 44. For comparative and structural information on the World Community of Al-Islam under the leadership of Wardith (Wallace) Muhammad see, e.g., Marsh, *From Black Muslims to Muslims,* chap. 6. See also: Lawrence H. Mamiya, "From Black Muslim to Bilalian: The Evolution of a Movement," *Journal for the Scientific Study of Religion* 4 (1982): 138–52.

126. Tate, *Little X,* 133.

127. Ibid., 132. For an early account see also Minister Lucioius X (Temple No. 4, Washington, D.C.), "Why I Believe in Islam," *Salaam* 1, no. 1 (July 1960): 26–29.

128. Gardell gives 1978 as the date for this name change (*In the Name of Elijah Muhammad,* 110).

129. Sterling X Hobbs, "Miracle Man of the Muslims," *Sepia* (May 1975): 28, quoted in Magida, *Prophet of Rage,* 31. Some claim that the Messenger had been informed of Walcott's presence in the audience.

130. Clegg, 249–52. Also see Magida, *Prophet of Rage.* Another biography, unauthorized, was recently published and is of interest for comparative reasons: Florence Hamlish Levinsohn, *Looking for Farrakhan* (Chicago: Ivan R. Dee, 1997). Levinsohn is concerned with the Nation as a "secret society" that may hold some benefits for the oppressed, but one that is also capable of great manipulation and misrepresentation. The question is how much of this view stems strictly from her personal inability to gain access secured by Magida and others.

Malcolm X, disillusioned by Elijah Muhammad's disregard for the very rules he had instituted, combined with his desire for more direct involvement in political efforts to transform society, left the Nation in 1964. This caused a leadership void that Louis X's charisma and knowledge allowed him to fill. From the time of Malcolm's assassination to the present there have been speculations concerning Louis X's and the Nation's involvement in Malcolm X's death. Although this concept is softened in public discourse, Malcolm X is still thought of as an ungrateful son who turned on his teacher. Whether this merits death is a question left to speculation. And whether the Nation (and Louis X and Elijah Muhammad Jr., who called for Malcolm's severed tongue, in particular) acted upon its anger with Malcolm is yet another unanswered question. It was known that the Nation often resolved internal conflict and breaches through violence, but that this would extend to the murder of Malcolm X is an unanswered question. In recent years Farrakhan has recognized Malcolm as a visionary whose ideas and plans were ahead of their time (within the Nation). See Richard Muhammad and Donald Muhammad, "A Step toward Healing," *The Final Call* 14, no. 15 (May 24, 1995): 3, 8–9.

131. For a very insightful treatment of these developments see Mamiya, "From Black Muslim to Bilalian."

132. Gardell, *In the Name of Elijah Muhammad,* 24.

133. Magida, *Prophet of Rage,* 123.

134. For more information on this see Mattias Gardell, "The Sun of Islam Will Rise in the West: Minister Farrakhan and the Nation of Islam in the Latter Days," 15–51, in Haddad and Smith, eds., *Muslim Communities in North America.*

135. Marsh, *From Black Muslims to Muslims,* 97–98.

136. Gardell, "The Sun of Islam Will Rise in the West: Minister Farrakhan and the Nation of Islam in the Latter Days," 26–27.

137. Quoted in McCloud, *African American Islam,* 78.

138. Gardell, *In the Name of Elijah Muhammad,* 131–32.

139. Ibid., 135, 137.

140. Lee, *The Nation of Islam,* 118–19, 121. This text is very useful for understanding the millenarian dimensions of the Nation and the links between this and its sense of nationalism,

although it does not provide an in-depth analysis of the implicitly theological motivations for the Nation's millenarian and nationalist tendencies.

141. Gardell, "Sun of Islam," 33. The Nation believes that there are two Qur'āns, one physically available, the other hidden and mathematically coded, and that the Nation has discovered the code (the key being the number 19) for the second Qur'ān and uses this knowledge to help the Original people (ibid., 34).

142. Louis Farrakhan, "Why Do They Blame Farrakhan?" in *Let Us Make Man: Select Men Only and Women Only Speeches*, ed. Brother Yusuf and Sister Shah'Keyah, (New York: Uprising Communications, 1996), 78.

143. Farrakhan, "As a Man Thinketh in His Heart," in *Let Us Make Man*, 47.

144. Farrakhan, *Torchlight for America* (Chicago: FCN Publishing Company, 1993). Also see *Back Where We Belong: Selected Speeches by Minister Louis Farrakhan*, Joseph D. Eure, and Richard M. Jerome, eds. (Philadelphia: PC International Press, 1989).

145. For reactions to the March see Kim Martin Sadler, ed., *Atonement: The Million Man March* (Cleveland: The Pilgrim Press, 1996); Garth Baker-Fletcher, ed., *Voices on the Future: Black Religion after the Million Man March* (Maryknoll, N.Y.: Orbis, 1998).

146. Farrakhan, *Torchlight for America*. Farrakhan's public appearances outside of the Nation include an appearance on "Donahue," October 10, 1995 ("Donahue" Transcript 4356, October 10, 1995, "Minister Farrakhan's Million Man March to Unify Black Men"). The Nation's current economic efforts include its line of POWER (People Organized and Working for Economic Rebirth) products, which include shampoo, etc. This line was launched in 1985–86. Financial assistance for this venture was provided by the Nation and by a loan from Libya.

147. An alternative is offered in the Nation's Three-Year Economic Program outlined in Farrakhan, *A Torchlight for America*, and Muhammad, *Message to the Black Man*.

148. Farrakhan, *A Torchlight for America*, 19.

149. Ibid., 23.

150. Ibid., 49–50.

151. Ibid., 82.

152. Muhammad, *Message to the Black Man*, 173.

153. The reader might be interested in comparing this phenomenological report with information concerning the early Nation's worship as found in, e.g., Louis E. Lomax, *A Report on Elijah Muhammad, Malcolm X, and the Black Muslim World: When the Word Is Given* (Westport, Conn.: Greenwood Press, 1963).

154. Interview with James Muhammad, December 20, 1997.

155. It was unclear from conversations with James Muhammad, whether the Minneapolis members of the Nation formed a mosque or a study group.

156. Interview with James Muhammad, December 1997.

157. Farrakhan, *Let Us Make Man*, 1.

158. As Gardell (*In the Name of Elijah Muhammad*) has reported, a mosque is officially registered with the Nation only after gaining and maintaining forty members and applying for a charter. In this letter, the members commit themselves to the teachings of the Nation and the regulations upheld by Farrakhan and the Nation's leadership. James Muhammad says that in age he is probably the senior member of the adult study group. If the group maintains the required membership and is consistent in maintaining prayer and the other requirements, it will become a mosque subject to "inspection" by the national headquarters. Interview with James Muhammad, December 20, 1997.

159. Gardell (*In the Name of Elijah Muhammad*, 149–51) is one of few scholars to give direct attention to the Nation of Islam's theology as an explicit response to the problem of evil or theodicy. However, my analysis of the problem of evil in the Nation's theology highlights the nature of Allah and of Yakub's creation in a manner not found in Gardell's account, which is weighted more heavily, I think, toward a historical and sociological depiction of theodicy. Michael Dyson also mentions theodicy in the Nation of Islam's thought; however, his discussion

is primarily concerned with Malcolm X and does not develop notions of moral evil in the same manner as presented in my work. See Dyson, *Making Malcolm*, Part III, chap. 3, particularly pp. 89–90.

160. Elijah Muhammad, *The Supreme Wisdom*, II, 74; quoted in Essiem-Udom, *Black Nationalism*, 132–33.

161. McCloud, *African American Islam*, 122.

162. Muhammad, *Message to the Black Man*, 24–25.

163. Muhammad, *Our Saviour Has Arrived*, 112.

164. Louis Farrakhan, *Let Us Make Man*, "How to Overcome the Pain," 65.

165. Elijah Muhammad, *Message to the Black Man*, 108.

166. Louis Farrakhan's appearance on C-SPAN, August 22, 1997.

167. Muhammad, *Our Saviour Has Arrived*, 199.

168. Gardell, "The Sun of Islam Will Rise in the West," 29. This argument is also contained in Gardell, *In the Name of Elijah Muhammad*.

169. See Muhammad, *Message to the Black Man*, 290–91.

170. Jabril Muhammad, "The Need for a Special Kind of Man—Farrakhan: The Traveler," *The Final Call* (April 26, 1995): 26–27.

171. Muhammad, *Message to the Black Man*, 304.

172. Louis Farrakhan, "Peace: The Fruit of Justice," *The Final Call* 16, no. 43 (August 26, 1997): 2. Also see Louis Farrakhan, "An Open Letter to the 3rd Popular Arab and Islamic Conference," *The Final Call* 14, no. 13 (April 26, 1995): 20–21.

173. Louis Farrakhan, "Toward a More Perfect Union," in *Let Us Make Man*, 138.

CHAPTER 4: WHAT IF GOD WERE ONE OF US?

1. Charles Trinkaus, "Italian Humanism and Scholastic Theology," in Albert Rabil, Jr., *Renaissance Humanism: Foundations, Forms, and Legacy,* vol. 3: *Humanism and the Disciplines* (Philadelphia: University of Pennsylvania Press, 1988), 327–28. An earlier and shorter version of this chapter is published as: "'Anybody There?': Reflections on African American Humanism and Its Praxis Sites," *Religious Humanism* (Spring 1998): 61–78.

2. Ibid., 329.

3. John F. D'Amico, "Humanism and Pre-Reformation Theology," in Rabil, *Renaissance Humanism* 3:349.

4. Ibid., 330.

5. Ibid., 350.

6. Ibid., 352.

7. Ibid., 370.

8. Corliss Lamont, *The Philosophy of Humanism* (New York: Frederick Ungar Publishing Company, 1965), 42.

9. Lewis W. Spitz, "Humanism and the Protestant Reformation," in Rabil, *Renaissance Humanism* 3:380.

10. Lamont, *Philosophy of Humanism,* 12.

11. Ibid., 15.

12. Ibid., 30. I attempt to take into consideration this problem of naming by holding to the definition of religion presented in the introduction to this book, a definition that allows me to work without differentiating between "religious" and "secular" expressions of humanism. Some will find this problematical. I do not suggest that mine is the only alternative, but I do hold that it is a reasonable way of understanding humanism, and the one most fitting for my purposes.

13. Ibid., 17–18.

14. Henry F. May, *The Enlightenment in America* (New York: Oxford University Press, 1976), 350.

15. John H. Dietrich, "Unitarianism and Humanism," in *What If the World Went Humanist? Ten Sermons*, selected by Mason Olds (Yellow Springs, Ohio: Fellowship of Religious Humanists, 1989), 58.

16. Ibid., 53. Also see *Humanist Manifestos I and II* (Buffalo, N.Y.: Prometheus, 1973). A copy of this manifesto is available in Lamont, *Philosophy of Humanism*.

17. Lamont, *Philosophy of Humanism*, 24, 25.

18. Donald H. Meyer, "Secular Transcendence: The American Religious Humanists," *American Quarterly* 34, no. 5 (Winter 1982): 531.

19. Meyer, "Secular Transcendence," 526.

20. Lamont, *Philosophy of Humanism*, 52.

21. Ibid., 53. Some argue that it was only logical that Unitarianism's distaste for religious doctrine, which downplayed human value and human life, would provide the grounding for a humanism that embraced the essential worth of humanity above all else. The reader should not think this theological openness was easily achieved. To the contrary, it was a result of ideological battle. Conflict between liberal Unitarians and religious humanists referred to as the "humanist-theist controversy" concluded with the above openness to both theism and humanism.

22. Mason Olds, "What Is Religious Humanism?" *Free Inquiry* 16, no. 4 (Fall 1996): 13.

23. Humanist organizations such as the American Humanist Association founded in 1934 also merit consideration. This organization has been extremely important, although it has not consistently given attention to overtly religious issues.

24. Meyer, "Secular Transcendence," 524–42.

25. Benjamin E. Mays, *The Negro's God as Reflected in His Literature* (New York: Atheneum, 1973), 255. Although I find Benjamin Mays' comments useful in the post–1920s section, his observation on the period prior to 1914 is incorrect. He writes: "It is significant to note that prior to 1914, one finds no ideas of God that imply doubt and repudiation" (244). The information I provide in this section refutes his claim. Also see, for example, Lawrence Levine, *Black Culture and Black Consciousness: Afro-American Folk Thought from Slavery to Freedom* (New York: Oxford University Press, 1978), and V. P. Franklin, *Black Self-Determination: A Cultural History of the Faith of the Fathers* (Westport, Conn.: Lawrence Hill and Co., 1984), 51–55. I am currently completing an anthology of Black Humanism that will further disprove May's statement: *By These Hands Alone! A Documentary History of African American Humanism* (New York: New York University Press, forthcoming).

26. Daniel Alexander Payne, "Daniel Payne's Protestation of Slavery," in *Lutheran Herald and Journal of the Franckean Synod* (August 1, 1839): 114–15.

27. Arthur Fauset, *Black Gods of the Metropolis: Negro Religious Cults of the Urban North* (Philadelphia: University of Pennsylvania Press, 1944), 7.

28. In Roy D. Morrison II, "The Emergence of Black Theology in America," *The A.M.E. Zion Quarterly Review*, vol. 94, no. 3 (October 1982): 6.

29. Eugene Levy, *James Weldon Johnson: Black Leader, Black Voice* (Chicago: University of Chicago Press), 15.

30. Ibid., 19.

31. James Baldwin, *The Fire Next Time* (New York: Dell Books), 42.

32. Ibid., 43–44.

33. Ibid., 47.

34. Ibid., 56–57. Also see pp. 64–67.

35. Ibid., 97.

36. Faith Berry, ed. *A Scholar's Conscience: Selected Writings of J. Saunders Redding, 1942–1977* (Louisville: University Press of Kentucky, 1992).

37. Ibid., 49.

38. Ibid.

39. Ibid., 52.

40. Ibid.

41. Ibid.

42. Ibid., 53–54.

43. Trudier Harris, "Three Black Women Writers and Humanism: A Folk Perspective," in R. Baxter Miller, ed., *African-American Literature and Humanism* (Lexington, Ky.: University Press of Kentucky), 54.

44. In ibid., 72. See Alice Walker, *The Color Purple: A Novel* (New York: Harcourt Brace Jovanovich, 1982); Alice Walker, *The Third Life of Grange Copeland* (New York: Harcourt, Brace, Jovanovich, 1970).

45. According to Alice Walker, "the only reason you want to go to heaven is that you have been driven out of your mind (off your land and out of your lover's arms): clear seeing inherited religion and reclaiming the pagan self" (*On the Issue* 6, no. 2 [Spring 1997]: 19–20).

46. Ibid., 23.

47. Mays, *The Negro's God,* 243.

48. Langston Hughes, "Goodbye Christ," quoted in ibid., 238.

49. See Langston Hughes, "Concerning 'Goodbye Christ,'" in *Good Morning Revolution: Uncollected Writings of Social Protest by Langston Hughes* (Carol Publishing Group, 1992), 147–49. Hughes also denies being an atheist in "Concerning Red Baiting," 159–61.

50. Hughes, *Good Morning,* xvi–xvii.

51. See Mark Naison, *Communists in Harlem During the Depression* (Urbana: University of Illinois Press, 1983).

52. Robin D. G. Kelley, "Comrades, Praise Gawd for Lenin and Them! Ideology and Culture among Black Communists in Alabama, 1930–1935," *Science and Society* 52, no. 1 (Spring 1988): 61–62. Also see Robin Kelley, "'Afric's Sons with Banners Red,'" in Sidney J. Lemelle and Robin D. G. Kelley, eds., *Imagining Home: Class, Culture, and Nationalism in the African Diaspora* (New York: Verso, 1994).

53. Kelley, "Comrades," 63.

54. Ibid., 64.

55. Ibid., 65–66.

56. Ibid., 133.

57. Nell Irvin Painter, *The Narrative of Hosea Hudson: His Life as a Negro Communist in the South* (Cambridge, Mass.: Harvard University Press, 1979), 133–34.

58. Ibid., 134.

59. Ibid., 134–35.

60. See Harold Cruse, "Jews and Negroes in the Communist Party," in *The Crisis of the Negro Intellectual: A Historical Analysis of the Failure of Black Leadership* (New York: William Morrow and Company/Quill, 1967, 1984), 147.

61. Others who combined humanism with political involvement include A. Philip Randolph, T. Thomas Fortune, and Paul Robeson. Harold Cruse's comment on Robeson's romanticization of the "negro worker" indirectly reveals Robeson's nontheistic leanings:

Robeson and [his] middle-class-leftwing ethos truly idealized . . . nice, upright Negro workers; who, even if they did go to church and worship God and not Russia, at least tilled the Southern soil as solid citizen sharecroppers. (Ibid., 236)

62. Rev. J. M. Lawson, Jr., "Statement of Purpose," *The Student Voice* 1, no. 1 (June 1960), in Clayborne Carson, ed., *The Student Voice, 1960–1965: Periodical of the Student Nonviolent Coordinating Committee* (Westport, Conn.: Meckler, 1990), 2.

63. Stokeley Carmichael and Charles Hamilton, *Black Power* (New York: Vintage Books, 1967), 44, quoted in Norman Harris, *Connecting Times: The Sixties in Afro-American Fiction* (Jackson, Miss.: University Press of Mississippi, 1988), 91.

64. James Forman, "Corrupt Black Preachers," in *The Making of Black Revolutionaries* (Washington, D.C.: Open Hand Publishing, 1985), 58.

65. James Forman., "God Is Dead: A Question of Power," in *The Making of Black Revolutionaries,* 80–81.

66. Ibid., 82.

67. Ibid., 83. Italics added.

68. Bobby Seale, *Seize the Time* (New York: Random House, 1991), 3. Although on the individual level the objectives often gave way to problematic and abusive behavior, the humanist tone of the Black Panther Party's platform is still noteworthy:

1. We want freedom. We want power to determine the destiny of our Black Community.

2. We want full employment for our people.

3. We want an end to the robbery by the white man of our Black Community.

4. We want decent housing, fit for shelter of human beings.

5. We want education for our people that exposes the true nature of this decadent American society. We want education that teaches us our true history and our role in the present-day society.

6. We want all black men to be exempt from military service.

7. We want an immediate end to POLICE BRUTALITY and MURDER of black people.

8. We want freedom for all black men held in federal, state, county and city prisons and jails.

9. We want all black people when brought to trial to be tried in court by a jury of their peer group or people from their black communities, as defined by the Constitution of the United States.

10. We want land, bread, housing, education, clothing, justice, and peace. And as our major political objective, a United Nations–supervised plebiscite to be held throughout the black colony in which only black colonial subjects will be allowed to participate, for the purpose of determining the will of black people as to their national destiny.

69. *To Die for the People: The Writings of Huey P. Newton*, ed. Toni Morrison (New York: Writers and Readers Publishing, Inc., 1995), 63–64.

70. Ibid., 64.

71. Eldridge Cleaver, "On Becoming," in *Soul on Ice* (New York: McGraw-Hill, 1967), 4–5.

72. Cleaver, "'The Christ' and His Teachings," in *Soul on Ice*, 34.

73. Seale, *Seize the Time,* 429.

74. Anthony B. Pinn, *Why, Lord? Suffering and Evil in Black Theology* (New York: Continuum Publishing Group, 1995), chaps. 5 and 6.

75. Unitarian Universalist Commission on Appraisal to the General Assembly, *Empowerment: One Denomination's Quest for Racial Justice, 1967–1982* (Boston: Unitarian Universalist Association, 1983), 24. Also see Unitarian Universalist Association, *Black Caucus Controversy II* (Boston: Unitarian Universalist Association, 1968).

76. Jacqui James and Mark Morrison-Reed, eds., *Been in the Storm So Long: Meditation Manual* (Boston: Skinner House Books, 1991), 1.

77. Mark D. Morrison-Reed, *Black Pioneers in a White Denomination*, 3d ed. (Boston: Skinner House Books, 1994), xii.

78. One of the greatest sources of information on the UUA is the UUA archive materials held at Harvard University Divinity School, Cambridge, Mass. Prior to the merger, the first Black Universalists brought into the ministry were Jeffrey Campbell and Francis Davis.

79. For information on racial debates in the UUA see, e.g., Mark Morrison-Reed, *Black Pioneers in a White Denomination,* 3d ed. (Boston: Skinner House Books, 1994).

80. Ibid., 91.

81. Ibid., 92.

82. Quoted in ibid., 94.

83. Ibid., 95.

84. Ibid., 65, 66.

85. Ibid., 130.

86. Ibid., 132–33.

87. Ibid., 120.

88. Quoted in ibid., 135.

89. Interview with Norm Allen, Jr., January 1997, in Amherst, New York.

90. Ibid.

91. Ibid.

92. Norm Allen, Jr., "Humanism in the Black Community," in *The Sunrays* 1, no. 1 (October–December 1991): 12.

93. "An African-American Humanist Declaration," in *Free Inquiry* 10, no. 2 (Spring 1990): 13.

94. Ibid., 14–15.

95. Don Cupitt, *After God: The Future of Religion* (New York: Basic Books, 1997), 82.

96. Dietrich, *What If the World Went Humanist?* 104.

97. Ibid., 134.

98. James Baldwin, *The Fire Next Time* (New York: Dell Books), 46.

99. For an extended discussion of humanism and the problem of evil, see William R. Jones, *Is God a White Racist? A Preamble to Black Theology*, 2d ed. (Boston: Beacon Press, 1997); Pinn, *Why, Lord?* chaps. 4 to 6.

100. Interview with Norm Allen, January 1997.

101. Ibid.

CHAPTER 5: HOW DO WE TALK ABOUT RELIGION?

1. Leland Ferguson, *Uncommon Ground: Archaeology and Early African America, 1650–1800* (Washington, D.C.: Smithsonian Institution Press, 1992), 123.

2. I should say a few words concerning my use of the term *artifact*. I understand all cultural production, once outside of the creative moment, as artifacts because they have become contextually uncertain. They are products of human activity completely open to historical conditioning; they are no longer "owned" by their creators. Historical placement, past and present, cannot be used to determine what is an artifact and what is not, because history is conditioned. One sees this contextual uncertainty, for example, in recent heated discussions of rap music. The fact that the rap artists, with few exceptions, are still present and producing has not lessened the debate over such issues as intentionality, meaning, and consequences.

The discussion contained in this chapter is more fully developed in a project on which I am currently working, *Earth Bound: Toward a Theology of Fragile Cultural Memory and Religious Diversity*. It will also be published by Fortress Press.

3. I use *cultural production* as a loose term for the various sites of cultural memory—the spots where history, circumstance, and creativity merge. In this sense cultural production is the "enactment" of this memory.

4. James Cone defines culture this way: "Black culture consists of the creative forms of expression as one reflects on history, endures pain, and experiences joy. It is the black community expressing itself in music, poetry, prose, and other art forms. . . . Culture refers to the way persons live and move in the world; it molds their thought forms." James Cone, *A Black Theology of Liberation*, 20th anniversary ed. (Maryknoll, N.Y.: Orbis, 1993), 27.

5. Ibid., 22, 23.

6. Cone does embrace, however, Barth's notion of the permanent and qualitative distinction between God and humanity. Cone, like Barth, wants to avoid the possibility of idolatry. He understands that human words cannot be radically understood as God's words without the danger of theology becoming mere ideology, with limited liberative potential.

7. Cecil Wayne Cone, *The Identity Crisis in Black Theology* (Nashville, Tenn.: AMEC, 1975).

8. Ibid., 18, 142.

9. Joseph Washington, "How Black Is Black Religion?" 22–43, in James J. Gardiner and J. Deotis Roberts, Sr., eds., *Quest for a Black Theology* (Philadelphia: Pilgrim Press, 1971).

10. Ibid., 28.

11. See, e.g., James Cone, *The Spirituals and the Blues: An Interpretation* (New York: The Seabury Press, 1972; repr. Maryknoll, N.Y.: Orbis, 1991); Riggins R. Earl, Jr., *Dark Symbols, Obscure Signs: God, Self, and Community in the Slave Mind* (Maryknoll, N.Y.: Orbis, 1993); Dwight N. Hopkins, *Shoes That Fit Our Feet: Sources for a Constructive Black Theology* (Maryknoll, N.Y.: Orbis, 1993); Emilie Townes, ed., *A Troubling in My Soul* (Maryknoll, N.Y.: Orbis, 1994).

12. For example, critiques of homophobia and heterosexism in Black churches and Black theology tend to revolve around rereadings of Scripture and the open nature of Black religious community. Why not give attention to, whether ultimately fruitful or not, homoeroticism in Black musical expression and other forms of Black cultural expression that critique homophobia and heterosexism? Why is not the assumed heterosexual norm of Black slave communities and relationships questioned? Does anyone explore possible cultural artifacts that point to homosexuality in slave communities? Or, are the images of mandingo, Jezebel, and the Mammie actually embraced in a bizarre and distorted reaction to white stereotypical depictions of Blacks?

13. Maurice Halbwachs, *On Collective Memory*, trans. and ed. Lewis A. Coser (Chicago: University of Chicago Press, 1992), 93.

14. I make this argument as an extension of comments made by Don Cupitt concerning theology done in light of an understanding of tradition as whole and perfect. He considers this theology an exercise in advocacy. See Don Cupitt, *After Religion: The Future of Religion* (New York: Basic Books, 1997), 106–18. Cupitt's comment concerning concepts of religion is applicable here:

This in turn shows how partial and unsatisfactory our concept of religion is: we are able to recognize with confidence as being "religious" only the developed type of religious system that we already know.

15. Dwight Hopkins, "Theological Method and Cultural Studies: Slave Religious Culture as Heuristic," in Dwight Hopkins and Sheila Devaney, eds., *Changing Conversations: Religious Reflection and Cultural Analysis* (New York: Routledge, 1996), 163–80.

16. Ibid., 165.

17. Ibid.

18. Cupitt, *After Religion*, xiii. For the purposes of this chapter, I do not consider it essential to distinguish sharply among folk, popular, and mass culture. My concern is with the function and format of collective cultural memory. Those interested in such distinctions, however, might find useful the concise definition offered by Susan Willis ("Memory and Mass Culture," in Fabre and O'Meally, eds., *History and Memory in African-American Culture* [New York: Oxford University Press, 1994], 179).

19. Cupitt, *After Religion*, 22–23.

20. Barry Schwartz offers a useful definition of collective memory: "a metaphor that formulates society's retention and loss of information about its past in the familiar terms of individual remembering and forgetting. Part of this collective memory is, in fact, defined by shared individual memories, but only a small fraction of society's past is experienced in this way. Every member of society, even the oldest, learns most of what he knows about the past through social institutions—through oral chronicles preserved by tradition, written chronicles stored in archives, and commemorative activities (making portraits, statues, and shrines, collecting relics, naming places, observing holidays and anniversaries) that enable institutions to distinguish significant events and people from the mundane, and so infuse the past with moral meaning." From "Iconography and Collective Memory: Lincoln's Image in the American Mind," *Sociological Quarterly* 32, no. 3 (1991): 302; cited in Michael Eric Dyson *Making Malcolm X: The Myth and Meaning of Malcolm X* (New York: Oxford University Press, 1995), 201, n. 1.

21. Michael Kammen, *Mystic Chords of Memory: The Transformation of Tradition in American Culture* (New York: Alfred A. Knopf, 1991), 51–53, 59.

22. Ibid., 87.

23. Ibid., 281–82.

24. Charles Long, "Assessment and New Departures for a Study of Black Religion in the United States of America," in Gayraud Wilmore, editor, *African American Religious Studies: An Interdisciplinary Anthology* (Durham: Duke University Press, 1989), 45.

25. Also of growing concern, and no doubt connected to the race-ing of memory, are discussions of the constitutive sources of collective memory: high culture, folk culture. The ramifications of cultural borrowing and cross-regional transmission were yet to be discussed. It is my opinion that during the WPA years, the collecting of tradition entailed concrete and pragmatic wrestling with these and related issues.

26. Cited in Kammen, *Mystic Chords of Memory*, 121.

27. It would be interesting to explore the manner in which immigration to the United States by various groups impacted the collective cultural memory. But that discussion is beyond the scope of this book.

A recognition of the importance of African American cultural memory hits home in the 1970s, particularly with the mega-media success of Alex Haley's TV series and book *Roots*. Households across the country read the book and were glued to the television when Haley's story aired. Yet, by the 1980s this surge was, for the most part, superficial.

28. I draw from Dyson's discussion of collective memory. Although he uses this framework as a way of assessing the importance of Malcolm X, I think the workings of collective (and I add cultural) memory help to explain more than the creation of African American heroes and heroic genius. See Dyson, *Making Malcolm X*, 149–50.

29. Fabre and O'Meally, eds., "Introduction," in *History and Memory in African-American Culture*, 7.

30. Evidence of this break in collective memory is found in problems with collective identity commonly sighted by African Americans; hence, a push toward conformity, toward "genuine" and "recognizable" Blackness. I think Jacques Le Goff speaks to this point when he observes that "the absence, or voluntary or involuntary loss, of collective memory among peoples and nations can cause serious problems of collective identity" (Jacques Le Goff, *History and Memory*, trans. Steven Rendall and Elizabeth Claman [New York: Columbia University Press, 1992], 53).

Other communities experience this as well. It is one of the defining characteristics of life in the "postmodern" world. Some work with respect to this is being done on Jewish and German collective memory after the Holocaust.

31. Toni Morrison, "The Site of Memory," in Cornel West et al., *Out There: Marginalization and Contemporary Cultures* (Cambridge, Mass.: MIT Press, 1994), 301.

32. Pierre Nora's work on memory and history, or sites of memory, is extremely helpful on this point. I am not as pessimistic, however; the availability of any cultural memory worth considering is still a somewhat open question for me. I am certain, nonetheless, that this memory is tattered and fragment. Pierre Nora, "Between Memory and History: Les Lieux de Mémoire," in Fabre and O'Meally, *History and Memory in African-American Culture*, 284.

33. Fabre and O'Meally, "Introduction," 8–9.

34. I consider current reactions to hip hop culture and rap music in particular an example of this fragile cultural memory. Many have criticized the oppressive language and scenarios commonly found in rap music. Yet these same critics fail to examine critically the lyrics of the Stagger Lee songs and stories. Nor do they critique the more sexist and homophobic lyrics of some blues tones. It is as if these critics regard rap music as dissimilar and unconnected to the larger body of African American music culture. This is a sign of fractured cultural memory on the individual and group level, the inability to place rap music in the larger framework of cultural artifacts. Cultural relativism has set in.

35. Karen Fields, "What One Cannot Remember Mistakenly," in Fabre and O'Meally, *History and Memory in African-American Culture*, 150.

36. Ibid., 150. Although Fields is, for the most part, talking in terms of individual memory, her comments are applicable with respect to collective memory.

37. Fanon recognized this connection:

The Negroes who live in the United States and in Central or Latin America in fact experience the need to attach themselves to a cultural matrix. Their problem is not fundamentally different from that of the Africans. The whites of America did not mete out to them any different treatment from that of the whites who ruled over the Africans. We have seen that the whites were used to putting all Negroes in the same bag (Frantz Fanon, *The Wretched of the Earth* [New York: Grove Weidenfeld, 1963], 215).

38. Frantz Fanon, *Black Skin, White Masks* (New York: Grove Press, 1967), 9, 10, 18.

39. Ibid., 128. Italics added.

40. I borrow this term from Fanon, *The Wretched of the Earth,* 210.

41. Fanon, *The Wretched of the Earth,* 223–24.

42. I drew this notion of human beings as ambiguous from the work of Lewis Gordon, who, in turn, borrows from such thinkers as Simone de Beauvoir. See Lewis Gordon, "Existential Dynamics of Theorizing Black Invisibility," in Lewis R. Gordon, ed., *Existence in Black: An Anthology of Black Existential Philosophy* (New York: Routledge, 1997), 72. I think this concept of ambiguity is nicely played out in certain movements in rap music, e.g., to ScarFace's words in "Mind Playin' Tricks on Me," Geto Boys, *Best Uncut Dope,* Rap-A-Lot Records Inc., 1992, and the updated "Mind Playin' Tricks on Me, 1994," ScarFace, *The Diary,* Rap-A-Lot Records Inc., 1994.

43. I draw from a discussion of Spiller's idea in G. M. James Gonzalez, "Of Property: On 'Captive' 'Bodies,' Hidden 'Flesh,' and Colonization," in Gordon, ed., *Existence in Black,* 129–33. One could also include here Toni Morrison's imagery concerning emotional memory housed in the inner body: "Writers are like that [water]: remembering where we were, what valley we ran through, what the banks were like, the light that was there and the route back to our original place. It is emotional memory—what the nerves and the skin remember as well as how it appeared," 305.

44. Fanon, *Black Skin, White Masks,* 232.

45. Fanon, *The Wretched of the Earth,* 209–10.

46. Richard Wright, *Black Boy* (New York: Harper & Row, 1937, 1996), 284.

47. Toni Morrison, "The Site of Memory," 302.

48. Ibid., 302. Italics added.

49. Also of interest is the "tracking" metaphor employed by Mark Taylor. Taylor's implicit questions ("Tracking Spirit: Theology as Cultural Critique in America," in Hopkins and Devaney, eds., *Changing Conversations,* 123–44) revolve around the gathering of cultural resources for world informed theological reflection. He asserts that theologians engaged in cultural critique must "at least shuttle between cultural words, be ready for some searching and journeying. The tracking metaphor seeks to respond to that demand." This is, he continues, in keeping with the task of theology because theology is the search for the evidence or tracks of spirit and those who have engaged in liberative struggle. Hence, it is the effort to (re)construct memories of healthy existence or liberation and of those who have fought to create a healthy world. But this is not an easy process, because with all tracking ventures it is necessary to fill in blanks, which requires a theological process of flexibility. Finally,

Good trackers do not simply think about or imagine the ones sought after as at a distance; they need also to read and feel themselves as distinct but in relation to the sought ones, and then set their feet and bodies in motion along the way they discern the ones sought after to have gone. They rarely imitate exactly the ways of the distant ones, but with their motions and presence, they seek to approximate those ways. (140)

Taylor provides a very useful metaphor pointing to a form of theological reflection comfortable with the challenges of the religious and cultural terrain. Nonetheless, I cannot help but suspect that this approach ultimately narrows the cultural terrain and can also narrow additional searches. Continuing his metaphor of tracking, such a process can, I think, result in the belief that portions of the terrain have been adequately explored and that there is a certain thing sought and found. In short, even with appeals to liminal space and time, it is too teleologically certain for my taste.

Tracking, although open to uncertainty on one level, is a rather certain process in that one knows what one is looking for. Bounty hunters or private investigators, for example, track a particular individual, and materials that do not lead to that particular person are considered useless. By extension, theological trackers are looking for particular evidence that speaks to a certain reality of liberation. Furthermore, tracking entails an investigation of evidence left by the trackee and assumes that this evidence is present and decipherable. But in many cases the existence of evidence or tracks to follow cannot be assumed. Oppressed communities are an example of this. What happens to material that does not point in the direction of sought-after Spirit? What happens to material that we, in the late twentieth century label non-life-affirming? It may be noted, but does it receive attention? Can trackers function without hardcore evidence or signs to follow? In short, this approach, while helpful in that it does require theological stretching, does not prevent a narrowing of the theological terrain. And I think it is important to keep the terrain wide and to consider all of the religious landscape necessary.

50. There is a natural link between archaeological inquiry and theological reflection. See Michael L. Blakey, "American Nationality and Ethnicity in the Depicted Past," in P. Gathercole and D. Lowenthal, eds., *The Politics of the Past* (Boston: Unwin Hyman, 1990), 38.

51. Glyn Daniel, *The Origins and Growth of Archaeology* (New York: Thomas Y. Crowell Company, 1967), 1, 3, 20.

52. Brian Fagan, *Time Detectives: How Archaeologists Use Technology to Recapture the Past* (New York: Simon and Schuster, 1995), 25.

53. Stephen Shennan, "Cultural Transmission and Cultural Change," in Robert W. Preucel and Ian Hodder, eds., *Contemporary Archaeology in Theory: A Reader* (Cambridge, Mass.: Blackwell Publishers, 1996), 282.

54. Gathercole and Lowenthal, eds, *The Politics of the Past*, 312.

55. Preucel and Hodder, eds., *Contemporary Archaeology*, 106. Political economy, in short, can be defined as the study of the creation and use of goods, services, and value (99).

56. See Charles E. Orser, Jr., "Beneath the Material Surface of Things: Commodities, Artifacts, and Slave Plantations," in Preucel and Hodder, eds., *Contemporary Archaeology*, 189–201.

57. William E. Montgomery, *Under Their Own Vine and Fig Tree: The African-American Church in the South, 1865–1900* (Baton Rouge: Louisiana State University Press, 1993), 34.

58. Ibid., 52–53.

59. Albert J. Raboteau, *Slave Religion: The "Invisible Institution" in the Antebellum South* (New York: Oxford University Press, 1978, 1980), section II, chap. 5.

60. Ibid., 212.

61. Ferguson, *Uncommon Ground*, 116. Also see 114–18.

62. Ibid., xxxvi.

63. Ibid., 117.

64. See Anthony B. Pinn, *Why, Lord? Suffering and Evil in Black Theology* (New York: Continuum, 1995), chap. 6. This chapter, with some alterations, also appears as "Message in the Music: On Interpreting the Contact Between Religion and Popular Culture," in Bruce Forbes and Jeffrey Mahan, eds., *Religion and Popular Culture in America* (University of California Press, forthcoming).

65. Pinn, *Why, Lord?* 116.

BIBLIOGRAPHY

BOOKS AND ARTICLES

Adefunmi I, H.R.H. Oseijeman. "Keynote Address," Columbia University, January 16, 1993. Unpublished manuscript.

————. *OLORISHA: A Guidebook into Yoruba Religion.* Oyotunji Village: Great Benin Books, 1982.

————. *The Gods of Africa.* Sheldon, S.C.: Great Benin Books, 1960.

"An African-American Humanist Declaration." *Free Inquiry*, vol. 10, no. 2 (Spring 1990).

Allen, Norm, Jr. "Humanism in the Black Community." *The Sunrays*, vol. 1, no. 1 (October–December 1991).

Ajayi, J. F. Ade, and Robert Smith. *Yoruba Warfare in the Nineteenth Century.* London: Cambridge University Press/Institute of African Studies of the University of Ibadan, 1964.

Anderson, John Q., "The New Orleans Voodoo Ritual Dance and Its Twentieth-Century Survivals," *The Southern Folklore Quarterly*, vol. 24 (1960): 35–43.

Ansaris, Zafar Ishaq. "Aspects of Black Muslim Theology." *Stuida Islamica* 53 (1981): 137–76.

Apter, Andrew. *Black Critics and Kings: The Hermeneutics of Power in Yoruba Society.* Chicago: University of Chicago Press, 1992.

Argyle, W. J. *The Fon of Dahomey: A History and Ethnography of the Old Kingdom.* Oxford: Clarendon Press, 1966.

Austin, Allan D. *African Muslims in Antebellum America: Transatlantic Stories and Spiritual Struggles.* New York: Routledge, 1997.

————. *African Muslims in Antebellum America: A Sourcebook.* New York, 1984.

Baer, Hans. *The Black Spiritualist Movement: A Religious Response to Racism.* Knoxville: University of Tennessee Press, 1984.

————, and Merrill Singer. *African-American Religion in the Twentieth Century: Varieties of Protest and Accommodation.* Knoxville: University of Tennessee Press, 1992.

Baldwin, James. *The Fire Next Time.* New York: Dell Books, 1963, 1988.

————. *Go Tell It on the Mountain.* New York: Dell, 1981, 1985.

Ball, Charles. *Slavery in the United States: A Narrative of the Life and Adventures of Charles Ball, a Black Man.* New York: Negro Universities Press, 1969; John S. Taylor, 1837.

Barnes, Sandra T. *Africa's Ogun: Old World and New.* Bloomington: Indiana University Press, 1989.

Bascom, William. *Sixteen Cowries: Yoruba Divination from Africa to the New World.* Bloomington: Indiana University Press, 1980.

————. *Ifa Divination: Communication between Gods and Men in West Africa.* Bloomington: Indiana University Press, 1969.

Beier, Ulli. *The Return of the Gods: The Sacred Art of Susanne Wenger.* New York: Cambridge University Press, 1975.

Belgun, Erik. *Voodoo: Opposing View Points.* San Diego: Greenhaven Press, 1991.

Berry, Jason. *The Spirit of Black Hawk: A Mystery of Africans and Indians.* Jackson: University Press of Mississippi, 1995.

Bethell, Leslie, ed. *Cuba: A Short History.* Cambridge, England: Cambridge University Press, 1993.

Beynon, Erdmann Doane. "The Voodoo Cult Among Negro Migrants in Detroit." *American Journal of Sociology* 43 (1938): 894–907. Also printed as *Master Fard Muhammad: Detroit History*, with commentary by Prince A. Cuba (n.p., n.d.)

Biobaku, S.O., ed., *Sources of Yoruba History*. Oxford: Clarendon Press, 1973.

Blakey, Michael L. "American Nationality and Ethnicity in the Depicted Past." In P. Gathercole and D. Lowenthal, eds. *The Politics of the Past*. Boston: Unwin Hyman, 1990, 38–48.

Bodin, Ron. *Voodoo: Past and Present*. Louisiana Life Series. Center for Louisiana Studies: University of Southwestern Louisiana, 1990.

Bontemps, Arna, and Jack Conroy. *Any Place but Here*. New York: Hill and Wang, 1966.

Bourguigeon, Erika. "Afro-American Religions: Traditions and Transformations," 191–202, in John F. Szwed, ed., *Black America*. New York: Basic Books, 1970.

Brandon, George. *Santeria from African to the New World*. Bloomington: Indiana University Press, 1993.

————. "African Religious Influences in Cuba, Puerto Rico and Hispaniola." *Journal of Caribbean Studies*, vol. 7, nos. 2–3 (Winter 1989–Spring 1990).

Breitman, George, ed. *By Any Means Necessary*. New York: Pathfinder, 1970.

Brotz, Howard. *The Black Jews of Harlem: Negro Nationalism and the Dilemmas of Negro Leadership*. New York: Schocken Books, 1970.

Brown, Karen McCarthy. *Mama Lola: A Vodou Priestess in Brooklyn*. Berkeley: University of California Press, 1991.

Burns, Sir Alan. *History of Nigeria*. London: George Allen and Unwin Ltd., 1972.

Canizares, Raul. *Walking with the Night: The Afro-Cuban World of Santeria*. Rochester, Vt.: Destiny Books, 1993.

Canet, Carlos. *Oyotunji*. Miami: Editorial AIP, n.d.

Carmichael, Stokeley, and Charles Hamilton. *Black Power*. New York: Vintage Books, 1967.

Carson, Clayborne, ed. *The Student Voice, 1960–1965: Periodical of the Student Nonviolent Coordinating Committee*. Westport, Conn.: Meckler, 1990.

Chireau, Yvonne P. "Hidden Traditions: Black Religion, Magic, and Alternative Spiritual Beliefs in Womanist Perspective." In Jacquelyn Grant, ed., *Perspectives on Womanist Theology*. Black Church Scholars Series 7. Atlanta: Interdenominational Theological Center Press, 1995.

Clapp, Stephen C. "A Reporter at Large: African Theological Arch-Ministry, Inc." New York Public Library: Schomburg Collection, 1966.

Clayton, Edward T. "The Truth about Voodoo." *Ebony* (April 1951): 54–61.

Cleaver, Eldridge. *Soul on Ice*. New York: McGraw-Hill, 1967.

Clegg, Claude. *An Original Man*. Boston: St. Martin's Press, 1996.

Cone, Cecil Wayne. *The Identity Crisis in Black Theology*. Nashville: African Methodist Episcopal Church, 1975.

Cone, James H. *A Black Theology of Liberation*. 20th anniversary edition. Maryknoll, N.Y.: Orbis Books, 1993.

————. *Martin and Malcolm and America: A Dream or a Nightmare?* Maryknoll, N.Y.: Orbis Books, 1991.

————. *The Spirituals and the Blues: An Interpretation*. New York: The Seabury Press, 1972.

Courlander, Harold. *The Drum and the Hoe: Life and Lore of the Haitian People*. Berkeley: University of California Press, 1960.

————, and Remy Bastien. *Religion and Politics in Haiti*. Washington, D.C.: Institute for Cross-cultural Research, 1966.

Cragg, Kenneth. *The Call of the Minaret*. 2d ed. Maryknoll, N.Y.: Orbis Books, 1985.

Creel, Margaret Washington. *"A Peculiar People": Slave Religion and Community-Culture among the Gullahs*. New York: New York University Press, 1988.

Cruse, Harold. *The Crisis of the Negro Intellectual: A Historical Analysis of the Failure of Black Leadership*. New York: William Morrow and Company/Quill, 1967, 1984.

Cupitt, Don. *After God: The Future of Religion*. New York: Basic Books, 1997.

Curry, Mary Elaine. "Making the Gods in New York: The Yoruba Religion in the Black Community." Ph.D. diss., City University of New York, 1991.

D'Amico, John F. "Humanism and Pre-Reformation Theology." In Albert Rabil, *Renaissance Humanism: Foundations, Forms, and Legacy.* Vol. 3, *Humanism and the Disciplines.* Philadelphia: University of Pennsylvania Press, 1988.

Daniel, Glyn. *The Origins and Growth of Archaeology.* New York: Thomas Y. Crowell Company, 1967.

Davis, Rod. "Children of Yoruba: The Religion the Bible Belt Wouldn't Allow Is Again Boiling to the Surface." *Southern Magazine* (February 1987): 35–41, 84–86.

Deren, Maya. *Divine Horsemen: The Living Gods of Haiti.* New York: McPherson & Company, 1953.

Desmangles, Leslie G. *The Faces of the Gods: Vodou and Roman Catholicism in Haiti.* Chapel Hill: University of North Carolina Press, 1992.

"Detroit's University of Islam." *Salaam,* vol. 1, no. 1 (July 1960).

Dietrich, John H. *What If the World Went Humanist? Ten Sermons,* selected by Mason Olds. Yellow Springs, Ohio: Fellowship of Religious Humanists, 1989.

Durham, Katherine. *Island Possessed.* Chicago: University of Chicago Press, 1969, 1994.

Dyson, Michael Eric. *Making Malcolm: The Myth and Meaning of Malcolm X.* New York: Oxford University Press, 1995.

Earl, Riggins R. *Dark Symbols, Obscure Signs: God, Self, and Community in the Slave Mind.* Maryknoll, N.Y.: Orbis Books, 1993.

Edwards, Gary, and John Mason. *Black Gods: Orisa Studies in the New World.* Brooklyn, N.Y.: Yoruba Theological Archministry, 1985.

El-Amin, Mustafa. *The Religion of Islam and the Nation of Islam: What Is the Difference?* Newark: El-Amin Productions, 1991.

Ellis, A. B. "On Vōdu-Worship." *The Popular Science Monthly* 38 (November 1890–April 1891): 651–63.

Endore, Guy S. *Babouk.* Rev. ed. New York: Monthly Review, 1991.

Essien-Udom, E. U. *Black Nationalism: A Search for Identity in America.* Chicago: University of Chicago Press, 1962.

Evans, James. *We Have Been Believers: An African-American Systematic Theology.* Minneapolis: Fortress Press, 1992.

Fabre, Genevieve, and Robert O'Meally, eds. *History and Memory in African-American Culture.* New York: Oxford University Press, 1994.

Fagan, Brian. *Time Detectives: How Archaeologists Use Technology to Recapture the Past.* New York: Simon and Schuster, 1995.

Fanon, Frantz. *The Wretched of the Earth.* New York: Grove Weidenfeld, 1963.

————. *Black Skin, White Masks.* New York: Grove Weidenfeld, 1967.

Farrakhan, Louis. *Let Us Make Man: Select Men Only and Women Only Speeches.* Edited by Brother Yusuf and Sister Shah'Keyah. New York: Uprising Communications, 1996.

————. *Torchlight for America.* Chicago: FCN Publishing Company, 1993.

————. *Back Where We Belong: Selected Speeches by Minister Louis Farrakhan.* Edited by Joseph D. Eure and Richard M. Jerome. Philadelphia: PC International Press, 1989.

Fauset, Arthur. *Black Gods of the Metropolis: Negro Religious Cults of the Urban North.* Philadelphia: University of Pennsylvania Press, 1944.

Ferguson, Leland. *Uncommon Ground: Archaeology and Early African America, 1650–1800.* Washington, D.C.: Smithsonian Institution Press, 1992.

Forman, James. *The Making of Black Revolutionaries.* Washington, D.C.: Open Hand Publishing, Inc., 1985.

Foucault, Michel. *The Archaeology of Knowledge and the Discourse on Language.* New York: Pantheon Books, 1972.

Franklin, V. P. *Black Self-Determination: A Cultural History of the Faith of the Fathers.* Westport, Conn.: Lawrence Hill and Co., 1984.

Gomez, Michael A. "Muslims in Early America." *The Journal of Southern History*, vol. 60, no. 4 (November 1994): 671–710.

González-Wippler, Migene. *Legends of Santeria*. St. Paul, Minn.: Llewellyn Publications, 1994.

_____. *The Santeria Experience: A Journey into the Miraculous*. St. Paul, Minn.: Llewellyn Publications, 1992.

Gordon, Lewis R., ed. *Existence in Black: An Anthology of Black Existential Philosophy*. New York: Routledge, 1997.

Grant, Douglass. *The Fortunate Slave: An Illustration of African Slavery in the Early 18th Century*. New York: Oxford University Press, 1968.

Gardell, Mattias. *In the Name of Elijah Muhammad: Louis Farrakhan and the Nation of Islam*. Durham, N.C.: Duke University Press, 1996.

Gregory, Steven. "Afro-Caribbean Religion in New York City: The Case of Santería." In Constance R. Sutton and Elsa M. Chaney, eds., *Caribbean Life in New York City: Sociocultural Dimensions*. New York: Center for Migration Studies of New York, Inc., 1994.

_____. "Santeria in New York City: A Study in Cultural Resistance." Ph.D. diss., New School for Social Research, 1986.

Guillaume, Alfred. *Islam*. New York: Penguin Books, 1986.

Haddad, Yvonne Yazbeck, and Byron Haines. *The Islamic Impact*. Syracuse: Syracuse University Press, 1984.

_____, and Jane Idleman Smith, eds. *Muslim Communities in North America*. Albany: State University of New York Press, 1994.

_____. *Mission to America: Five Islamic Sectarian Communities in North America*. Gainesville: University Press of Florida, 1993.

Halbwachs, Maurice. *On Collective Memory*. Translated and edited by Lewis A. Coser. Chicago: University of Chicago Press, 1992.

Hallgren, Roland. *The Vital Force: A Study of Ase in the Traditional and Neo-traditional Culture of the Yoruba People*. Lund, Sweden: University of Lund, 1995.

Harris, Norman. *Connecting Times: The Sixties in Afro-American Fiction*. Jackson, Miss.: University Press of Mississippi, 1988.

Harris, Trudier. "Three Black Women Writers and Humanism: A Folk Perspective." In R. Baxter Miller, ed., *African-American Literature and Humanism*. Lexington, Ky.: University Press of Kentucky, 1981.

Haskins, James. *Voodoo and Hoodoo: Their Tradition and Craft as Related by Actual Practitioners*. New York: Stein and Day, 1978.

Herskovits, Melville J. *Dahomey: An Ancient West African Kingdom*. 2 volumes. Evanston, Ill.: Northwestern University Press, 1967.

Hobbs, Sterling X. "Miracle Man of the Muslims." *Sepia* (May 1975): 24–30.

Hodgkin, Thomas. *Nigerian Perspectives: An Historical Anthology*. London: Oxford University Press, 1960.

Hopkins, Dwight N. "Theological Method and Cultural Studies: Slave Religious Culture as a Heuristic." In Dwight N. Hopkins and Sheila Devaney, eds., *Changing Conversations: Religious Reflection and Cultural Analysis*. New York: Routledge, 1996, 163–80.

_____. *Shoes That Fit Our Feets: Sources for a Constructive Black Theology*. Maryknoll, N.Y.: Orbis Books, 1993.

Hughes, Langston. *Good Morning Revolution: Uncollected Writings of Social Protest by Langston Hughes*. Edited by Faith Berry. Carol Publishing Group, 1992.

Humanist Manifestos I and II. Buffalo, N.Y.: Prometheus, 1973.

Hunt, Carl M. *Oyotunji Village: The Yoruba Movement in America*. Washington, D.C.: University Press of America, 1979.

Hurbon, Laennec. *Voodoo: Search for the Spirit*. Translated by Lory Frankel. New York: Harry N. Abrams, 1995.

Hurston, Zora Neale. *Moses: Man of the Mountain*. New York: HarperPerennial, 1939, 1991.

_____. *Mules and Men.* 1935; New York: Harper & Row, 1990.

_____. "Hoodoo in America." *The Journal of American Folklore*, vol. 44, no. 174 (October–December 1931): 317–417.

Hyatt, Harry Middleton. *Hoodoo—Conjuration—Witchcraft—Rootwork: Beliefs Accepted by Many Negroes and White Persons These Being Orally Recorded among Blacks and Whites.* 2 volumes. Washington, D.C.: Distributed by American University Bookstore, 1970 (Hannibal, Mo.: Western Publishing).

IBIE, C. Osamaro. *Ifism: The Complete Work of Orunmila.* Lagos, Nigeria: Efehi Ltd., 1986.

Ídòwú, E. Bóláji. *Olódùmarè: God in Yorùbá Belief.* 1962; New York: Wazobia, 1994.

Jacobs, Claude F., and Andrew J. Kaslow. *The Spiritual Churches of New Orleans: Origins, Beliefs, and Rituals of an African American Religion.* Knoxville: University of Tennessee Press, 1991.

James, C. L. R. *The Black Jacobins: Toussaint L'Ouverture and the San Domingo Revolution.* 2d ed. New York: Vintage Books, 1963, 1989.

James, Jacqui, and Mark Morrison-Reed, eds. *Been in the Storm So Long: Mediation Manual.* Boston: Skinner House Books, 1991.

Jenkins, Ulysses, *Ancient African Religion and the African American Church.* Jacksonville, N.C.: Flame International, 1978.

Johnson, James Weldon. *Along This Way: The Autobiography of James Weldon Johnson.* New York: Da Capo Press, 1933, 1973.

Jones, William R. *Is God a White Racist? A Preamble to Black Theology.* 2d ed. Boston: Beacon Press, 1997.

Joyner, Charles. "'Believer I Know': The Emergence of African-American Christianity." In David G. Hackett, ed. *Religion and American Culture: A Reader.* New York: Routledge, 1995.

Jules-Rosette, Bennetta. "Creative Spirituality from Africa to America: Cross-Cultural Influences in Contemporary Religious Forms." *The Western Journal of Black Studies*, vol. 4, no. 4 (Winter 1980): 273–85.

Kammen, Michael. *Mystic Chords of Memory: The Transformation of Tradition in American Culture* New York: Alfred A. Knopf, 1991.

Kaufman, Gordon. *God, Mystery, Diversity: Christian Theology in a Pluralistic World.* Minneapolis: Fortress Press, 1996.

_____. *An Essay on Theological Method.* Rev. ed. Missoula, Mont.: Scholars Press, 1975, 1979, 1995.

_____. *In Face of Mystery: A Constructive Theology* Cambridge, Mass.: Harvard University Press, 1993.

Kelley, Robin, D. G. "'Afric's Sons with Banners Red.'" In Sidney J. Lemelle and Robin D. G. Kelley, eds. *Imagining Home: Class, Culture, and Nationalism in the African Diaspora.* New York: Verso, 1994.

_____. "Comrades, Praise Gawd for Lenin and Them! Ideology and Culture among Black Communists in Alabama, 1930–1935." *Science and Society*, vol. 52, no. 1 (Spring 1988): 59–82.

Kiple, Kenneth F. *Blacks in Colonial Cuba, 1774–1899.* Gainesville: University of Florida Press, 1976.

Klein, Herbert S. *Slavery in the Americas: A Comparative Study of Virginia and Cuba.* Chicago: University of Chicago Press, 1967.

Laguerre, Michel S. *Voodoo Heritage.* Sage Library of Social Research 98. Beverly Hills: Sage Publications, 1980.

Lamont, Corliss. *The Philosophy of Humanism.* New York: Frederick Ungar Publishing, Co., 1965.

Lee, Martha. *The Nation of Islam: An American Millenarian Movement.* Lewiston, N.Y.: Edwin Mellen Press, 1988; Syracuse University Press, 1991.

Levine, Lawrence W. *Black Culture and Black Consciousness: Afro-American Folk Thought from Slavery to Freedom.* New York: Oxford University Press, 1977.

Levy, Eugene. *James Weldon Johnson: Black Leader, Black Voice.* Chicago: University of Chicago Press, 1973.

Lincoln, C. Eric. *The Black Muslims in America.* 3d ed. Grand Rapids: Wm. B. Eerdmans, 1994.

Lomax, Louis E. *A Report on Elijah Muhammad, Malcolm X, and the Black Muslim World: When the Word Is Given.* Westport, Conn.: Greenwood Press, 1963.

Long, Charles. "Assessment and New Departures for a Study of Black Religion in the United States of America." In Gayraud Wilmore, ed., *African American Religious Studies: An Interdisciplinary Anthology.* Durham, N.C.: Duke University Press, 1989, 34–49.

_____. *Significations.* Philadelphia: Fortress Press, 1986.

Lucioius X. "Why I Believe in Islam." *Salaam,* vol. 1, no. 1 (July 1960): 26–29.

Lyell, Sir Charles. *A Second Visit to the United States of North America.* Vol. 1 New York: Harper & Brothers, 1849.

McCartney, John T. *Black Power Ideologies: An Essay in African-American Political Thought.* Philadelphia: Temple University Press, 1992.

McCloud, Aminah Beverly. *African American Islam.* New York: Routledge, 1995.

Maduro, Renaldo J. "Hoodoo Possession in San Francisco: Notes on Therapeutic Aspects of Regression." *Ethos,* vol. 3, no. 3 (Fall 1975): 425–47.

Magida, Arthur J. *Prophet of Rage: A Life of Louis Farrakhan and His Nation.* New York: Basic Books, 1996.

Malcolm X. *Yakub History: The Nation of Islam Speech.* Stone Mountain, Ga.: T.U.T. Publications, 1997.

_____. *The Autobiography, As Told to Alex Haley.* New York: Ballantine Books, 1965.

Mamiya, Lawrence H. "From Black Muslim to Bilalian: The Evolution of a Movement." *Journal for the Scientific Study of Religion,* vol. 21, no. 2 (June 1982): 138–52.

Marsh, Clifton E. *From Black Muslims to Muslims: The Resurrection, Transformation, and Change of the Lost-Found Nation of Islam in America, 1930–1995.* 2d ed. Lanham, Md: Scarecrow Press, Inc., 1996.

Mason, John. *Orin Òrìsà: Songs for Selected Heads.* Brooklyn, N.Y.: Yoruba Theological Archministry, 1992.

May, Henry F. *The Enlightenment in America.* New York: Oxford University Press, 1976.

Mays, Benjamin E. *The Negro's God as Reflected in His Literature.* New York: Atheneum, 1973.

Metraux, Alfred. *Voodoo in Haiti.* Translated by Hugo Charteris. New York: Oxford University Press, 1959.

Meyer, Donald H. "Secular Transcendence: The American Religious Humanists." *American Quarterly,* vol. 34 no. 5 (Winter 1982): 524–42.

Montgomery, William E. *Under Their Own Vine and Fig Tree: The African-American Church in the South, 1865–1900.* Baton Rouge: Louisiana State University Press, 1993.

Morrison, Toni. "The Site of Memory." In Cornel West et al., *Out There: Marginalization and Contemporary Cultures.* Cambridge, Mass.: MIT Press, 1994.

Morrison, Roy D., "The Emergence of Black Theology in America." *The AME Zion Quarterly Review,* vol. 94, no. 3 (October 1982): 2–17.

Morrison-Reed, Mark D. *Black Pioneers in a White Denomination.* 3d ed. Boston: Skinner House Books, 1994.

Moses, Wilson Jeremiah. *The Wings of Ethiopia: Studies in African American Life and Letters.* Ames, Iowa: Iowa State University Press, 1990.

Muhammad, Akbar. "Muslims in the United States: An Overview of Organizations, Doctrines, and Problems." In Yvonne Yazbeck Haddad, Byron Haines, and Ellison Findly, eds. *The Islamic Impact.* Syracuse, N.Y.: Syracuse University Press, 1984, 195–217.

Muhammad, Elijah. *The True History of Master Fard Muhammad.* Compiled and edited by Minister Nasir Makr Hakim. Atlanta: Messenger Elijah Muhammad Propagation Society, 1996.

_____. *Our Saviour Has Arrived.* Newport News, Va.: United Brothers Communications Systems, 1996.

_____. *How to Eat to Live.* Chicago: Muhammad's Temple of Islam no. 2, 1967.

_____. *Message to the Black Man in America.* Philadelphia: Haim's Publications, 1965.

_____. "Mr. Muhammad Speaks." *Salaam,* vol. 1, no. 1 (July 1960): 14–15.

Muhammad, W. Deen. *Challenges That Face Man Today.* Chicago: W. D. Muhammad Publications, 1985.

_____. "Self-Government in the New World." *Bilalian News,* vol. 1 no. 19 (March 19, 1976): 23–26. Reprinted in Milton Sernett, ed. *Afro-American Religious History.* Durham, N.C.: Duke University Press, 1985, 413–20.

Mulira, Jessie Gaston. "The Case of Voodoo in New Orleans." In Joseph E. Holloway, ed. *Africanisms in American Culture.* Bloomington: Indiana University Press, 1990.

Mullin, Michael. *Africa in America: Slave Acculturation and Resistance in the American South and the British Caribbean, 1726–1831.* Chicago: University of Illinois Press, 1992.

Murphy, Joseph. *Working the Spirit: Ceremonies of the African Diaspora.* Boston: Beacon Press, 1994.

_____. *Santería: African Spirits in America.* Boston: Beacon Press, 1988, 1993.

Murray, Chalmers S. "Edisto Negroes Close to Spirits." Chalmers S. Murray Papers, Charleston: South Carolina Historical Society.

_____. "Voodoo Gods Yet Alive in Islands." Chalmers S. Murray Papers, Charleston: South Carolina Historical Society.

_____. "Voodoo Survivals Traced on Edisto." Chalmers S. Murray Papers, Charleston: South Carolina Historical Society.

Naipaul, Shiva. *Love and Death in a Hot Country.* New York: Penguin, 1985.

Naison, Mark. *Communists in Harlem During the Depression.* Urbana: University of Illinois Press, 1983.

Neimark, Philip John. *The Way of the Orisa: Empowering Your Life Through the Ancient African Religion of Ifa.* San Francisco: HarperSanFrancisco, 1993.

Newton, Huey P. *To Die for the People: The Writings of Huey P. Newton.* Edited by Toni Morrison. New York: Writers and Readers Publishing, Inc., 1995.

Nichols, G. W. "Six Weeks in Florida." *Harper's New Monthly Magazine,* vol. 41 (1870): 657–67.

Núñez, Luis Manuel. *Santería: A Practical Guide to Afro-Caribbean Magic.* Dallas: Spring Publications, 1992.

Olds, Mason. "What Is Religious Humanism?" *Free Inquiry,* vol. 16, no. 4 (Fall 1996): 11–14.

Olupona, Jacob K. "The Study of Yoruba Religious Tradition in Historical Perspective." *NUMEN* 40 (1993): 240–71.

_____, ed., *African Traditional Religions: In Contemporary Society.* New York: Paragon House, 1991.

Ortiz, Antonio Dominguez. *The Golden Age of Spain, 1516–1659.* New York: Basic Books, 1971.

Ott, Thomas O. *The Haitian Revolution, 1789–1804.* Nashville: University of Tennessee Press, 1973.

Oyotunji African Village. "Biographical Sketch of Oba Adefunmi I," n.p., n.d.

Painter, Nell Irvin. *The Narrative of Hosea Hudson: His Life as a Negro Communist in the South.* Cambridge, Mass.: Harvard University Press, 1979.

Parenti, Michael. "The Black Muslims from Revolution to Institution." *Social Research* 31 (1964): 975–94.

Paris, Peter. *The Spirituality of African Peoples: The Search for a Common Moral Discourse.* Minneapolis: Fortress Press, 1992.

Payne, Daniel Alexander. "Daniel Payne's Protestation of Slavery." In *Lutheran Herald and Journal of the Franckean Synod* (August 1, 1839): 113–15.

Perry, Bruce, ed. *Malcolm: The Life of a Man Who Changed Black America.* Barrytown, N.Y.: Stations Hill Press, 1991.

_____. *Malcolm X: The Last Speeches.* New York: Pathfinder, 1989.

Piersen, William D. *Black Yankees: The Development of an Afro-American Subculture in Eighteenth-Century New England.* Amherst, Mass.: University of Massachusetts Press, 1988.

Pinn, Anthony Bernard. "Rethinking the Nature and Tasks of African American Theology: A Pragmatic Perspective." In *American Journal of Theology and Philosophy*, vol. 19, no. 2 (May 1998): 191–208.

_____. "Keep On Keepin' On: Reflections on 'Get on the Bus' and the Language of Movement," 58–67. In Garth Kasimu Baker-Fletcher, ed., *Black Religion after the Million Man March: Voices on the Future.* Maryknoll, N.Y.: Orbis, 1998.

_____. *Why, Lord? Suffering and Evil in Black Theology.* New York: Continuum Publishing Company, 1995.

Preucel, Robert W., and Ian Hodder, eds. *Contemporary Archaeology in Theory: A Reader.* Cambridge, Mass.: Blackwell, 1996.

Raboteau, Albert J. "The Afro-American Traditions." In Ronald and Darrel W. Amundsen, eds. *Caring and Curing: Health and Medicine in the Western Religious Traditions.* New York: Macmillan, 1986.

_____. *Slave Religion: The "Invisible Institution" in the Antebellum South.* New York: Oxford University Press, 1978.

Redding, J. Saunders. *A Scholar's Conscience: Selected Writings of J. Saunders Redding, 1942–1977.* Edited with an introduction by Faith Berry. Louisville: University Press of Kentucky, 1992.

Religion, Scriptures & Spirituality Audio Classics Series, "African & African-American Religions." Nashville: Knowledge Products, 1994.

Rigaud, Milo. *Secrets of Voodoo.* Translated by Robert Cross. San Francisco: City Lights Books, 1953.

Rhodes, Jewell Parker. *Voodoo Dreams: A Novel of Marie Laveau.* New York: Picador USA, 1993.

Sadler, Kim Martin. *Atonement: The Million Man March.* Cleveland: Pilgrim Press, 1996.

Savannah Unit, Georgia Writers' Project, Work Projects Administration. *Drums and Shadows: Survival Studies Among the Georgia Coastal Negroes.* Garden City, N.Y.: Anchor Books, 1972.

Seale, Bobby. *Seize the Time: The Story of the Black Panther Party and Huey P. Newton.* New York: Random House, 1970.

Van Sertima, Ivan, ed. *African Presence in Early America.* New Brunswick, N.J.: Transaction Books, 1987.

_____. *They Came Before Columbus.* New York: Random House, 1976.

Simpson, George Eaton. *Religious Cults of the Caribbean: Trinidad, Jamaica, and Haiti.* Rio Piedras, Puerto Rico: Institute of Caribbean Studies, University of Puerto Rico, 1980.

Smith, Theophus H. *Conjuring Culture: Biblical Formations of Black America.* New York: Oxford University Press, 1994.

Snow, Loudell F. "I Was Born Just Exactly with the Gift: An Interview with a Voodoo Practitioner." *Journal of American Folklore*, vol. 86, no. 341 (July–September 1973): 272–81.

Spitz, Lewis W. "Humanism and the Protestant Reformation." In Albert Rabil, *Renaissance Humanism: Foundations, Forms, and Legacy.* Vol. 3, *Humanism and the Disciplines.* Philadelphia: University of Pennsylvania Press, 1988.

Suchlicki, Jaime. *Cuba: From Columbus to Castro and Beyond.* 4th ed. Washington, D.C.: Brassey's, 1997.

Tallant, Robert. *Voodoo in New Orleans.* New York: Collier Books, 1946; Macmillan Co., 1971.

Tate, Sonsyrea. *Little X: Growing Up in the Nation of Islam.* San Francisco: HarperCollins, 1997.

Teish, Luisah. *Carnival of the Spirit: Seasonal Celebrations and Rites of Passage.* San Francisco: HarperSanFrancisco, 1994.

_____. *Jambalaya.* San Francisco: Harper & Row, 1985.

Thompson, Robert Farris. *Flash of the Spirit: African and Afro-American Art and Philosophy.* New York: Random House, 1983.

Touchstone, Blake. "Voodoo in New Orleans." *Louisiana History*, vol. 4, no. 13 (1972): 371–86.

Townes, Emilie, ed. *A Troubling in My Soul: Womanist Perspectives on Evil and Suffering.* Maryknoll, N.Y.: Orbis Books, 1993.

Trinkaus, Charles. "Italian Humanism and Scholastic Theology." In Albert Rabil, *Renaissance Humanism: Foundations, Forms, and Legacy.* Vol. 3, *Humanism and the Disciplines.* Philadelphia: University of Pennsylvania Press, 1988.

Turner, Richard Brent. *Islam in the African-American Experience.* Indianapolis: Indiana University Press, 1997.

Unitarian Universalist Commission on Appraisal to the General Assembly. *Empowerment: One Denomination's Quest for Racial Justice, 1967–1982.* Boston: UUA, 1984.

_____. *Black Caucus Controversy II.* Boston: UUA, 1968.

Vega, Marta Moreno. "The Yoruba Orisha Tradition Comes to New York City." *African American Review*, vol. 29, no. 2 (1995): 201–6.

Walker, Alice. "the only reason you want to go to heaven is that you have been driven out of your mind off your land and out of your lover's arms: clear seeing inherited religion and reclaiming the pagan self." *On the Issue*, vol. 6, no. 2 (Spring 1997): 16–23, 54–55.

_____. *The Color of Purple: A Novel.* New York: Harcourt, Brace, Jovanovich, 1982.

_____. *The Third Life of Grange Copeland.* New York: Harcourt, Brace, Jovanovich, 1970.

Walker, Sheila S. *Ceremonial Spirit Possession in Africa and Afro-America.* Leiden: Brill, 1972.

Washington, Joseph. "How Black Is Black Religion?" In James J. Gardiner and J. Deotis Roberts, Sr., eds., *Quest for a Black Theology.* Philadelphia: Pilgrim Press, 1971.

Welch, Alford T., and Pierre Cachia, eds. *Islam: Past Influence and Present Challenge.* Albany: State University of New York Press, 1979.

Whitten, Norma E. "Contemporary Patterns of Malign Occultism among Negroes in North Carolina," *The Journal of American Folk-lore* 75 (1962): 311–25.

Wilmore, Gayraud. *Black Religion and Black Radicalism: An Interpretation of the Religious History of Afro-American People.* 2d ed. Maryknoll, N.Y.: Orbis Books, 1983.

Wormser, Richard. *American Islam: Growing Up Muslim in America.* New York: Walker and Company, 1994.

Wright, Richard. *The Outsider.* 1st Perennial Library Edition. New York: Harper & Row, 1965, 1989.

_____. *Black Boy.* New York: Harper & Row, 1937, 1996.

Wyhte, Abbie. "Christian Elements in Negro American Muslim Religious Beliefs." *Phylon*, 24 (Winter 1964): 382–88.

NEWSPAPERS AND NEWSLETTERS

Chicago Tribune, February 21, 1977.
Final Call, 1995–1997, Chicago.
Inquirer, December 8, 1996, Buffalo.
Voodoo Realists Newsletter, 1995–1997, New Orleans.
Washington Post, May 1989; July 2, 1995

INTERVIEWS WITH AUTHOR

Adefunmi I, H.R.H. Oseijeman. Oyotunji African Village, April 1996.
Allen, Norm, Jr. Buffalo, N.Y., January 1997.
Ajamu, Chief. Oyotunji African Village, April 1996.
Chamani, Priestess Miriam. New Orleans, La., May 1996.
Muhammad, Minister James. St. Paul, Minn., December 1997.
Zannu, Medahochi K. O. Milwaukee, Wisc., March 1995.

INDEX